MW00978886

# FIAT LUX

## Volume I

# FIAT LUX

*Winners of the*
*Certificate of Literature of the*
*Philalethes Society*

## Volume I: 1956–1986

Edited by
Jack Buta, FPS

Philalethes Society
·2009·

www.freemasonry.org

ISBN 978-0-9841494-0-7

# CONTENTS

# PREFACE

The *Philalethes Magazine* was first published in 1946 and has a back catalogue of over 60 years worth of articles. This prompted me to consider that reprinting a selection of the very best would make quality and interesting reading.

The Philalethes Society has been fortunate that throughout its publication masonic writers and researchers of excellence have been happy to have their material published in the Philalethes.

Each year the society awards the Certificate of Literature to the best qualifying article each year. I say qualifying because no one can win the award more than once and no officer of the society is eligible. This award is not easily won and in some years is not awarded.

The first award, and now the first paper in this anthology, is by James R Case. Among the 38 papers there are 26 recipients of this award and among the authors are Roscoe Pound, Allen E Roberts, Alphonse Cerza, Dwight Smith, Louis C King, Harold B Voorhis and Wallace McLeod.

You might not agree with all the views expressed, some may have changed after new evidence, or our perspective changed. However the papers read as comfortably and well as when they were first printed

This volume is planned to be the first of several, it only covers the period to 1986. There are plenty of other papers worth a reprise.

As you might have guessed, a project such as this involves a great deal of scanning, transcription and editing and any errors are mine. Have a great read and buy the next volume when it is published.

While these works of the past are valuable treasures, our best work is yet to be done.

**_Jack Buta, FPS_**
1st VP (2009–2011)
Philalethes Society

# INTRODUCTION

Dear Reader,

In your hands you hold one of the finest collections of masonic essays produced in the United States in the last 60 years. The Philalethes Society, through its magazine, has dedicated itself to being a forum for the current research and the dissemination of the best available writings to its members, and the readers of the magazine. It has prided itself that it is able to discuss the issues of the day simply because it has the advantage of being independent.

Through the diligent labouring 'in the quarry' of Jack Buta FPS, our societies 1st Vice President we have selected some of the very best that we have published from 1956 through 1986. A second volume is being planned covering the period till 2007 and other volumes may follow.

From the Volume of the Sacred Law we are constantly reminded to *"Remember the former things of old...."* (Isaiah 46.9) Memory is important because it reminds us that we stand in an endless line of splendor indebted to those who have gone before us. It also reminds us that we are part of a much larger story and that we also have our part to play in that story. In this post-modern world, where so much emphasis is on finding or inventing your own concept of meaning and significance, it is encouraging to remember that as Masons we have a legacy of moral and philosophical truth which has made substantial contributions to our world and social order. We are different. We know who we are. We cannot be like so many people today, for whom Karl Marx's dictum remains all too true, "A people without a heritage are easily persuaded."

The Philalethes Society has been going since 1928 and the *Magazine* published since 1946. This is a remarkable achievement given that the run of most masonic periodicals is less than a decade. The years to come will be exciting ones, good times to be a part of a forward looking society. We would hope that you find enough here in this book for you to consider joining the society. Visit our website and members have a closed email list where they can exchange news and discuss matters of interest. We do believe that email lists are the way to get to know other brothers, not for us forums as the current software dictates but realtime exchange of views, a place to make friends.

So do join us, the Philalethes Society, we are part of the tapestry of Masonic life in this country. You will be welcome.

Fraternally yours,

**Terry L. Tilton, FPS,**
President (2009–2011)
Philalethes Society

# THE HAMILTON BI-CENTENNIAL

## James R. Case, FPS

*1956 Certificate of Literature*

JANUARY 11, 1957, is the 200th anniversary of the birth of Alexander Hamilton, a great American.

Born in the British West Indies, a student at King's College, now Columbia University, a soldier of the Revolution, "principal and most confidential aide of Washington," legislator in the Congress of the Confederation, ardent Federalist, essayist and first Secretary of the Treasury, lawyer and politician in New York City, he had the unenviable distinction of being shot to death by a Vice President of the United States.

He will be extolled by Masonic writers during this anniversary year, as his name was eagerly seized a half century ago by a writer who made him a Freemason, "sight unseen." And the error has been compounded and so dignified by repetition, that now it will be difficult to refute, because so many want to believe it.

The minutes of American Union, the famous traveling Lodge held in the Connecticut Line regiments of the Continental army, include many distinguished names of both members and visitors, among others that of Hamilton. The present-day American Union Lodge at Marietta, Ohio, has many of the original records in its archives. A study of *Freemasonry in Morristown in the Revolution-*

*ary War* was made by Edmund D. Halsey many years ago, and published in 1900 as Appendix A to the Proceedings of the Grand Lodge of New Jersey. The author, Halsey, who apparently was not himself a Freemason, categorically stated it was Alexander Hamilton who visited American Union Lodge on December 27, 1779, and March 6, 1780.

Sidney Hayden, in his book *Washington and His Masonic Compeers*, first published in 1866, makes no mention of Hamilton. This book has been remarkably free from criticism concerning either error or omission. It is generally accepted as authentic as far as it goes, and omission of the name of Alexander Hamilton, of course, does not prove or disprove anything.

Since the appearance of the Halsey story, the identification of Alexander Hamilton as a Freemason has been made a matter of record in many articles and publications. The 1946 edition of Mackey's Revised Encyclopedia of Freemasonry goes so far as to state that it was Alexander who was present at Morristown, "identified because the only one of that name then holding a commission in the army." This broad statement can readily be refuted by reference to Heitmann's Register of Continental Officers where no less than twenty-two Hamiltons are listed. The DAR Ancestral Register contains at least forty Hamiltons and SAR records have mere than twice as many. The Hamiltons were extensively patriotic.

William Coleman. editor of the New York Post and a close friend, printed a *Collection of the Facts and Documents Relating to the Death of Alexander Hamilton* just a short time after the sad event which followed the duel with Aaron Burr July 11, 1804. Hamilton had opposed Burr for the presidency in 1800 and for the governor's chair in 1804, and political differences had developed to such a point they could not be otherwise resolved. The burial was conducted by the Society of the Cincinnati, of which Hamilton was the president general, and other societies attending included those of Saint Andrew, Tammany, the Mechanics and the Mariners. No mention is made of the Freemasons. It is inconceivable that a man of such prominence as Alexander Hamilton could have been a member of the Fraternity, and not have been accorded the last sad rites due a distinguished Brother, but such apparently was the case.

Hamilton himself wrote voluminously and much of his correspondence, as well as his *Federalist Papers* and many political essays have been printed. The indexes do not reveal a single mention of Freemasonry, nor does the text give any clue to his possible attachment to the Fraternity. Yet consider the many references and direct testimony which Washington left in his writings.

Who, then, was the Hamilton who visited American Union Lodges? At the December meeting Washington himself was a visitor, and alongside him are listed Captain Caleb Gibbs, who commanded his Life Guard, and Thomas Kinney, joint proprietor with Jeremiah Bruen of the Arnold Tavern where the meeting was held. Hamilton was far away, listed among the Brethren from Pennsylvania. At the March meeting Washington did not attend, but Hamilton is listed between James Bruff of Baltimore and Charles Graham of New York.

Among the manuscripts known as the *Otho Holland Williams Papers* in the Collections of the Maryland Historical Society in Baltimore are several of Masonic interest, but in connection with our subject, the following *Delegation of Authority* was uncovered:

> The Subscribers, Antient, Free and Accepted Masons serving in the Military Lines of the States of Maryland and Delaware, Do hereby nominate and appoint our Worthy Brother Mordecai Gist, Past Master Mason, for the State of Maryland, and our Worthy Brother Otho Holland Williams, Master Mason of the State for Delaware to appear in Convention of Masons in Morris Town on Monday the seventh Day of February Instant, and Represent us the Brethren of the aforesaid States. To take into consideration the Present Condition of our Lodges, and to prepare an Humble Address to the several Grand Masters Presiding in each of the respective States Beseeching them to adopt and pursue the most necessary and effective measures for procuring an Appointment of a Right Worshipful Grand Master to Preside over all the lodges of The United States of America and to recommend such a mode for obtaining the same

as to them. Our said Representatives in Convention shall seem Eligible. In Testimony whereof, we have hereunto put our name this fifth day of the second Month Anno Mundi 5780.

> John Willson MM , Lodge No. 18 Delaware
>
> Walker Muse W.M., Lodge No. 16 Maryland
>
> J. Bruff MM , 7th Maryland
>
> T. B. Hugou MM, 11th Pensila. Lodge
>
> Elijah Skillington MM, Lodge No. 18 Delaware
>
> Edw. Dyer MM, State Maryland
>
> John Lynch, Maryland, – Lodge No. 6
>
> John Hamilton, Maryland, do
>
> Archd Anderson MM, Lodge No. 5 Delaware

Of the names represented by the above signers, Bruff and Hamilton were listed at the December 27, 1779, meeting at Morristown. At the March 6, 1780, "Convention Lodge" all of the signers except Dyer and Lynch are among those listed.

Lacking any evidence whatsoever that Alexander Hamilton was a Freemason any such claim can hardly be based solely on the Morristown listing of his last name alone. But from the facts cited above it can be safely deduced that the one who was at Morristown was none other than John Hamilton (1749–1795), a Lieutenant in the 1st Maryland Regiment, member of Lodge No. 6 in Maryland, and later a member of Military Lodge No. 29, AYM, both chartered under Pennsylvania.

By due trial, strict examination, and legal Masonic information, as well as the application of good research working tools that dig deep, we may be able to clear up other misrepresentations. No blame however, can rest upon those whose great names have earned them posthumous—and fictitious—Masonic honors. But enthusiasm should never excuse a substitution for the facts.

# IMPORTANCE OF THE
# FELLOW CRAFT'S DEGREE

## Allen Cabaniss, MPS

*1957 Certificate of Literature*

IN THE SYMBOLISM of the first three degrees of Ancient Craft Masonry, the first degree represents birth, the entry into life. We see light for the first time. We see the Lodge for the first time, extending "from east to west, between north and south, from earth to heaven, and from the surface to the center," its covering "no less than a clouded canopy or starry decked heaven," a great emblem "of human life, checkered with good and evil." And we take our first step.

The third degree is a beautiful drama of the end of life. Death, yes, but far more than death—for "the Master Mason is suddenly revived by the ever-green and everliving sprig of faith in the merits of the Lion of the tribe of Judah, which strengthens him, with confidence and composure, to look forward to a blessed immortality."

The first degree then teaches us about the beginning of life; the third, about the end of life. Between the beginning and the end, there is life itself—and that is the important teaching of the second degree. Or, as our Monitor says, "In Youth, as Entered Apprentices, we ought industriously to occupy our minds in the attainment of useful knowledge; in Manhood, as Fellow Crafts, we should apply our knowledge to the discharge of our respective duties to God, our neighbor, and ourselves, so that in Age, as Master Masons, we may enjoy the happy reflection consequent on a well spent life and die in the hope of a glorious immortality."

The Fellow Craft's degree is perhaps the most neglected degree, yet in many ways the most significant. What does it teach about life, life itself as lived every day, not the beginning of life nor the end of life, but just life? It gives us two important suggestions, that life is made up of work and study, or, phrased differently, life, like Freemasonry itself, is both operative and speculative, not one or the other, but both together.

It is well for us to be frequently reminded of that teaching. But since most of us are aware that life is work, I want to single out the special teaching of the second degree that life, to be worthwhile, is also study. Remember the stress of this degree on the five senses of human nature; then recall that everything we know is derived from perceptions coming to us through one or more of those senses. Above all, remember the stress on the seven liberal arts and sciences.

(1) Grammar, or the framework of language. Language is the distinctive characteristic of man and is the chief feature which distinguishes him from the rest of the animal world. Without grammar, no Bible, no Shakespeare, no Freemasonry. How important is grammar or the framework of language!

(2) Rhetoric, or the use of language. Correct communication is the basis of understanding in our world in small affairs as well as in great affairs of state, from the correct wording of a recipe to the correct wording of a treaty between nations. A failure in rhetoric may mean a failure in cooking and a failure in international peace.

(3) Logic, or reasonableness. "Come, let us reason together" is a message of Masonry as well as of the prophet. Reading, writ-

ing, reasoning should be our "three R's"—reading with compre-hension; writing legibly and intelligibly; and reasoning so that our communication may be clearly understood.

These three arts and sciences are basic; the others rest on them.

(4) Arithmetic, or counting. What would we do without it in cal-culating days, years, or even votes?

(5) Geometry, or measurement. Architects, generals, and astron-omers need this science, but so do we—in the measurement of cloth, paper, land, hats, socks, and dogfood.

(6) Music, or the study of harmony. Not only the relation of one musical note to another, but also the relation of one man to another, one nation to another, this world to the next.

(7) Astronomy, or the study of worlds beyond our own. Not only the stars, planets, and comets, but even beyond them to their Almighty Creator.

In sum, then, the second degree puts before us as in a nut-shell all of knowledge as the proper sphere of a Freemason's study. Obviously, the ultimate purpose of the second degree cannot be exhausted by that degree alone. But that degree gives us the direc-tion. It points us to the schools, from the first grade through college and university, and reminds us that Freemasonry stands for more and more and more study and learning. And it reminds us also that study and learning go far beyond all schools—it is a lifelong process which should never end. It is as much a part of life itself as work is.

For we can learn—and should study and learn—from everything around us: from life in the family, life in the community, life in our vocation. We are, or should be, always learners. In that process of lifelong study and learning Freemasonry itself is one of our teach-ers, is one of our schools. I think that most of us who take Masonry seriously actually do learn something new every time we are pres-ent at the conferring of a degree. There is always a new word we have not noticed before, a new thought, a new action or movement. Or, the ritual may evoke a strong sense of a deep past and we may quite suddenly become aware that we are the inheritors of long-dead worthies who worked and struggled and died for us.

Again the ritual may cause our minds to wander throughout the present world and bring before us the realization of a worldwide brotherhood that already exists.

As a matter of fact one of the most impressive evidences of the ability of Freemasonry to teach us often comes after the degree-work is over and the Worshipful Master calls on various Brethren to speak a few words. There are Brothers present who would never dream of standing up in any other meeting to say anything. Yet they feel free to stand up in a Masonic meeting and express their thoughts. Moreover, they not only feel free to do so, but they feel that they must say something, at least express appreciation of the work. It is really one of the most surprising and yet most satisfying experiences to see that Masonry has taught its members to speak up, say something, express themselves—the truest of all forms of freedom of speech.

Above all, however, the second degree teaches us that the most important things in our world are not the great things that draw the headlines of newspapers—they pass away—but the quiet work of attentive ears listening to instructive tongues and treasuring the precepts in faithful breasts—these alone endure for ever.

Freemasonry, pursuing its quiet way of hearing, teaching, learning, studying, preserving, has still survived. So, too, have the Bible, Shakespeare, Plato—and learning itself—been kept alive by students here and there over the world. "And thus through a succession of ages are transmitted, unimpaired," not only "the most excellent tenets of our institution," but also of all the learning mentioned and emphasized by our beautiful Fellow Craft's degree.

# NOTES ON A LIST OF
# SOME CONJECTURED
# AMERICAN FREEMASONS

## Ronald E. Heaton, FPS

### *1958 Certificate of Literature*

SOME YEARS AGO, while visiting the Masonic Museum at Fredericksburg I saw a framed picture the wall which read in part:

Of the 29 major generals in Washington's army, 24 were Masons; of the 37 brigadiers 30 were Master Masons; of the 56 signers of the Declaration of Independence 53 were Master Masons.

As a Master Mason of relatively short duration at that time, I felt proud that any organization could attract to its membership such an outstanding group of patriots. Inquisitive as I am, I wanted to learn who the fifty-three signers were, Thus I set out on what has turned out to be a most interesting venture, one which I thought would be easy, nothing to do but read some standard reference books and copy down what others had already laboriously dug out of the records which I thought certainly existed.

But the records were non-existent, vague, or fragmentary, and the writers had already repeated tradition and wishful thinking for fact, to lead to contradictions, blind alleys, and dark trails.

The list of 130 names was set down—the 56 signers of the Declaration of Independence, General Washington and his general officers of the Continental Army—29 major generals and 44 brigadier generals. An effort was to be made to document fully the Masonic membership of as many of these as possible.

Now, after two years, some progress can be reported. Here is the report to the present time:

42 can be shown to have been members of the Masonic Fraternity. 38 have been claimed to be members, but evidence is only traditional, or impossible to document. 50 apparently have had no connection with the Fraternity, although claims of membership have been made in some cases.

Much of the work done so far has been to check and verify claims made by previous Masonic writers; in other cases some new data has been located. Similarity of names, the free and easy phonetic spelling of the times have been confusing. Nor can the birthplace of the individual or his residence be of much help in tracing the Masonic membership of these early patriots. Certainly, Washington, Franklin, and Hancock, were members of Masonic Lodges in their home towns, and their membership can be fully documented. But others became Masons far afield from their native state.

Possibly some of the work done may be of some interest. For example, a little-known brigadier general in the Continental Army, James Hogun, of North Carolina. Born in Ireland, served in Georgia and North Carolina Militia, appointed brigadier general January 9, 1779; taken prisoner at Charleston, South Carolina, May 12, 1780, and died in captivity January 4, 1781.

While reading the By-Laws of Lodge No.3 of Philadelphia, I located the name James H-O-G-A-N as a member, under date of April 13, 1779. In the meantime reference was found in Douglass Scott Freeman's Life of Washington that Brig. Gen. James Hogun was in Philadelphia in the spring of 1779.

The original minutes of Lodge No. 3, in the library of the Grand Lodge of Pennsylvania, show that Hogan was entered April 13, passed on the 15th, and raised April 17, 1779. He signed the By Laws of the Lodge on April 16, 1779, as James *Hogun,* although the minutes refer to him as *Hogan.*

Thus, on this chance reference, we find three of Washington's general officers members of this same Lodge, with the complete record of the dates on which all three degrees were conferred.

Brigadier General John Peter Gabrial Muhlenberg was the second of the three officers, he receiving his degrees simultaneously with Hogun. The third officer was William Thompson, of Pennsylvania.

Thompson received his three degrees at one time, while a prisoner on parole, enroute to New York.

Thomas Jefferson is another example of unverified membership which we have discussed before.

Claims have been made by writers that he was and was not a Mason.

An article in a *Bulletin of The American Philosophical Society* for 1953 lists him as a Foreign Member of La Loge des Neuf Soeurs for 1776–1792, with *indirect evidence* of membership. Dr. Brown states "there is considerable contemporary evidence to indicate that Jefferson was himself a Mason," while Boyden says "No positive evidence of where or when he was made a Mason." His presence at a cornerstone laying at the University of Virginia is no proof that he was a Mason. But there is this from *The Masonic Review* of August 1851 p. 338, on the occasion of the anniversary of St. John's Day, June 24, 5851 … volunteer toasts given, one by D. W. C. Dunwell, "Whilst Masons can boast of a Washington, a Lafayette, a Jefferson, and a Jackson as brethren, they have just cause to be proud of their Order."

Or take Thomas Nelson, Jr., of Virginia, supposedly a visitor with Washington and Lafayette to Lodge No.9 at Yorktown, after the siege there that ended the Revolutionary War. Quoting from *Great American Masons,* by George W. Baird, 1924, Washington, p. 63: "When the cornerstone of the Washington monument was

laid in Richmond about the year 1830, the then Grand Master of
Masons, Robert G. Scott, said:

> The campaign of this year is ever memorial for the capture of Corn-
> wallis at Yorktown. In that village was Lodge No.9, where after the
> siege was ended, Washington, Lafayette, Marshall, Nelson came
> together and by their union bore abiding testimony to the beautiful
> tenets of Masonry.

"There are no other records of the visit of Nelson to Lodge 9 on
that occasion, but as Grand Master Scott and hosts of other Masons
who enjoyed a personal and intimate acquaintance with Nelson,
were living at that time, there can be no question of the accuracy
of the information." Was Thomas Nelson, Jr., then a Mason?

A Report on Foreign Correspondence, 1908, p. 13, in the Proceedings of the Grand Lodge of New Jersey, relates that 52 out of
56 signers were Masons, but on the next page, page 14, is this: "It
happens, so far as careful examination of Grand Lodge records can
show the facts that only five Freemasons signed the Declaration
of Independence, namely: Franklin, Hancock, Hooper, Livingston,
and Nelson."

Nine signers are included among the 42 I have documented.

George Read, a signer from Delaware, is another name almost
fully documented. While P. A. Roth says, "there is no record of his
having been a Mason," records in Philadelphia indicate the possibility that he was. There is a record in Philadelphia of a George
Read being admitted a member of Lodge No.3 on December 7,
1782. A dues ledger is also shown for him. He was admitted as
a member of Lodge No. 33, New Castle, Delaware, February 2,
1792, and his dues record is complete to December 1798, with
notation at that time 'of six years and nine months membership.
Since he died September 21, 1798, it could be this is the man we
are searching for, but the Secretary of the Lodge and Read himself
signed the name George Reid. I believe further research will clear
this up and prove this George Read to have been a Mason.

James Smith, also of Pennsylvania. To attempt to pin-point a James Smith, among the many others of that name, appears to be almost hopeless. Yet in the Grand Lodge of Pennsylvania's library there is a record of a James Smith belonging to Lodge No. 2 of Philadelphia, being raised on the 27th of December in 1754. Since this Smith was born in 1719 it could well be the man we are trying to track down. Roth in his book, *Masonry in the Formation of Our Government,* 1761–1799, relates that Smith was made a Mason in Lodge No. 2 Philadelphia, on September 11, 1754. Brother Paterson, the librarian and curator, in Philadelphia, writes on March 21, 1957: "We have made several inquiries about Robert Morris and James Smith, signers, and the answer we receive, that these two men were not members of the Masonic Fraternity." More work is needed here, too.

Others, have been claimed as Masons, or to have attended Lodge after they died. Others have been made Masons in one place when records indicate they were in some other place at that time. As, for example, John Witherspoon, of New Jersey, said to have conducted a Masonic church service in Ryegate, Vermont, on June 24, 1782, when the records of the Continental Congress show him to have been present in Philadelphia, attending sessions of Congress on Friday, the 22nd of June, 1782, and on Monday, the 25th of June. I believe, too, Lafayette was claimed to have been made a Mason at Valley Forge while he was still in France!

Several statements have been noted that Freemasonry needs not reach out and attempt to bring into its membership individuals whose background renders membership unlikely, or whose record would not lend support to the possibility of their being Masons. But there does appear to be too much undocumented material being published, individually and unfortunately, by or under the auspices of Masonic Culture Committees of Grand Lodges. Article after article appears in which names of early Americans are listed and claimed to have been Masons. When trying to authenticate these writings, the reply is invariably, "Unfortunately Brother So and So did not document his material."

I have set up three rather arbitrary and strict classifications for myself, and each of the 130 names fall into one of these groupings.

In the first group are those individuals for whom documentary information is available, in the form of original Lodge minutes or Proceedings of Grand Lodges.

The second group comprises those who have been claimed as Masons, but for which definite documentary information is now lacking. Much traditional information is available, contemporary writing of friends and neighbors, presumption on the part of later writers, and assumption due to the fact that Grand Lodge officers may have had a part in a dedication ceremony, as the laying of a cornerstone or even words on a grave monument. But until further research does prove definitely the membership of these individuals, they should be left out.

The third group, of course, is the remainder, and is made up of those for whom no information, even traditional, is available, or on whom "negative" information has been found, like John and Samuel Adams. Available information appears to be very clear that neither were Freemasons. Roger Sherman and his Masonic apron, Robert Morris and the mention of his having been a member of a "Keystone Lodge," and others, all point to the need for continuing and intensive research in the future.

# WHAT IS LAW?

## Roscoe Pound, FPS

### *1959 Certificate of Literature*

WHEN THE GENTILES, which have not the law do by nature the things contained in the law, these, having not the law, are a law unto themselves: " Epistle to the Romans, 2:14.

"If any one thinks [a question of lawmaking policy] can be settled deductively, or once for all, I can say that I think he is theoretically wrong, and that I am certain that his conclusion will not be aceepted in practice semper ubique et ab omnibus." Holmes, ;."The Path of the Law," 10 Harvard Law Review, 457.

"Nothing is more certain than that in modern society there are no absolutes." Dennis v. United States, 341 U.S. 494, 508.

Today the difficult questions of conduct have become not questions of individual conduct in relations of individual men but of conduct in the relation of organized groups of men with other such groups, in which we no longer have the situation of which St. Paul wrote. The conscience, sense of justice, and reason of the individual man could operate to guide or check individual conduct in the simpler conditions of individual relations and activities before the industrial era.

Group personality is perhaps the most vexed problem of the science of law today.

How far can there be a group conscience, a group reason, a clear group sense of justice in the complicated relations and complex activities of present-day industry? A collective conscience is something much more than the sum of the individual consciences of a million members of the International Brotherhood of Teamsters or the thousands of shareholders of the Bethlehem Steel Corporation.

The complicated relationships of these aggregations of capital and of collective activity cannot be treated on the analogy of two neighbors in a simple rural community settling liability for a trespassing cow or bargaining over sale of a horse.

I do not deny that there are absolutes, starting points for reasoning upon the problems of just conduct in the relations with one's fellow men in every day life. But when we rely upon what we take as an absolute we must make sure that we are starting from a principle, not from a rule—from a proposition attaching a definite detailed consequence to a definite detailed state of fact which may or may not be the exact state of fact to which we apply it.

When men seek to formulate universal principles for complex and unwonted relations and situations of fact they have often in effect put a narrowly conceived principle in the form of a rule set in a theological, historical, political or economic strait-jacket.

Two conspicuous examples may be seen in the development of legal doctrine as to liability, that is, obligation to repair injuries suffered by others and obligation to fulfill expectations created in others.

As to the first down to the seventeenth century our common law knew only of injuries due to intentional aggression by one man upon another. The remedy was an action of trespass in which the writ set forth an attack by a plaintiff upon a defendant with "swords, knives, and staves." Accordingly the answer seemed simple. It was a universal proposition of right and justice that a wrongdoer should be required to repair injuries due to his intentional wrongdoing.

In a simple economic order all injuries stemmed from intentional aggression. Knives and staves did not go off half cocked and even arrows shot from bows had a short range.

The advent of gunpowder led to a new theoretical foundation. In 1616 in a skirmishing drill a member of a military company unintentionally wounded another member of the company by careless discharge of his musket. He was held liable as for a battery—intentional violence to another's person. The court would not allow a plea that the injury was due to a chance accident. There the matter stood for a while. But at the end of the eighteenth century a new theory of liability was formulated. When one had been injured, the person through whose fault the injury occurred must repair it. The basis of liability for what in our law we call negligence was so put in the French Civil Code of 1804 and became established doctrine

So long as injuries to the person were either intentionally inflicted or imposed by carelessly subjecting another to an unreasonable risk, the whole matter of liability could be treated on a principle of culpable causing of harm—or requirement of answering for the results of moral wrong. This was the doctrine taught to my generation when I entered law school in 1889.

Liability for fault was taken to mean liability for fault only. In the latter part of the nineteenth century we came to see that we could not stop where we had come by the opening of the century. The every day injuries to life and limb were no longer due to simple culpable conduct of one man inflicting harm on another. The most numerous and serious injuries were incident to industrial undertakings—often of great extent and involving many who were in the nature of the undertaking exposed to risks that were not culpably caused. It came to be felt more and more that the undertaking instead of some determined culpable person ought to respond. The undertaking was generally a corporation, and came generally to be insured, so that a feeling of injustice done to an individual defendant gradually made less appeal. We could talk of "spreading the loss." But rules formulated by the modes of thought of the time when we knew only of intentionally inflicted injury by aggression of one individual upon another still embarrass our Anglo-American law of torts.

A like story may be told of what in a broad sense we may call the law of contract. The condition of consent to be bound to some performance or of assuming specific duties are very different from what they were in pioneer, frontier America.

This has been brought out strikingly in the development of what we are now calling labor law. Adjustment of wages, hours, conditions of employment is no longer a matter of bargain between two individuals on a footing of relative equality. It has become one of reconciling the demands and expectations and needs of huge organized bodies of men conscious of power and confidently seeking economic advantage. The judges at the end of the last century who interpreted due process of law in terms of the farmer and an ambitious hired man looking forward to being himself a farmer and employing a hired man, were just and learned men but are now discredited. But those who discredit them make the same mistake of judging economic and social conditions of today by the analogies of the law of our formative era.

Of no less significance is the development in the present century of standard clauses and what the French call contracts of adhesion. Many of the most important transactions of today are not had between single individuals. They are between single individuals on one hand and great financial organizations on the other. The increasing risks involved in every day life in the crowded, mechanically operated world of our time make insurance a necessity for every one. But few can risk being their own insurers. In procuring insurance, however, the individual is not dealing with another upon an equality. The insurer is a wealthy super-corporation with a well trained force of specialist lawyers, a force of expert investigators, and is able to secure the advice and procure the services and the expert opinions and testimony of the most experienced and skillful medical practitioners. The insurer writes the policy and shapes its terms and conditions skillfully in its own interest.

As the number of insurers is limited by economic considerations while almost every one needs some sort of insurance protection, the insurance companies have what in the law of public service we call a virtual monopoly.

Nor is this situation confined to contracts of insurance. It is marked also in contracts for transportation and in marketing of agricultural products.

Hence today legislation prescribes standard insurance policies, standard contracts for an increasing number of transactions, and standard clauses for many forms of special contracts. The complete freedom of contract which was believed fundamental in the nineteenth century has been superseded by a regime of state-prescribed transactions whenever the single individual must deal with highly organized institutions controlling necessary or at least highly convenient transactions. A large measure of state control of business transactions has become a matter of course. Free contract as understood yesterday is no longer an absolute. But is not this because it had ceased to be an actual freedom under changed economic conditions? But did not a better conceived freedom remain as an absolute?

What seemed absolute to the judges who applied the Fourteenth Amendment to labor conditions and business transactions of the last quarter of the nineteenth century we now perceive was too narrowly conceived.

St. Paul saw that there were principles behind the Jewish law that could be and were perceived by intelligent Gentiles who did by the light of natural reason what the Jews did because Moses had so taught them. As he put it the Gentiles show "the work of the law written in their hearts, their consciences also bearing witness."

It took a long time to show the ancient world "the work of the law written in their hearts." It took a long time for this to be achieved for the world of yesterday. We cannot hope it to be achieved over night for the world of today. But the one absolute of which we are assured is the eternal that makes for righteousness.

# MASONIC BACKGROUND

## Dr. William I. Cummings, FPS

### *1960 Certificate of Literature*

IT HAS BEEN APTLY SAID that Freemasonry is the "no-man's land of history." Perhaps no other subject has been so badly handled or so thoroughly buried under the rubble of guesswork and unfounded speculation.

There is no lack of theories. One school, which probably has the greatest number of adherents, insists that our present-day Speculative Freemasonry is a direct outgrowth of the trade guilds of the Middle Ages—the Operative Masonry of the cathedral-building days. Another goes to equal length to prove that the system arose out of certain groups commonly referred to under the generic name of Rosicrucians, who are supposed to have indulged in mystical and occult teachings. Still another, the so-called Anthropological School, traces Freemasonry to the rites and practices of primitive and barbarous tribes. The Ancient Mysteries, the Comacine Builders and so on ad infinitum have been declared to be the only original and true starting points.

Each of these groups has bent history almost to the breaking point to prove that theirs is the only correct solution. All have committed the fundamental error of treating Freemasonry as if it was an isolated phenomenon and have entirely overlooked the fact that it was and is a purely natural sequence of the social, economic, political and religious thought of the period that gave it birth. They have attempted to explain an effect without for a single moment dealing with the cause or causes which brought it about.

It is my thesis that things do not just happen; that back of every effect there is an adequate and impelling cause, and that this is just as true of social movements as of what may be termed more material things; that the true origin of Freemasonry as we know it today lies in the general conditions of the period when it came into existence—in the ideas and thought that had come down to the men of the early eighteenth century from former ages. In other words in the "background" which forms the title of this paper.

This is simply a recognition of what is termed by scholars the Unity of History, which may be defined as meaning that the past determines the present and the present the future; that events occurring at any particular time are dependent upon and the result of what has happened before and that things as they are today will determine those of the future—the unvarying law of cause and effect.

By intensive study any event or movement can be traced back through the centuries until the trail vanishes in the darkness of unrecorded history. Ideas are imperishable. They may disappear from view over a longer or shorter period, but sooner or later the train they set in motion will again break to the surface and exert its effect on the thought of that time.

Just as the strength and beauty of a fabric is the result of the combination and interweaving of many threads, so the thought and action of today is the result of the combination of many causes and events. There is no isolated strand in history. Each thread is interwoven with many others in a kind of mingled network which must be patiently and carefully untangled to follow a particular one through its devious course.

To arrive at anything like definite and logical conclusions regarding Masonic origins a somewhat comprehensive study of English history must be made. We must know something of the conditions in Saxon England, of the feudal system set up by the Norman conquerors which persisted to a greater or lesser extent up to the sixteenth century, of its gradual decline as the result of the Crusades which reduced many of the barons to comparative poverty and the "Black Death" of 1348–1349 which destroyed practically half the population of England and thus completely revolutionized conditions of agricultural labor by bringing about the landlord and tenant system in place of the formal system of villenage. We must trace the gradual progress of political freedom from its inception in 1215 when, at Runnymede, the barons wrested from King John much of his former power and forced him to grant the Magna Charta and closely follow succeeding events which resulted in the abolition of the theory of the Divine Right of Kings, the slow but constant lessening of the authority of the throne and the putting of more and more power into the hands of the people, thus changing England from a practically complete autocracy to a strongly parliamentary form of government.

Among the events which tended to crystallize the thought and ideas of their periods to stand out in broad perspective and demand special attention—the invention of printing and the Protestant Reformation, the former of which completely revolutionized the intellectual status of the English people and the latter which gradually freed them from the existing evils of priestcraft and religious persecution. Although neither was immediate in its effect their influence over the centuries cannot be overestimated.

Printing from movable types invented by Gutenberg, in Germany, in 1438, was introduced into England by William Caxton circa 1471. This invention which one of the writers of the day said "Gave the death-blow to the superstition of the Middle Ages," made the dissemination and preservation of thought easy, stimulated scholarship and exercised a vast influence toward increasing literacy and promoting education.

Prior to the invention of printing, literacy was confined largely to the clergy and a small fraction of the nobility or ruling class.

Such works as existed were in manuscript and written in Latin, a language wholly unknown to the common people. These consisted chiefly of religious liturgies and copies of the Scriptures. With the production of books in the mother tongue, particularly translations of the Bible, more and more of the people learned to read. Despite the opposition of the Church which made the possession or even the reading of the Bible a capital crime, men came to study and to put their own interpretation upon its teachings, something the most rigorous opposition of the ecclesiastics was unable to suppress. Such freedom of thought along religious lines could not have failed to develop ideas of political and economic freedom.

Although the Protestant Reformation did not become an established fact until November 1534, under the reign of Henry VIII, its roots go back more than two centuries earlier. From the days of Henry III (1217–1371), the English had resented the exactions of the Papacy. In the reign of Edward III (1327–1371) two great statutes were enacted, the one forbidding Papal appointments to ecclesiastical positions in England, the other forbidding appeals from the civil to the Papal Court. The Reformation was both religious and political in its intention and effect.

The Reformation did not immediately bring about anything like complete religious freedom. There was still a state religion to which the entire population of the country was required to conform and for a long period persecutions for nonconformity went on. It is highly important to follow the slow but constant growth of freedom to think and worship in accordance with one's own conscience.

As time went on, the struggle for freedom of thought in religious matters progressed, with the result that breaking away from the Established Church and the setting up of other forms of worship became common. It came about that there was no common denominator of religious belief, each of the separatist groups maintaining that theirs was the only true interpretation of the Scriptures.

We must not overlook the great advances in education during the sixteenth and seventeenth centuries. Literature flourished and such writers as Sir Francis Bacon and John Locke produced works which revolutionized education and laid the foundation for modern scientific methods. Shakespeare, Ben Johnson and various other writers greatly enriched the language with their matchless productions. The teachings of earlier times were being rapidly discarded. Old lines were loosened, the chain of tradition was breaking at practically every link, a spirit of inquiry was abroad and almost daily new facts were discrediting old methods.

In this age of progress, of change and of great intellectual activity, it is not surprising that the idea of the importance of the individual should come in for its share of attention. It was then that the seeds which ultimately developed into the idea of an organization such as Speculative Freemasonry began to germinate.

The revival of learning had been illuminating and enlarging the intellectual horizon; the Reformation and succeeding events had removed those checks which had hindered freedom of inquiry on speculative subjects, and by the time of William and Mary that which in earlier times could be practiced only in the privacy of the study could now without hindrance or danger be proclaimed from the house tops and discussed freely in the market place. Words and actions which in earlier days would have brought the ones speaking or performing them to the gibbet or the stake now met little or no opposition.

The revolution in religious thought and practice was closely followed by a general revolt against the old philosophical authorities whose teachings—chiefly those of Aristotle—they had perverted and disfigured. Progress in scientific lines was constantly being made. The Royal Society, formed in 1662, arose from the realization that more could be accomplished by men working in concert rather than individually.

Alongside the progress in strictly material lines there had arisen a school of thought which had to do with the relation of man to the universe, his duty to God and to his fellow-man. Practical ethics came to occupy a far larger place in the public mind than at any preceding period. Men had come to differentiate between religion and theology and this thought which found expression in the article on "God and Religion" in the Constitutions adopted by the premier Grand Lodge lies at and forms the foundation of the greater progress toward the unity and solidarity of the human race in the realm of history. It put into words and into effect for the first time the idea of genuine brotherhood, based not upon creed nor dogma, but on the importance of the individual and the inalienable right of thought and belief which opened a field where all might labor together for the benefit of all.

Just as the Royal Society was designed to encourage the study of the natural sciences, so Speculative Freemasonry, which arose from the same thought of working in concert, was instituted to promote the investigation of moral science and to inculcate in the hearts and minds of its adherents that as children of a common parent all men are brothers.

The true origin of Freemasonry will not be found in any of the far-fetched theories of the past. It arose not from a single cause but from the combination of many causes and events. So many streams have fed the lake of the Institution that no single one can be correctly designated as the only or even the principal source from which it came. Speculative Freemasonry is definitely and distinctly an English Institution, born and bred upon English soil, a child of the progress of English thought and ideas over the centuries during which the English People progressed from feudalism and villenage to a full measure of religious, political and economic freedom.

The formation of the Grand Lodge of England, on June 24, 1717, which is generally recognized as the beginning of organized Speculative Freemasonry, was not the result of a momentary impulse, but instead the culmination of a movement which began centuries earlier.

The early eighteenth century was an era of organization. So-called clubs were formed for almost every possible and impossible purpose. Most of these had but an ephemeral existence, but Freemasonry had within it that indefinable something which guaranteed its permanent existence and its spread over the entire civilized world.

It is my sincere conviction that something of the kind was bound to happen at this particular time. Had it not been that some of those interested in the movement had become members of the fast-decaying Operative Lodges it might have been known by a different name, but its philosophy would have been the same; its symbolism might have been built up around something else but there would have been the same teaching, that of the Brotherhood of Man, first promulgated by the ancient Greeks but lost through the Dark Ages, again brought to light in eighteenth-century England, when on St. John's day in 1717, was laid the foundation on which future generations have erected the vast Masonic superstructure of today.

# MASONRY UNDER TWO FLAGS

## Allen E. Roberts, FPS

*1961 Certificate of Literature*

### Freemasonry Attempts to Prevent the Civil War

FREEMASONS AND FREEMASONRY had tremendous connections with the Civil War and the peaceful overtures prior to the outbreak of hostilities. How much will never be learned. The thousands of volumes written specifically about the period mention nothing about the role of Freemasonry before or after the needless war.

Close to four hundred generals on both sides of the conflict were Masons; both Congresses had many Masons in their ranks; Masons were in both Cabinets; Masons made up about eleven per cent of the armed forces of both the United and Confederate States—after the efforts for peace ended in a dismal failure.

For more than thirty years the American Civil War was in the making; for over thirty years Freemasons were in the forefront of those who desired a peaceful solution to the differences between the so-called Slave and Free States. Perhaps not so strangely, the men who had been taught tolerance in Masonic Lodges were the men who strove hardest to reconcile the opposing forces.

Henry Clay, who had been Grand Master of Kentucky in 1820, used his influence to preserve peace when Andrew Jackson, also a Mason, threatened to use force to back up revenue officers in the

South. The tariff acts of 1828 met wholehearted disapproval in the southern section of the nation, particularly in South Carolina. Jackson planned on sending an army into that state if his tax collectors met resistance, but Clay's compromise was adopted and harsh feelings for a time were lessened.

Radicals like the South's Barnwell Rhett and William Yancey, and the North's Wendell Philips and William Garrison, were more than a match for the compromising Masons such as Clay, Thomas Benton, Stephen Douglas, John Crittenden, and others. The northern abolitionists and the southern fanatics raged constantly; never accurate with their statements; always twisting the truth to suit their purpose—to precipitate "a little blood-letting."

Even the fair sex helped spill "a little blood." The most famous of them was Harriet Beecher Stowe. Although the little wife of a northern minister had never been in the South, and knew nothing from her own experience about slavery, her Uncle Tom's Cabin did much to hasten bloodshed between fathers, sons, and brothers. Lincoln, when he met Mrs. Stowe in 1862, left no doubt about her role when he greeted her with: "So you're the little woman who wrote the book that made this great war."

John Brown had spilled "a little blood" at Pottawatomie, Kansas, and decided to try his hand in Virginia. Brown had once belonged to a Masonic Lodge in Pennsylvania, but renounced the Order soon after the anti-Masonic period was ushered in, toward the close of 1826. He did what so many weak-kneed Masons did when the press, churches, and politicians, spoke against the "secret" Order of Freemasonry. And from that day on, he did all he could to harm the organization.

Brown felt that immediate emancipation of the slaves could never be brought about at the ballot box. He knew, as the politicians knew, but would never admit, that the vast majority of the citizens of the United States wanted to be left alone. So he considered a little killing was necessary to achieve his end.

John Brown committed treason against his government when he captured the United States arsenal at Harper' Ferry on October 16, 1859. Even the man who was to become President of the United States, Abraham Lincoln, stated that whatever Brown's reasons "that cannot excuse violence, bloodshed and treason." After Brown was captured by United States troops, he was placed on trial and on November 2nd found guilty.

The trial could have been averted, for the defense had written evidence of his insanity, but he would not repudiate himself. So one month later, the Masonic governor of Virginia, Henry A. Wise (who was to become a general in the Confederate army), having refused to commute his sentence, Brown was hanged by the neck until dead. His body began mouldering in the grave.

Love S. Cornwell, Grand Master of Masons in Missouri in 1856, asked: "Is there a Mason hailing from the land of the Puritans, who so far forgets his duty as to set laws at defiance, and attempt to propagate his political creed by force of arms ... or is there a Mason hailing from the sunny South, proverbial for honor, generosity and benevolence, who is willing to sacrifice this temple of freedom, upon the altar of ambition?" Within a period of two years from the day he spoke, many Grand Masters and individual Masons asked the same question. All of them pleaded for understanding—and peace.

Known instances of Masons helping one another, although on opposing sides, occurred in the War of Independence. Many instances occurred in Kansas while blood was being shed because of the passage of Stephen Douglas' Kansas-Nebraska Bill. Douglas had submitted his bill in an attempt to still the talk of hostilities then running rampant. It had the opposite effect, which caused the Grand Lodge of New York to send a sympathizing letter to the Grand Lodge of Kansas. The letter called for Masonry to "Let her do her kind offices in mitigating the severities of civil war, which in the days of other years, have marked her career through far more fearful and protracted scenes and come out unscathed, unsullied, and without 'the smell of fire upon her garments,' and stood forth luminous, the admiration of the moral world."

President James Buchanan, a Past Master of a Pennsylvania Lodge, during the dedication ceremonies of the Equestrian Statue of Washington pleaded for understanding between the opposing factions. The applause he received indicated the citizens of the country agreed with his sentiments. Not so the fanatics. Their activities were increased. They were not interested in peace. They wanted what they expected to be just "a little blood-letting." No one dreamed their activities would start a war that cost the United States more men than the nation was to lose in the two world wars to follow.

A paradox occurred when a Military Lodge was abandoned because of the war clouds on the horizon. It was a paradox, for during the four years of war over two hundred Military Lodges were to come into being due to the conflict. The Lodge that turned over its records to the Grand Lodge of Missouri prior to the outbreak of the Civil War was Rocky Mountain Lodge No. 205, Utah Territory.

Early in 1858, President Buchanan had ordered troops into Utah Territory to uphold the laws of the United States of America. It would appear that the Mormons had been accused of defying the laws of the District Courts, and the President wanted them enforced. A group of Masons were among the troops that ended up at Camp Floyd, under the command of a general considered by many to be a Mason, Albert Sidney Johnston. The Freemasons there wrote to the Grand Lodge of Missouri requesting a dispensation to organize a Masonic Lodge. The request was granted by the Grand Master, Samuel H. Saunders.

The first Master of the Lodge, John C. Robinson, was to later become a Union general and meet a fellow member, Henry Heth, who became a Confederate general, during the Battle of Gettysburg. Both of them, as well as many of the other members of Rocky Mountain Lodge, were to distinguish themselves numerous times on numberless fields of battle.

The Reverend Thomas Taylor, Grand Orator of the Grand Lodge of Tennessee, in October 1860, was more prophetic than either he or his listeners realized, saying:

> Now is the time when every true Mason should seek to guide the Ship of State with a well-directed hand, and be sure to mingle his lessons of prudence in all he says and does.
>
> I must be permitted to say, that should our nation remain prosperous and happy—should her gates be enlarged and her stakes be strengthened—it will be done by Masonic hands, by principles embodied in our Order. It is my opinion, that when the last political cord shall be broken, there will be one still stronger uniting us together, which is indissoluble.

The Grand Lodge of Arkansas met on November 5, 1860, and the eminent Mason. Albert Pike, presented his credentials as Representative of the Grand Lodge of Kansas near the Grand Lodge of Arkansas saying he knew those present agreed with him in hoping "that the bonds of friendship and good neighborhood may be reknit and strengthened, and anger and recrimination cease, and that all the great moral and social influences of Masonry may be exerted, honestly and unceasingly, for the restoration of harmony, the maintenance of peace." Pike was to become a Confederate general, and while fighting away from his home have his library saved by the Grand Master of Iowa, Thomas Benton, a Union colonel.

The Grand Master of North Carolina, Lewis L. Williams, a month later asked his members to "invoke the Genius of Masonry to endue us with that spirit of brotherly love which will lead us to a discharge of those high duties entrusted to our care with that noble emulation of who can best work and agree."

John Dove told the Grand Chapter of Royal Arch Masons meeting in Richmond, Virginia: "If separation must come, if the Bird of Jove is driven from his splendid eyre, let him not be harrowed with the mortifying reflection, as he flies to some mountain height to die, that his own wing furnished the feather which gave the deadly aim of the envenomed arrow. But rather, when we have exhausted every effort at compromise and reconciliation, and the very last ray of hope is about departing from the patriot stateman's vision in the western horizon, and the black and rayless night of anarchy is about to shroud his mind with gloomy forebodings of the future, ... let us agree to separate amicably, as brothers

The Grand Master of Massachusetts, Dr. Winslow Lewis, remembering a visit he had made to Richmond, wrote a letter to the Grand Master of Virginia, asking: "Is it too late to avert the calamity? Is there nought remains of conservatism to be tried? Have we not an institution which binds us together not only as fellow citizens but as Brothers, and as Brothers can we lacerate those pledges, the foundation of our Faith and Practice?"

Eleven days after South Carolina had seceded from the Union, John R. McDaniel answered: "As a body we can do nothing; but did every individual brother possess, and yield to the dictates of so true and fraternal a heart as beats in your bosom, much could be done as individuals—indeed this state of things would never have existed.... The blood of the Old Confederacy is upon the intriguing and unprincipled politicians, and the wolves in Christian clothing...."

Not all of the politicians were "unprincipled," for John J. Crittenden, in an eleventh hour bid to avert the threatening war, submitted a whole parcel of compromises to the Senate. That parcel was turned over to a Committee of Thirteen. The committee, with the endorsement of Lincoln and his "let there be no compromise" statement, killed what the New York Tribune called "the most considerate and conciliatory" proposal of "our opponents." So the white-haired Mason from Kentucky, backed by two other Masons, the "Little Giant" Douglas and the Southern "fire-eater" Robert Toombs, lost his fight to preserve the Union.

Peace conventions, many of them led by Masons, were unable to halt the struggle. The pleas of Grand Masters, Grand Lodges, and individual Masons for sanity were ignored. And although the vast majority of the people of the country wanted peace, the fanatics, in a last-ditch stand, won; the citizens of the United States lost.

Ironically, the opposing commanders in the first battle of the Civil War were Masons. The Confederate Mason, Pierre G. T. Beauregard, fired into a fort on a ledge made of Vermont granite, manned by troops under the command of Robert Anderson, a member of Mercer Lodge No. 50, Trenton, New Jersey. The war of words had ended—a shooting war had started.

## Freemasonry During the Early Weeks of the Civil War

While Freemasons and Freemasonry teamed with other peace-seeking elements in the United States of America in an endeavor to prevent war, the radicals, both North and South, increased their propaganda. Those who sought war, or at least the separation of the two sections of the country, realized time was running out for them during the early days of 1861. The sentiments of the people were for compromise—not bloodshed.

James Buchanan had waited—and was condemned for inaction. He, like his successor, Abraham Lincoln who also waited, had no other choice. The people, not wanting war, placed them in the same predicament Franklin Roosevelt was to be in eighty years later before Pearl Harbor was bombed. They were in a dilemma! As far as the federal government was concerned, it was necessary for the Confederacy to fire upon the American flag!

Lincoln proved he knew that to be true when he wrote to Gustavus Fox: "You and I both anticipated that the course of the country would be advanced by making the attempt to provision Fort Sumter, even if it should fail, and it is no small consolation now to feel that our anticipation is justified by the result."

The radicals of the North knew their one hope of achieving their end was to force the issue at Fort Sumter. While Lincoln's Cabinet urged him to let Sumter go, the agitators insisted he must strike a vigorous blow if he was to win the Northern states for his administration. The Southern radicals warned Davis to take some strong action or see the Confederate States of America crumble around him.

The die was cast! Fort Sumter was to be provisioned—the American flag was to be fired upon—the fanatics had overruled the vast majority of the citizens of the once united states.

The Commanding officers facing each other at Charleston, South Carolina, were Freemasons. The Confederate commander, Pierre Gustave Toutant Beauregard, is reported to have said early in 1861: "If the [blank] politicians will get out of the way and leave the issues to us Masons, we will settle the difficulty." In that fateful April of 1861 he was forced to ask his former instructor, Robert Anderson, to surrender his fort. Anderson refused. Under orders from the President of the Confederate States, the "battle" at Fort Sumter was started at four-thirty on the morning of April 12th, as the first gray light of dawn appeared on the horizon. Beauregard fired upon the American flag!

Among the Masons in the fort was Peter Hart, a man who had been out of the army for many years. Mrs. Eliza Anderson became alarmed over the talk about Fort Sumter being the focal point in the war of words and decided to help her husband. She searched for Hart, who had been Major Anderson's devoted orderly during the Mexican War. She found him on the New York Police force. He was eager to join the major, so Mrs. Anderson accompanied him to Charleston.

During the bombardment, the high flagstaff on the fort was severed. Hart grabbed a long spar, nailed the American flag to it, and raised it again "while shot and shell were pouring all around him in a hissing shower." Although the American flag was lowered on the fourteenth, the story of that flag, Robert Anderson, and Peter Hart, had not ended. All three were to meet again exactly four years later in exactly the same place. Once more Hart was to attach the same battle-scarred flag to the halyards, then salute as Anderson raised it atop Fort Sumter.

Lincoln immediately called for 75,000 troops to "suppress" the Confederate States "and to cause the laws to be duly executed." That order enraged the South. Among the Masonic governors who refused to comply, were John W. Ellis of North Carolina and Isham G. Harris of Tennessee.

Many Northerners rushed to obey Lincoln's order. Feelings ran high, even among the fair sex. Mrs. Maria Gove, wife of Jesse Gove, a member of Rocky Mountain Lodge, No. 205, wrote to her sister in New Hampshire: "I have hung a flag in my parlour. I never was so proud of my being a Northerner, and I tell all who come in they must salute the Stars and Stripes...." She also felt "it is high time" for those who "glory with the South in their rebellion" to get out of Utah Territory.

James McCallum, Grand Master of Tennessee, sent a letter to every Grand Lodge seeking "for some means of escape from the dire calamity that seems so certainly impending over us as a people." Other Grand Bodies were unsuccessfully looking for a peaceful solution, even though all hope of peace appeared lost.

An example of the harm suffered by Freemasonry over a situation it could not control occurred in Arkansas. For years the Grand Lodge had worked to open a Masonic college. It was finally successful only to have its school, Saint John's College, close its doors eighteen months after classes had commenced. The trustees claimed: "Mr. Lincoln's proclamation of war upon the South came, and there was a call to arms, the larger students, prompted by that ardent and impulsive patriotism ... laid aside their books, deserted the college, and rushed into service, and the president and professors ... followed the boys to the war." No one was left to teach or be taught.

The outbreak of hostilities disrupted the "Representative System" which was then in its infancy. The Grand Masters of each section were hesitant to appoint Representatives of the "other side." John C. Breckinridge, the fourteenth Vice-President of the United States, was "fired" as the Grand Representative of the Grand Lodge of Iowa Near the Grand Lodge of Kentucky. He had a particularly hard row to hoe as he was expelled from the Senate for defending the Confederacy in December 1861; during the same year he was suspended from Good Samaritan Lodge No. 174, Lexington, Kentucky. It was ten years later before he was reinstated.

During the Battle of Manassas, or Bull Run, on July 21st, Colonel W. H. Raynor, of the First Ohio Regiment, and Colonel Benjamin Wood, of New York, were saved because they were Masons. Colonel John B. Slocum and Sullivan Ballou, Rhode Island Masons, were not as fortunate; both were killed during the battle. So was Bernard B. Bee, who gave Jackson the immortal name of "Stonewall." A short time later a Military Lodge was authorized by the Grand Lodge of Virginia in honor of Bee. It held a special communication in his memory the following year on the anniversary of the battle in which he died.

The Union disaster at Manassas caused Lincoln to replace McDowell with a Mason named George B. McClellan. McClellan earned the love and respect of his men during the time he was in command. He was heartily disliked by those who wanted a quick victory at any cost. To some he was a great general and a master strategist; others felt just the opposite.

While McClellan was strengthening the Union forces, the Masonic governor of Missouri, Hamilton R. Gamble, was doing everything possible to save his state for the Union. His efforts proved troublesome for a Confederate general, and Mason, Sterling Price, who was called "Pap" by his men. Federal troops occupied Lexington early in 1861 to keep the Union lifeline to the Missouri River open. In September Price attacked their stronghold—the Masonic college and the bluffs surrounding it. The Confederates, with superior forces won the battle.

During the fighting, the home of Oliver Anderson, a Mason who had moved to Lexington from Kentucky, which was being used as a federal hospital, was captured. Union forces recaptured the house, trapping six Confederates, three of whom were shot, one escaped, one hid in this attic. The other crawled into bed with a federal Mason thereby escaping death.

One of the most unusual legends of the war, as far as Masonry was concerned, took place in Missouri in August 1861. A company of the First Iowa Regiment was guarding a railroad bridge at Mozelle Mills when a group of Confederate guerrillas attacked. The Iowa troops drove the attackers off and chased them to a farm house. The guerrillas set fire to the house, evidently to divert the Federals. But three of the party that set the fire were captured and sentenced to die by a "drum-head court-martial."

One of the guerrillas, a boy with an Irish brogue, pleaded for his life, but his pleas went unheeded. Then, a girl of about eighteen burst upon the scene exclaiming: "Oh soldiers! Oh Holy Mother! gentlemen! for the love of Jesus, do not kill him. He is innocent, he is my brother!" She clasped the boy in her arms, defending him from his executioners. In attempting to break her grasp on her brother, the coat sleeve of one of the Iowans was torn and a Masonic pin was disclosed fastened to his shirt sleeve. She suddenly became calm, and in a confident tone said: "Soldiers, let me make one more effort for my brother."

She turned her back to the young man, and faced the soldiers and gave a sign familiar to all Masons. The Masons in that group were startled; the captain called his officers into a huddle. A few moments later he called out in a loud voice: "Owing to the distress and interference of the young woman, the execution will be postponed until nine o'clock tomorrow morning."

The Masons in the company, it is claimed, met with the girl in the captain's quarters, where they examined her carefully and found that she possessed all of the secrets of a Master Mason. It would appear that her father had been Master of a Lodge in Ireland, but how she had become a "Mason" none of those present could determine. The next morning she and her brother were found missing. They had made their escape although the guard had been doubled during the night.

While both sides were building up their military might, Grand Lodges and Freemasons were still fighting for peace—a peace that would be four years in the future.

**Freemasonry in the Fall of 1861**
There was to be little to be happy about during the early days of the Civil War, but a pleasant note was struck in a Masonic Lodge in Minnesota. A baby boy was born in the hall of Monticello Lodge No. 16!

Samuel Adams, who owned a general merchandise store in Monticello, rented the upstairs portion to the Lodge. On the night of September 15, 1861, he moved Mrs. Adams into the Lodge room. The downstairs quarters were too crowded for the privacy she needed. Soon after the expectant mother was settled in her new quarters, Dr. James W. Mulvey, the Junior Warden of the Lodge, was hurriedly called. He brought into the troubled world Henry Rice Adams, who was destined to have as unusual a Masonic career as was the place of his birth.

Twenty-three years later, Henry Adams was made a Mason in the room in which he was born. In 1903, he became Grand Master of Masons in Minnesota. Twenty-four years from then, he was fatally stricken while attending a communication of Minnesota Lodge No. 224. Thus, a highly successful Masonic life ended as it had started—in a Masonic Lodge

After the battle at the Masonic College in Lexington, Missouri, General Sterling Price moved to Neosho, where he protected Claiborne Jackson and forty-nine members of the Missouri Legislature during their secession meeting in the Masonic hall. The session declared on October 28th "… war exists between Missouri and the Federal government and is incompatible with the continuance of our union." The statement, plus the Ordinance of Secession, was greeted with cannon fire and shouts of joy from Price's men.

There was only one thing wrong with the "Ordinance of Secession" adopted in the Masonic hall in Neosho—the governor and his legislators had been declared "fugitives" before they left the capital. But Richmond recognized it; so did thousands of Missourians; all of which led to many unusual Masonic experiences during the long and bitter struggle.

Kentucky, another border state, had its troubles, also. The Breckinridge family offers an example of how the Masonic members of many families were split over the politics of the day. Robert J. was an eminent Presbyterian minister, and strongly in favor of the Union; his son, William C.P., went into the Confederate army, along with his cousin, John C.; Joseph C., not known to be a Mason another son of Robert's, served in the Union forces.

The scope of war conditions in the state was illustrated in October by the Grand Master of Kentucky, Lewis Landram:

> We have met under circumstances of a peculiar character. Our beloved commonwealth is the theater of civil strife, and where a few months since all was peace and quiet, the stirring drum and deep mouthed cannon now breathe forth their tones of war. It is with no ordinary feelings of sadness that we look upon these empty seats, once filled by brethren from distant parts of our noble State; and, whilst we can but mourn the absence of many of those we have been accustomed to meet, we can but trust, that amid all the vicissitudes of life, they may ever prove faithful to the trusts confided to their care.

R. S. Alden, Grand High Priest of the Grand Chapter of Minnesota, took note of the war, during his address in October. He, like all Masons, was unhappy about the political status of the country. He set forth the goal of the Craft when he stated: "We meddle with no political organizations, have no sectional objects to promote, nor can revolutions, dismemberment of states, or even the overthrow of civil government, and the prevalence of anarchy, sunder these indissoluble ties which bind the hearts of the royal craft in a beautiful and eternal union."

The Grand Master of the District of Columbia, Charles F. Stansbury, on November 5th, claimed: "I hope to die—as I shall try to

live—a Mason; but above and beyond all other hopes, is the heart-
felt aspiration that I may retain to my latest breath, and transmit
unimpaired to my children, that proudest title that humanity can
boast—the title of an American citizen." His Committee on Foreign
Correspondence did not care for a Mason like Albert Pike being
"engaged in the diabolical purpose of arming the fierce and bloodthirsty savages with tomahawk and scalping knife to carry desola-
tion and death to our homes and firesides."

General Albert Pike, who knew the Indians of his area extremely
well, armed three regiments from the Choctow, Chickasaw, Chero-
kee, Creek, and Seminole nations, or tribes. They were to serve in
the Indian Territory, but did fight against Federal troops in the West.
During the Battle of Pea Ridge in March 1862, Pike and his Indians fought. The battle found two Masonic generals opposing each
other; Samuel R. Curtis, for the Union, and Sterling Price, for the
Confederacy. The Indians were charged with scalping and mutilat-
ing the bodies of the Federal troops; charges that gave the Northern
press a field day.

When Albert Pike heard about the charges placed against his
men, he called in his surgeon for his report. The surgeon reported
one Federal body had been scalped, so Pike issued an order
denouncing the act in the strongest possible language. A copy was
sent to Curtis, and it claimed none of the Indians could have been
responsible; the scalping had been done at night in a "quarter of the
field not occupied by the Indian troops under Pike's command."

In California, far away from the scene of war, the effects of the
strife was felt among the Masonic Lodges. In some cases Lodges
were split and new ones formed in an endeavor to keep Masonry
alive and civic feelings outside the walls.

Anti-Southern feelings had been running high in Wisconsin for
some years, causing one Lodge never to request a charter. The Lodge
was Nemadjii of Superior, which had been granted a dispensation
in 1856. Later, the Grand Lodge of Wisconsin received a report that
some of the officers of Nemadjii, being Southern sympathizers, with-

drew their association with the other members. Their withdrawal dealt a death-blow to all hopes of forming a Lodge that would prove successful, so Nemadjii Lodge never became a reality.

During the first three years of the Civil War, six Lodges in Wisconsin were forced to give up their charters because of the number of their officers and members serving in the armed forces. Nineteen new Lodges were chartered during the same time, making that the first boom period in the history of Wisconsin Freemasonry.

Many vexing problems arose in Missouri, a state where there appeared to be as many people for the South as for the North. Among the most perplexing was a situation that took place in Clarksville Lodge No. 17. In April 1861, J.W. Hemphill was reinstalled Master by the Rev. L.R. Downing. During the installation, the Master refused to assent to certain ancient charges, according to a letter sent to the District Deputy Grand Master, and signed by the Junior Warden, Secretary, and Junior Deacon of the Lodge. The Grand Master, William R. Penick, ordered the District Deputy to investigate the charges.

John F. L. Jacoby, also a member of Clarksville Lodge, investigated. He found the Master had assented to all of the charges of installation, but readily admitted he had certain political reservations of his own—those he planned on retaining. He denied the right of the District Deputy to go into them. Jacoby removed the Master from his office, and on November 16th, he took away the charter of the Lodge. A plotter against the government had been present in the Lodge a week earlier, he stated. The "plotter" was a member of the Lodge who had served as an officer with Sterling Price.

The Grand Lodge of Missouri acted. There was no reservation in its statement that "the Grand Lodge and every Grand Officer, as such, are prohibited by all the teachings of our noble institution from any interference in the heart-rending strife now desolating our beloved country." The Grand Lodge was unhappy about the conflicting opinions held by so many of its members, "but as Masons we hope the day will never come when our lodge rooms will be closed against a worthy brother on account alone of such conflicting opinions."

The actions of the District Deputy were repudiated in the strongest terms. "Fraternity must at all times inspire us," the report concluded, then the Grand Lodge adopted a resolution declaring the acts of Jacoby illegal. The charter was restored to Clarksville Lodge No. 17.

Even the Grand Master was taken gently to task for letting "politics" enter his address and actions during the year. It was recommended that the political portions of Penick's speech be omitted from the published Proceedings. The Grand Lodge was "looking alone to the future welfare and prosperity of our noble fraternity." So the "political" portions were omitted.

A thousand miles away, a letter was written from McHenry, Maryland, to the Grand Master of the state. The letter was from J.H. Chase, "Lt. and R. Quartermaster, 3d N.Y. Vols., and P.M. Temple Lodge No. 14, Albany, N.Y." The regiment was "encamped in June last at Camp Hamilton, Va., some two miles from Fortress Monroe, and about a mile from the village of Hampton." The village had been deserted by the people living there shortly before Federal troops arrived.

Chase learned there was a Masonic Temple in Hampton "exposed to the pillage and plunder of the hordes of negroes who congregated there immediately on the departure of the citizens." Fearing for the safety of the contents of the Masonic Lodge, he reported to General Benjamin F. Butler, also a Mason, asked for and received permission to take "a sufficient force, proceed to Hampton and take possession of such property belonging to the Masonic Order, as was thought proper and report to him [Butler]."

A detachment of soldiers, including five Masons, went to the Temple of St. Tarnmany Lodge No. 5, took several articles, including "the Records and Warrents," and returned to their regiment. A short time later, the whole village, including the Lodge, was burned by Confederates so Federal troops could not use it for winter quarters. The articles saved were sent to the Grand Lodge of Maryland, along with the letter, with the request they be returned to the Grand Lodge of Virginia as soon as convenient. Chase feelingly closed his letter with: "we come not to wage war upon an Order expressly founded to inculcate the exercise of Brotherly Love, Relief and Truth."

Shortly after Federal forces entered North Carolina, General Order No. 38, of Butler's department, was issued, containing the same sentiments as expressed by Chase: "... the Government of the United States in its efforts for the preservation of the Union, is not warring upon charitable benevolent organizations." As a result, the Lodge in Newburn was returned to the "quiet possession" of its trustees.

The Grand Master of Alabama, Stephen F. Hale, was unable to be present when his Grand Lodge met on December 2, 1861. He was serving in the Confederate army near Centerville, Virginia. A letter he had written two weeks earlier was read, in which he apologized for being unable to attend to his official duties during his year as Grand Master. He had been busy working for the cause of the Southern States. On July 18, 1862, Hale gave his life for that cause, after he was mortally wounded "in the Great Battle before Richmond." During the annual communication of his Grand Lodge, suitable resolutions were prepared. It was readily agreed that "his brilliant intellect" would be keenly missed in "the bar, the legislature and the congress hall, and the Lodge of which he was at once the member and the ornament."

John R. McDaniel, the Grand Master of Virginia, told his members in December: "We are bound to protect our property, our families and ourselves. Should the Square and Compasses glitter on the breast of an advancing foe, use it as a mark, and bring the invader to the dust. He fights under false colors; he violates the fundamental objects of the Order; he is unworthy of your confidence and protection; he uses the symbols of the Order for mercenary purposes and would prostitute its Holy principles."

Those were harsh words—excusable, perhaps, when a person's family and home are in danger. But McDaniel returned to the principles of Freemasonry by issuing a kind edict: "The battle over, visit the held of carnage and give the most extended scope to your Masonic feelings—administer to the sufferers all the comforts at your command; treat kindly those whom the fortunes of war have thrown in your power, regarding that a fallen and prostrate foe is no longer our enemy; but conquered, he should excite our pity."

The Grand Lodge of Pennsylvania met on St. John the Evangelist's Day, December 27th, and the Grand Master, John Thomson, alluded briefly to what was transpiring in "this once united and happy country." He feared Masonry could not still the storm hovering over the country: "Yet, if Masonry is powerless to heal and unite this bleeding and distracted nation, it is also at the same time powerful to relieve, commiserate with, and succor individual brethren on either side, engaged in this fratricidal strife."

On the same day, the Grand Lodge of the District of Columbia heard an unusual, yet fraternal, letter read. A group of Medical Doctors had opened an office in Washington "for the purpose of embalming and preserving the bodies of such brother Masons, citizens or soldiers who may be so unfortunate as to die or be killed, while at the seat of war and away from their families and friends."

The letter went on to describe the process employed, which was simply: "that of merely injecting fluid which contains no arsenic or other poison, and which instantly arrests decomposition and gradually hardens the body into a marble-like mass." The Doctors offered to preserve the bodies of Masons "free of cost" when they were notified. A person could "immediately appreciate the advantage of having the body of a deceased friend or relative returned to its sacred home free from the taint and ghastly discolor of a decaying corpse." Under their system, a body could go for "months or years without the necessity of immediate burial."

The year 1861 closed and found Freemasonry affected but little by the events which had transpired since the war began. Feelings

were strained in some cases; the work in a few Lodges was interrupted, but the full effects were to be felt in the succeeding years.
The annual communications of all Grand Lodges were held as
scheduled. The legislation passed and the words spoken were, as a
whole, surprisingly tolerant; a situation that was to exist throughout
the long conflict.

On the fields of battle, Masons had proven their patriotism.
They had fought valiantly and well for the side they happened to
represent. They had also proven the teachings of Freemasonry were
more deeply lodged in their hearts than anyone would have sus-
pected months earlier. That would hold true even though the war
was intensified the following year.

## Masons on the Tennessee and Cumberland

"Let us rigidly live up to the requirements of justice, but do not let
us fling away the mantle of charity," said the Grand Lodge Committee on Foreign Correspondence of the Grand Lodge of Vermont,
early in January 1862. Its report had earlier proven that "every
Grand Lodge has acted" during the first months of the Civil War,
"dispassionately, and in an eminent spirit of conservatism."

The same type of committee for Michigan also claimed the
"brotherly tie" had not been forgotten during the "asperities naturally engendered by the lamentable state of facts now existing."
The Grand Master of the state, Horace S. Roberts, although a member of the Union forces, prayed that Masonry would do all it could
to retain the respect of the world. His letter, written at "Annapolis
Junction, Maryland," called for Masonry not to meddle "with questions which do not concern it."

Roberts had offered his services to the governor when Fort Sumter fell. He then raised a company that came to be known as the
"Michigan Huzzars." At the end of the three months term of service,
he helped reorganize it for a three-year term and became its lieutenant colonel. Eight months later, he was commissioned a full colonel and was placed in charge of his regiment. He was in command

when he lost his life during the Second Battle of Bull Run on August 30, 1862. Before entering the battle he told his chaplain, "I trust Michigan will believe that I tried to do my duty." His Masonic Brethren believed it. Although his body was never found, they erected a monument in Elmwood Cemetery in Detroit in his honor.

George McClellan was busy in Washington raising, equipping, and training the greatest army the world had ever seen. Twenty-five miles away, in Manassas, Virginia, the Confederates were trying to do the same. They were to do an excellent job with what they had, but men and supplies were limited. Guns, powder, and bullets were so scarce, the noise for celebrations had to be confined to the beating of drums.

Affairs in the West were no better for the Confederates. Albert Sidney Johnston, considered one of the ablest soldiers of the Confederacy, was forced to maintain a military line extending from the mountains to the Mississippi. Before spring his line was to be penetrated repeatedly.

David G. Farragut, a well-liked naval officer and Mason, was asked to take command of the federal navy. Early in the war, being a Virginian, he had been asked to take charge of the Confederate navy—something that did not exist. He refused, choosing to remain with the government he had served since 1810, when he had entered the service at the age of nine. He accepted the challenge and went on to build a strong naval attacking force from vessels of all types, descriptions, and sizes.

The value of Farragut's navy was firmly established on February 6th when the Tennessee River was turned red with the blood of Americans. Gunboats steamed up the river and captured the poorly located Fort Henry after two hours of bombardment. So hopeless had been the battle, General Tilghman had kept it going only long enough to enable his garrison to escape to Fort Donelson, twelve miles away.

When Admiral Walke entered the fort, he was appalled at the devastation. The cheers of his men were sharply cut-off by the sight of the blood of the dead and wounded "intermingled with the earth and their implements of war."

Among the Masons who took part in the capture of Fort Henry was William D. Porter, commander of the Essex. He, along with John A. Logan and Edwin S. McCook, also Masons, was to go on to the more heavily fortified and manned Fort Donelson. There they were to fight with, and against, dozens of other Masons. One of them was the now world-famous General Lewis (Lew) Wallace.

Wallace, one of Grant's divisional commanders, was contemplating writing a book during the time he was fighting. A chance meeting years later with Robert G. Ingersoll, a man who had earned the title of "The Great Agnostic," was what determined him to put "Christ into the story." He "resolved to fill the book with accessory incidents which should tend to give the reader an idea of the moral, social and political condition of the world at that period; out of which shrewd minds might evolve one of the most powerful arguments for the divinity of Christ."

All movie-goers know the results of Wallace's book, Ben Hur. After it had been read by thousands of people throughout the years, it was made into a picture that received as much acclaim as Gone With the Wind, a story about the Civil War.

The battle for Fort Donelson was costly for both the North and the South. Grant decided to take it by force; the day of the siege had not then arrived. The Confederates hoped for reinforcements. When they did not arrive, the generals in the fort determined to capitulate rather than subject their men to a needless massacre. Simon B. Buckner, a Mason, was left to receive the "unconditional surrenders terms that made a relatively unknown Union general famous.

Lew Wallace wrote about another Mason in the fort: "Colonel [Nathan B.] Forrest was present at the council, and when the final resolution was taken, he promptly announced that he neither could nor would surrender his command. The bold trooper had no Qualms upon the subject. He assembled his arms all as hardy as himself, and ... moved out and plunged into a slough formed from the river. An icy crust covered its surface, the wind blew fiercely, and the darkness was unrelieved by a star.... He was next heard of at Nashville."

The surrender of Fort Donelson on February 16th opened the Tennessee River to Farragut's fleet; Johnston's left was cut from his center; and the South lost one-third of its coal supply plus large amounts of iron ore. The fort's new commander was also a Mason, Stephen A. Hurlbut, who was to be promoted to major general for meritorious conduct at Shiloh.

Early in February, Pierre G.T. Beauregard stopped at Nashville on his way to join Albert S. Johnston. While in the city he made public addresses in the Masonic auditorium. He joined with Father Abram Ryan in encouraging the Tennesseans not to give up hope for the cause they considered just.

On George Washington's Birthday the permanent Confederate government was inaugerated in Richmond, Virginia. The ceremonies took place at the foot of the equestrian statue of Washington, the cornerstone of which had been laid by the Grand Lodge of Virginia twelve years earlier. The same Grand Lodge had dedicated it just four years before President Jefferson Davis received the oath of office in the midst of a large group of citizens which included the clergy, members of the press, members of his cabinet, city and state officials, and "the Masons and other benevolent societies."

Davis became the first and last President of a country that was to be recognized by no political entity. The government of the United States never dealt with it except militarily. The European countries looked with favor on the Confederacy until after the fall of Donelson. The Confederate commissioners, under their Secretary of State, Robert Toombs, a Mason, continued doing what little they could toward obtaining recognition—to no avail.

The Grand Master of South Carolina, David Ramsey, sent a lengthy letter to the members of his Jurisdiction. He pleaded with them to remember their Masonic obligations and to help their Brother Masons "in darkness or light; in health and sickness; in wealth or want; in peril or safety; in prison, escape or freedom; in charity or evil-mindedness; armed or unarmed; friend or seeming foe."

Another Mason, John Hunt Morgan, raided the suburbs of Nashville on the day the Battle of Pea Ridge ended. Morgan had begun the raids that were to make him famous in the South and feared in the North. He went on to destroy millions of dollars worth of federal military stores, capture and burn dozens of railroad trains, tear up miles of track, burn scores of bridges, and continually harrass Northern officers until his death on September 4, 1864, near Greeneville, Tennessee.

On the same day, March 8, 1862, a cumbersome raft-like ship, called the Virginia, steamed up Hampton Roads on a trial run. Its commander sent the workmen ashore after he had decided to turn the trip away from a routine cruise and attack the federal vessels lying at anchor across the channel. She rammed the Cumberland, then headed for the Congress, which struck her colors an hour after the battle had started. Aboard the Congress was Joseph B. Smith, a member of National Lodge No. 12, District of Columbia. When his father, a rear admiral, heard of the ship's surrender, he exclaimed, "Then Joe is dead!" He was.

The consternation caused in Washington by the success of the Confederate iron-clad, was eased the next day when a Mason commanding a federal iron-clad met and battled the Virginia. John L. Worden fought the Confederate ship for over six hours and revolutionized naval warfare for all time. The battle between the Monitor and Virginia (better known as the Merrimac) ended in a draw, but it saved the blockade. It also made it safe for George McClellan to continue with his plans to destroy the Confederate capital in Richmond.

Prior to the Battle of Shiloh, or Pittsburg Landing, Lieutenant-Colonel Murray, in command of the "3d Ohio Cavalry," took possession of Lawrenceburgh, Tennessee. Murray ordered his men to search all the houses, arrest all the men, and confiscate all arms; no woman or child was to be harmed or insulted. He found some of his men looting the Masonic Hall and ordered them to return everything they had taken. An act that later saved his life.

During the Battle of Shiloh, a Confederate surgeon was captured by the "3d Ohio Cavalry." The surgeon asked Murray if he was not the officer who had saved the Masonic Lodge from being ransacked and was informed he was. The doctor then told him it was that fact alone that saved him from an ambush. He had been recognized by a Mason who had witnessed his generous act at Lawrenceburgh. The Southerners had been ordered to lower their guns and let him pass in safety.

Captain G.A. Strong, an officer in one of the Michigan regiments, found a wounded captain of a company of Texas Rangers. As Strong approached the wounded man, he saw a Masonic emblem on his coat, and ordered the Texan carried to a tent where he bound up his wounds as carefully as he could. The Union soldier could not leave a Brother "Mason, though a rebel, and in arms against his government ... with such a talisman of peace intervening between them."

Early in the Battle of Shiloh, the shot that has been called the most fateful of the war was fired. That missile severed an artery in the leg of Albert Sidney Johnston. Because he was so intent on pressing the battle, he bled to death in the saddle.

From Washington to Shiloh; from Maine to California; from the North and the South, East and West, the brotherhood of Americans gleamed through the light of Masonry. Many men were to attest before the war ended, Freemasonry held the hearts of men together although guns were keeping them apart.

### Masonry in the Spring of 1862

Lincoln had assumed control of much of the Northern railroad system on the day he declared a state of rebellion existed. Early in 1862, Daniel C. McCallum, a member of Valley Lodge No. 109, New York, was appointed military director and superintendent of railroads for the Federal government. The organization he established helped pave the way for the ultimate victory for Union forces.

In an attempt to disrupt the Confederate railroad between Atlanta and Chattanooga, a group of Ohio soldiers, led by a civilian spy named James J. Andrews, captured a train call the General. The tenacity of the conductor of the General, William A. Fuller, foiled the bridge-burning plans of the raiders. They were all captured within a week after the train had been stolen from Big Shanty, Georgia.

Among the raiders was Marion A. Ross, of whom William Pittenger, another member of the "train stealers," wrote: "Ross was a Freemason, and some of the members of the fraternity visited him, and gave him assurances of friendship, together with some small sums of money, which he generously used to procure us all a little greatly-needed addition to our food."

Ross, along with Andrews and six other raiders, was executed. The others were never brought to trial. At their first opportunity they attempted to escape by attacking their guard in "broad daylight." All but six were successful, and those six who were recaptured were exchanged in March 1863. All of the survivors of the expedition were the first to receive the newly created Congressional Medal of Honor. The other soldiers were awarded the medal posthumously, except for one whose relatives could not be located.

After five days of bombarding Forts Jackson and St. Phillip at the mouth of the Mississippi, Flag Officer David G. Farragut ordered the vessels under his command to heave up their anchors. At two o'clock on the morning of April 24th the ships set sail; an hour later they were under fire by Confederate shore batteries, gunboats, and rams. "In one hour and ten minutes after the vessels of the fleet had weighed anchor, the affair was virtually over." The boldness of Farragut's feat was something the Southern forces had not expected, and he went on to take New Orleans. The way was paved for a Mason named Benjamin Butler to become the most unpopular man in that city.

Butler issued his "General Orders 28" on May 15th stating any woman who insulted his soldiers would "be regarded and held liable to be treated as a woman about town plying her avocation." The order created so much controversy he had to defend it by claiming the real ladies of New Orleans did not interfere with his troops; the prostitutes, and would be "street walkers" would spit in his soldiers' faces, call them "monkeys" and other terms not too lady-like.

Throughout the war Butler remained a controversial figure. To some he was cruel, a despot and everything unsavory; to others he was an efficient administrator and general. The controversy did not end with the war; it continued into the reconstruction period. He was to help lead the fight to impeach Andrew Johnson; help pass bills submitted by the "Radical" Republicans to keep the South subjugated; all of which was to make the term "Republican" a nasty word in the vocabulary of the former Confederacy for the next one hundred years, and "Southerner" just as vile to the Northern press and politicians.

An episode occurred between the Mason Farragut and Winfield Schley who was to become a member of Benjamin B. French Lodge, No. 15, District of Columbia. Soon after the commander had sent Schley up the Mississippi in the little gunboat Winona to do some reconnaissance, he heard heavy gun fire. He signalled Schley to cease firing and return, but the sound of shots continued. After the Winona had returned, its commanding officer was ordered aboard the flagship. When he had arrived, Farragut lashed him verbally for disobeying his command. Then he turned to his subordinate and said, "Now, young man, come into the cabin with me, I have something more to say."

Inside the cabin, Farragut produced two glasses, a bottle of sherry, and the statement: "Young man, if I commanded a gunboat and got into a mixup with the enemy, and was getting the better of him, I'll be damned if I'd see a signal, either!"

While McClellan was marching up the Peninsula toward the capital of the Confederate States of America, the Grand Lodge of

Connecticut met. The Grand Master, Alvan P. Hyde, took note of what was transpiring in the South: "This terrible civil war is still raging, desolating our country, and causing Brothers of different jurisdictions to meet each other in battle array."

Ariel Ballou, Grand Master of Rhode Island, told his Grand Lodge he did not care for the proposal for a Masonic convention to try to pour oil on the troubled waters of the country. He felt any convention of Masons would "place our order in a false position, and render it open to the charge of being a selfish and political institution of which our enemies would not be slow to avail themselves."

General George Stoneman, a Mason, made a balloon ascension from Gaines' Mill on May 21st. He reached the unheard of altitude of 500 feet and had a complete view of Richmond "with the aid of a glass."

Two days later, the First Maryland, commanded by John R. Kenly, a Mason, was attacked at Front Royal, Virginia, by Jackson's forces. Nathaniel P. Banks, another Mason, was informed that the Confederates planned to encircle and destroy his army, so he retreated through Winchester into Maryland.

Nathan B. Forrest was in Mississippi on the same day, May 23rd, harassing the Federals. He took time out to answer a letter he had received from a member of his Lodge, Angerona, No. 168, Memphis, Tennessee. Forrest proved the fighting men were not always careful of their phrasing or language when he wrote: "I had a small brush with the Enemy on yesterday I suceded in gaining their rear and got in to thir entrenchments 8 miles from hamburg and 5 behind farmington and Burned a portion of thir camp at that place they wair not looking for me I taken them by Surprise they run like Suns of Biches I captured the Rev Dr Warin from Illanois and one fin Sorel Stud...."

The Grand Secretary of Missouri Anthony O'Sullivan, was particularly thankful for many of the Masons in the Union army who, while in St. Louis, "discharged their duties as soldiers, [but] never forgot their covenants as Masons." He later took to task a writer from another grand jurisdiction who had written phrases O'Sullivan considered un-Masonic.

The Masonic governor of Pennsylvania, Andrew G. Curtin, issued an order stopping the enlistment of three months' volunteers. He congratulated the people because "the emergency which seemed to require them" had passed. Two months later he issued a proclamation calling for more troops. He then instituted a system of caring for the children of men killed during the war, and thereafter became known as "the soldiers' friend."

Beauregard evacuated Corinth, Mississippi, on May 30th, leaving the city to the forces of Halleck. The following day, McClellan's forces crossed a winding, swampy stream called the Chickahominy, and arrived in sight of the church spires of Richmond. Johnston, expecting McClellan to be reinforced by McDowell, which was never to happen because of Lincoln's perpetual fear of an invasion of Washington, attacked the Federal forces near Seven Pines and Fair Oaks Station.

Late in the afternoon of May 31st Johnston was severely wounded. At two o'clock on June 1st, General R.E. Lee was given command of the Army of Northern Virginia. Among the generals fighting with Jackson in the Shenandoah Valley was Turner Ashby, "a man of striking personal appearance, about five feet ten inches tall, with a well-proportioned figure, graceful and compact, black eyes, black hair, and a flowing black beard.... He seemed to have been left over by the Knights of the Golden Horseshoe."

As the sun set in the west on June 6th, covering the Blue Ridge Mountains with a deeper blue, one that was almost purple. Turner Ashby. the daring Confederate general and a well-liked Mason, lost his life. He was shot two days before the Battle of Cross Keys when he endeavored to drive off a Federal advance party.

Ashby's body was buried in the cemetery at the University of Virginia; four years later it was "disinterred by the Faculty and Students ... to be taken to Winchester, Virginia, where it was to find its final rest in the Stonewall Cemetery, October 25, 1866." During the reinterment, "the Masonic Fraternity, representing 15 Lodges, and numbering 300 members," preceded the hearse to the grave. There Masonic services were held with ten thousand people looking on. The master of Winchester Hiram Lodge No. 21, William R. Denny, conducted the Masonic funeral which was concluded by Rev. James B. Avirett, a Mason who was also chaplain of the "Ashby Brigade."

A verse from the poem entitled *Ashby*, would be suitable for many a Mason before the bitter strife had ended:

> Earth, that all too soon hath bound him,
>    Gently wrap his clay,
> Linger lovingly around him,
>    Light of dying day,
> Softly, the summer showers,
> Birds and bees among the flowers
>    Make the gloom seem gay.

An episode of a different nature occurred after a battle at James Island, South Carolina. Major Sissons of the 3rd Rhode Island, bearing a flag of truce, and accompanied by three officers, all of them Masons, approached a group of Confederates. The Major remarked to the Southern officer who approached: "I suppose by the tools you carry I have the honor of meeting a Craftsman, as well as an enemy in war?"

The Confederate officer replied: "You do, and I am happy to meet you as such." He then sent for some of his fellow Masons. They "cracked a bottle of wine" and drank to "the health of the Craftsmen, whether in peace or in war."

The Grand Master of New York, Finlay M. King, took the Confederacy to task. He did not think the South should have left the Union just because Abraham Lincoln had been elected. "He is not of my choice any more than he is of yours.... I did all I could, in my capacity as a citizen, to prevent his election … but he was elected! … [He] is the President of the United States, and I bow with all deference and due solemnity, as all good Masons ought to bow, to the majesty and power and irrevocable decrees of those authorities. "

Only 45 Lodges were represented when the Grand Lodge of Texas met on June 9, 1862. Grand Master George W. Van Vleck graphically described the conditions that existed: "Our once prosperous and happy country has almost become desolate War, with all its trials, suffering and carnage, sweeps over our loved land."

The Grand Lodge of Wisconsin heard the Committee on Foreign Correspondence say on the following day: "When we pronounce the sentence of ex-communication against our brethren, and undertake to place them beyond the pale of recognition for other than purely Masonic reasons, we expose ourselves to like indignities at the hands of others, and jeopardise the prosperity, if not the very existence of our institutions."

In the meantime, George B. McClellan and his Army of the Potomac, was knocking at the gates of Richmond. The North prayed for his success, so bloodshed would cease; families would be reunited; and Masons could meet once again about the altars of their Mother Lodges.

**Masonic Rites for the Enemy**
The prayers of the North and the South for a quick peace were not answered as the Mason, George B. McClellan attempted to take Richmond in the early months of the war. Many factors contributed to the successful Confederate defense of the capital. Not the least of which was the fear in Washington of the capture of the Federal capital in a Southern counter-move.

McClellan was bombarded with false information about the superior strength of his enemy by Allan Pinkerton's intelligence squad. A master strategist named R. E. Lee, commander of the Army of Northern Virginia, secured accurate information about the Northern forces. He sent J.E.B. Stuart, the "eyes of the Southern

Army," clear around the entire Federal army before the outbreak of the Seven Days Battle.

The London Times called the war a scandal to humanity, the London Herald "declared the Union a nuisance among nations." A war correspondent for the Cincinnati Commercial reported, on July 2, 1862, at the close of the Seven Days Battle: "The soil of Virginia is now sacred. It is bathed with the reddest blood of this broad land. Every rood of it from Upper Chickahominy to the base of Malvern Hill, is crimsoned with the blood of your brave brethren." The blood of dozens of Masons, North and South, helped deepen the natural red of the clay of the Old Dominion.

On July 9th the first reports of the raids in Kentucky by the Confederate General, and Mason, John Hunt Morgan reached the Northern newspapers. On the same day the Grand Master of Canada, T. Douglas Harrington, took note of what was transpiring across the border. "It is our duty as fellowmen, and our privilege as brethren, to pray and hope for peace," he told his members.

Daniel Butterfield, a member of Metropolitan Lodge No. 273, New York City, was a businessman turned soldier. He did not appreciate the way the bugle calls were causing his regiment no end of confusion, so he decided to do something about it. At Harrison's Landing one night in July, 1862, he composed a new call because the final one of the day, "Extinguish Lights," sounded "too formal." His composition became the now famous "Taps." Its popularity was not confined to the Union forces; it also became a welcome sound in the Confederate camps.

General Nathaniel P. Banks, a member of Monitor Lodge, Massachusetts, was highly commended by General Pope for his action against "Stonewall" Jackson at Cedar Mountain on August 9th. Later in the month the second battle of Manassas, or Bull Run, was fought. Among the men left behind after the retreat of Pope's army were three members of the Tenth Regiment New York Volunteers. The men, Captains Robert A. Dimmick and Thomas D. Mosscrop, and Corporal Edward A. Dubey, were severely wounded. For two days their cries for help went unheeded. Then Captain Hugh Barr of the 5th Regiment of Virginia Riflemen stumbled upon the Federal soldiers. While aiding them he noticed a Masonic emblem on the shirt of Mosscrop. From that moment on the Confederate soldier and his companions redoubled their efforts to assist the Union troopers.

Nineteen years later the three New York Masons recorded for posterity the kind act of the Virginia Mason who, regarding a fallen foe as a friend in need, did all in his power to successfully save their lives.

John Edwin Mason, a war correspondent who was a Knight Templar, wrote about the Battle of South Mountain and of a Mason who fell mortally wounded at twilight: "When night had drawn around her sable mantle, and the roar of battle ceased, and all was still save the groans and low moaning of the wounded and dying lying on the field, two Generals again embraced each other; they were Brig. Gen. Samuel D. Sturgis and our dying hero, Maj. Gen. Jesse L. Reno. They were classmates at West Point, but there was something stronger than early friendship that bound them together. It was Freemasonry."

The Correspondent went on to tell of a Confederate officer whose life he had saved. When the Southerner asked him why he had helped him, the writer replied: "Because you are a Freemason—yes, a Royal Arch Mason."

"But," said the Confederate, "I have been fighting against you, and all such as you for a year." Mason told him to "go and sin no more." As the Surgeon walked up to them the South Carolinian promised, "I will never cease to love the flag I honored in boyhood, until we three, or three such as we, meet together in heaven."

During the Battle of Antietam a soldier handed Colonel Edward E. Cross, a member of North Star Lodge No. 8, New Hampshire, a slip of paper on which a sign had been crudely made with blood. The colonel sent for several Masons in the company and in a short time Lieutenant Edon of the Alabama volunteers was carried to the hospital of the 5th New Hampshire. Before the battle ended the

stable turned into a hospital contained ten Federal and two Confederate Masons. For several days they were cared for by Surgeon
William Child and Chaplain Milo M. Ransom, both Masons from
the Granite State.

On November 3, 1862 the Grand Lodge of Colorado had not
been charitable about an organization within Masonry called "The
Conservator's Association." It was termed a corrupt organization and
the Grand Lodge adopted this resolution: "Hereafter no Grand Officer, and no officer of any subordinate Lodge, shall be installed until
he shall have made a solemn pledge, in open Lodge, that on his
honor as a Mason he repudiates and condemns the said association."
Fires that had been smoldering broke into raging flames to cause a
division in the ranks of Freemasonry more severe than the war.

Robert Morris, a Past Grand Master of Kentucky, who had short-
ened his given name to "Rob" to keep him from being confused
with another man, was the head of the association. Whether or not
it was good for Masonry was debated all through its existence. From
the day it was born June 24, 1860, until it was dissolved on June
24, 1865, it plagued almost every Grand Lodge in America. Some
defended it, but far more denounced it—and its "Chief Conservator" Rob Morris. Soon after its demise all was forgiven and today
Morris is remembered as the "Poet Laureate of Freemasonry," and as
the author of a ritual and founder of the Order of the Eastern Star.

Monitor Lodge, U.D. was granted permission to organize
because of the Conservators. Several Nebraska Masons requested
a dispensation for a Lodge from their Grand Master, G.H. Wheeler,
because "the Grand Lodge of Missouri has passed resolutions
requiring all who visit their lodges to take an extra oath, which in
our opinion does not in the least appertain to Masonry." During its
duration from July 20, 1863 to June 21, 1866, the Lodge was an
asset to the Fraternity.

"This day will long be remembered by many as the day of the
'Great Ozaukee Draft Riot,' " claim the minutes of Ozaukee Lodge
No. 17, Port Washington, Wisconsin, for November 10, 1862.

They might well have stated, "This day will long be remembered as the day Freemasonry was blamed for the draft." That is what happened. The Lodge room was almost destroyed by a mob who felt Masonry was "the cause of the draft." The destroyers were so violent troops finally had to quell the riot in the county, for the violence did not stop at the Lodge; the crowd "turned around and wreaked vengeance upon several eminent citizens," each of whom was a Mason.

Less than a year later what has been described as the greatest riot in American history broke out in New York City because of the draft. Among the men who were finally successful in halting it was William T. Coleman, a Californian. Shortly after order had been restored he was made a Mason in Holland Lodge No. 8, New York.

Both the North and the South had trouble with draftees and "substitutes." They deserted both armies in wholesale lots. General Lee wrote President Davis: "Nothing will remedy this great evil which so much endangers our cause except rigid enforcement of the death penalty in future cases of conviction."

When the Grand Lodge of Virginia met in December Grand Master Lewis B. Williams told his members: "Since the last meeting of this Grand Body, seven Dispensations or Warrents have been granted for Military or Travelling Lodges." He was perturbed because Virginia had received Proceedings from only Confederate states. The Grand Lodge of Pennsylvania had received them from states adhering to the Union. Both felt the ties of Masonry should not be broken because of the war. But it was the fault of the split in the postal service between the two countries that kept the periodicals from being delivered. Masonry was not at fault.

Many of the communications for the South had to be carried by blockade-runners under difficult and dangerous conditions. Even Biblical publications were brought in by that means by men like Dr. Moses D. Hoge, a Presbyterian Minister in Richmond, Virginia. Dr. Hoge was not a Mason during the Civil War, but because of his love for the organization he was made a Mason on his death-bed.

On November 22, 1898, Dove Lodge No. 51, with the assistance of R.T.W. Duke, Jr., the Grand Master of Virginia, fulfilled the life-long desire of the Reverend, "dispensing with such portions of the ceremony as ... the physical condition of the candidate required."

John B. Magruder, an Entered Apprentice of San Diego Lodge No. 35, California, took over as commander of the Confederate forces in Texas. He decided to open the port at Galveston to Southern trade, and on the night of January 1, 1863, he attacked by land and sea. The Confederates were successful in capturing the port city.

During the engagement Captain I.W. Wainwright of the Harriet Lane was killed. Harmony Lodge No. 6 of Galveston was called into a "Lodge of Emergency to bury the dead" on the following day. P.C. Tucker, the Master of the Lodge and who was on the staff of General Magruder, answered the pleas of the Federal Masons who had been captured. They "asked nothing for themselves as Masons, but in behalf of their late Commander and brother," they requested a Masonic funeral. "Appreciating the spirit and force of Masonic ties" and determining that it would not "conflict with their duties as patriotic citizens to respond to calls of mercy by a prostrate political foe, or to administer the last rites of the Order to the remains of a Mason of moral worth, although yesterday they met as an armed enemy in mortal combat in which the deceased parted with his life," the Lodge approved the action of the Master.

Issac Van Wagoner, on January 21, 1863, told the members of the Grand Lodge of New Jersey: "Numerous instances are on record of the benignant influences that the teachings of Masonry have produced on the minds of its votaries. The heart-stirring revulsion of bitter and deadly feeling, caused by the utterance of the talismanic words, 'I am a Mason,' has saved many a gallant brother's life, relieved his sufferings when wounded, ministered to his wants when needed, and alleviated the miseries of his captivity."

Grand High Priest George H. Thatcher of the Grand Chapter of New York during the convocation of February 3rd, explained why the uninitiated are amazed at the power of Masonry: "Those whose hearts have not been touched by … the eternal fire that falls from heaven upon the mystic altar, know nothing of the sublime faith with which the true mason gazes upon the turbulence of the outer world, and that, too, when he is himself an actual participant in its conflicts. Nor can they understand why it is that, in the hour of general peril, when the very foundations of society seem to be breaking up, an institution, composed of men of different political and religious sentiments, of different associations and positions, preserves within itself such perfect accord, and holds its members together with such strong bonds of unity and friendship."

Grant, on his way to join in the siege of Vicksburg, passed through a railroad center in Mississippi. Stephen H. Johnson, the Grand High Priest, did not appreciate the destruction caused by Grant's men in Jackson. But near West Point a Mason's home was saved from being burned when Federal troops discovered a Masonic apron "of curious workmanship and material that had been in the Brame family since 1676."

Grand Master John B. Fravel of Indiana informed his members on May 23rd he had refused to let a Lodge expel one of its members because he had joined the Confederate army. A committee claimed he should have said: "Expel him, and expel him quickly; and should you ever catch him engaged in his unholy purposes, treat him just as you would the assassin who, in the dead hour of night would with stealth enter your bedchamber, and there, while carrying out his purposes of robbery, plunge the dagger to the heart of the wife reposing on your bosom." But the Grand Lodge chose to side with the more moderate view of its head.

The Sixth Michigan Infantry was stationed at Manchac Pass, Louisiana, during the month of May, 1863. Its commanding officer was Colonel Thomas Scott Clark, a member of Eureka Lodge No. 107, Monroe, Michigan. Clark sent a detachment of troops to Ponchatoula to burn a bridge near the town. The assignment was carried out successfully. But among the plunder brought back to the

Pass were the silver jewels of Livingston Lodge No. 60. The commander ordered them returned immediately under a flag of truce.

The kindness of the Federal Mason has been remembered throughout the years. It became an important part of the Centennial celebration of Livingston Lodge (now located in Hammond, Louisiana) in May, 1959.

Many similar acts took place during the war and for a hundred years after it was over. The love shown by Masons during and after the conflict, not only for members of the Craft, but for all human beings, was all that stood between a successful re-union and disaster.

## Brotherhood in Practice

"It is of inestimable benefit to both parties in the present civil war, that our Masonic relations should still continue in the same healthful condition as at present. I may go still further, and say that every honorable means should be used which would have a tendency to strengthen the fraternal bond between the Masons of the North and those of the South." So spoke the Grand Master of New York, John J. Crane, on June 2, 1863.

On the same day the Grand Lodge of Iowa met with its Grand Master absent. Thomas H. Benton was a colonel in the army of the United States. When he occupied Little Rock, Arkansas, two months later he placed a guard about the home of the Confederate General Albert Pike to save it from being looted and burned.

When Grand Master Samuel Mathers of Texas addressed his Grand Lodge on June 8th, only forty-nine Lodges were represented. He recited a verse of poetry to illustrate how happy he would be when peace reigned once again;

> "All hail to the morning that bids us rejoice
>     The Cap Stone completed, exalt high each voice,
> The Temple is finished, our labors are o'er,
>     And War with its horrors shall hail us no more."

The citizens of St. Francisville, Louisiana, were amazed when they saw a small boat from the USS Albatross approaching the shore under a flag of truce. The guns of that ship had been firing into the town at will. They were even more surprised later to witness Northern and Southern men dressed in Masonic regalia escort the body of the commander of the gunboat to the cemetery of Grace Episcopal Church—the church and cemetery which were pock-marked with exploded shells from the guns of the deceased.

Under a brilliant Southern sun on June 13, 1863, the ancient funeral rites of Masonry were held for Lt. Comdr. John E. Hart, a member of St. George's Lodge No. 6, New York. The acting Master was William W. Leake, Senior Warden of Feliciana Lodge No. 31, Louisiana. He was also a captain in the Confederate army. When informed of the request for a Masonic funeral for his enemy, Leake state: "As a Mason I know it be my duty to accord Masonic burial to the remains of a Brother Mason, without taking into account the nature of his relations in the outer world."

The war stood still in that part of the world while the magic rays of the brotherhood of Freemasonry flashed in all their brilliance through the dark clouds of bitterness to illuminate all those around. The rays continued to spread warmth; ninety-three years later the Grand Lodge of Louisiana placed a permanent marker over Hart's grave with the beautiful phrase: "This monument is dedicated in loving tribute to the universality of Freemasonry."

Lee's Army of Northern Virginia moved into the North during the latter part of June, and on the first day of July General Henry Heth, the last Senior Warden of Rocky Mountain Lodge No. 205, leading the Confederate advance met the lead forces of General Meade and pushed them back through the streets of Gettysburg. The Federal troops were rallied by General Winfield S. Hancock, a member of Charity Lodge No. 190, Pennsylvania, on the heights near Evergreen Cemetery.

The fighting raged furiously for three days and culminated in an infantry charge the likes of which the world had never seen. Three

Confederate generals who were Virginia Masons played an important role in the charge up Cemetery Ridge: George E. Pickett of Petersburg No. 15, Lewis A. Armistead of Alexandria Washington Lodge No. 22, and James L. Kemper, a Past Master of Linn Banks Lodge No. 126. Through a hail of death they and their thousands of men charged to die or straggle back. The Union lines held. The three day battle was over.

General Armistead reached the top only to fall mortally wounded. His friend, General Hancock, sent another Mason, Colonel (later General) Henry H. Bingham, to his assistance. But during the nigh Armistead died.

Lieutenant Stephen F. Brown of Seventy-Six Lodge No. 14, Vermont, fought throughout Pickett's Charge with a small camp hatchet. His side arms had been taken from him when General George J. Stannard, a member of Franklin Lodge No. 4, Vermont, ordered him placed under arrest. Brown had left his regiment during a forced march to the battlefield to fill several canteens with water for his fainting men. He had violated the general's order not to break ranks for any reason. When they reached Gettysburg the lieutenant was released to fight and the hatchet was the only weapon readily available.

On the day the crippled Army of Northern Virginia headed back toward the swollen Potomac River, this letter was written:

Hd. qrs 37th Ills
Below Vicksburg, Miss
July 4th 1863

Dear Mother

Vicksburg surrendered at 10 o'c this A.M. Glory, Glory, Glory! This is the beginning of the end. All is well. All are well.

Will is doing finely has not been touched. My arm is doing well. Not a man of Co "K" 37th Ills—is touched. Glory for the Stars & Stripes, & for old U.S. Grant.

*Charles*

P.S. Although constantly under the hottest fire, doing more than a fair proportion of work, & always in the front, but one (1) man of the entire rgt. has been wounded, he but slightly.

*Charles*

The author of the letter was Colonel (later General) John Charles Black (maternal grandfather of John Black Vrooman, Editor of the Philalethes), and a member of Olive Branch Lodge No. 38, Illinois. He had enlisted when Sumter fell and fought in the part of Virginia now known as West Virginia on July 11, 1861. During the Battle of Pea Ridge he was severely wounded. He fought in the Battle of Prairie Grove on December 7, 1862, and for his bravery he was awarded the Congressional Medal of Honor. Although he was once more severely wounded, he recovered to continue fighting until the war had ended.

T. Douglas Harrington, Grand Master of the Grand Lodge of Canada, told his members he had been invited to attend a national Masonic convention in New York. He had declined the invitation because his "attendance might have been looked upon as an unauthorized interference in a domestic quarrel with which Canada has nothing to do; and—secondly, because no Southern Brethren could have an opportunity of giving an expression to their feelings."

General John Hunt Morgan, a member of Daviess Lodge No. 22, Kentucky, kept the hopes of the South alive after the disasters at Gettysburg and Vicksburg. But not for long, for on July 26th he and many of his men were captured in Ohio. Morgan and sixty-nine of his officers and men were sent to the state penitentiary at Columbus. While there, a master Confederate spy named Thomas H. Hines, who had resigned from the staff of the Masonic University at LaGrange, Kentucky, at the outbreak of the war, planned a means of escape. For over twenty days they dug a tunnel and on the night of November 27th Morgan, Hines, and four others managed to leave their prison behind.

The others captured with Morgan were sent to Johnson's Island, situated at the mouth of Sandusky Bay, overlooking Lake Erie.

Among the Masons in the group was Major James Wilson. He reported the Masons were well treated while there; they had their own "Masonic mess"; every two weeks a Lodge meeting was held; they never knew what it was to be hungry, perhaps because the officer of the prison was also a Mason.

In the early 1900's the United Daughters of the Confederacy asked several Grand Lodges to contribute money to save from "desecration the Confederate grave-yard at Johnson's Island, Ohio, where lie 206 brave American soldiers in sadly neglected graves. " It was estimated that one hundred fifty-two of that number had been members of the Craft.

Mrs. Marie Merval was heartily thanked by the Masonic Monthly, a Massachusetts publication, for the work she and other "Union-loving ladies" of New Orleans did for Northern Masons. "She was the wife of a Mason whose sympathies were with the South, though he was not of the number of venomous rebels who defied and ill-treated Union soldiers in the streets."

Guerrillas under the command of Quantrell ransacked the buildings and stripped the people of their valuables at Lawrence, Kansas, on August 21st. Jacob Saqui told the Grand Lodge of Kansas in October the invaders made the village "a ruin, red with the blood of her unoffending citizens; and among the victims were a number of our brothers and fellows." He had requested the Lodges in Kansas to send aid to Lawrence. They responded whole-heartedly, even though many in the southern portion of the state had suffered in the same manner.

Union Lodge No. 7 was born because of a conflict of opinions among the members of Denver Lodge No. 5. Northern and Southern sympathizers appeared to be evenly divided, so Denver Lodge agreed to recommend to the Grand Lodge of Colorado that a charter be granted to the petitioners of Union Lodge. The charter was granted—and not a single member of the older Lodge demitted to join the new one. They had discovered it was not necessary for all Masons to think alike to maintain peace and harmony.

In December the Grand Lodge of Virginia was informed that thirteen Military Lodges had been issued warrants. A special committee reported five Lodges had been ransacked by Union troops and one by Confederates. But, even so, "in no portion of the world had the Masonic fraternity been so closely united as in this," the committee claimed. Although a bitter war was being fought, Masonry North and South was still united.

The Grand Lodge of Pennsylvania was still alarmed over the number of Grand Lodges that had not sent in their Proceedings. What reports it had received indicated "the vindictiveness and unmasonic bitterness which upon occasions were shown during the first outburst of the Rebellion, and led us to think that some of our brethren had forgotten the teachings of the altar, have for the most part passed away."

The year 1863 drew to a close and found the Confederacy in dire straits. Money was practically worthless; food was scarce, as were all of the necessities of life. The Confederate States were cut off from all outside intercourse except for a rare blockade-runner managing to escape the United States naval vessels.

In every Grand Lodge and most subordinate Lodges prayers continued for the restoration of peace. Masons from the North and South were no longer ashamed or afraid to fraternize with each other when the rules of war would permit. Assistance was more freely extended to each other. With the fighting becoming more fierce—brotherly love was being practiced—not merely with words, but by deeds.

### The Romance of Freemasonry

Medicine and surgical instruments were scarce. All of which caused Southerners no end of trouble. But the North suffered indirectly. Federal prisoners-of-war, who in most cases received the same rations and care as the Confederates, had to do without many of the things they really needed.

On January 8, 1864 the Masonic College at Little Rock, Arkansas, was the scene of a tragedy. David O. Dodd, charged with being a Confederate spy, was executed in front of it. Five days later J. Eastman Johnson, Grand Master of the Grand Master of the Grand Lodge of Michigan, said he had issued dispensations for one hundred and thirty-three candidates to receive their degrees in a shorter time than provided by law. It was done through patriotism and because "they have discovered what to them was the discovery of a new world, that this ray was the light of Masonry."

On January 26th a report was written that highly praised a Mason named Christoper "Kit" Carson for the success of Union forces in New Mexico. General James H. Carleton, another Mason, was also most complimentary of Carson's ability.

The 16th Army Corps, under the command of Stephen A. Hurlbut, a Mason, left Vicksburg on February 3rd in what has come to be known as "Sherman's Mississippi Expedition." In March he wrote: "we staid at Meridian a week, and made the most complete destruction of railroads ever beheld."

Not only railroads were destroyed. Homes and other property of the civilians in the area were also wrecked. At Marion, some five miles from where the Federal troops were encamped at Meridian, the home of Mrs. Margaret Rea was ransacked. According to her son, Richard, his mother had received "the side degrees of Masonry, similar to the Eastern Star of the present day" some years before the outbreak of war. Her association stood her in good stead, for as the troopers were about to make off with their loot she put in her appearance and "made the Masonic sign of distress." A "Wisconsin captain and others drew their swords and pistols and surrounded the robbers." Every piece that had been taken was returned. All of which caused Richard to state; "As to whether Masonry is a protection in the hour of danger, I know it is from actual experience.'

Nathan Bedford Forrest, who had been promoted to major-general and left without an army to command after Chickamauga, had recruited a new one from the western parts of Tennessee and Kentucky. Then he captured Union supplies and arms to equip his new force. He had done so well his men were able to keep General William Smith from joining Sherman at Meridian. Smith was fought to a standstill and ended up back in Memphis.

Forrest went on to raid throughout Kentucky and on April 12th he attacked Fort Pillow, about forty miles from Memphis. The Confederates stormed the fort and twenty minutes after the bugle sounded the charge the fighting was over. But the political fury lasted for months. President Lincoln called it a "massacre" and said it should be amply retaliated. Sherman was ordered to investigate and what he discovered evidently did not substantiate the findings of the Congressional Committee, for no "retaliation" ever took place.

A Confederate prison camp was hastily thrown together during February at Andersonville, Georgia. It was filled even before it was completed. It was needed to hold the overflow of Federal prisoners that had accumulated due to the Union government's refusal to exchange them. The overflow became so great that in November the Confederacy began returning them to the North without a man for man exchange.

Joseph McElroy, who was not a Mason, wrote that the Masonic Order "was the sole recognition on the part of any of our foes of our claims to human kinship. The churches of all denominations— except the solitary Catholic priest, Father Hamilton—ignored us as wholly as if we were dumb beasts."

Another prison camp located in Savannah was a "paradise compared to others in the South," claimed General J. Madison Drake. He wrote about a Confederate captain who helped a fellow Mason obtain lumber for a bed. When it was delivered there was so much, his "joy was so great that he divided the lumber among his friends, reserving scarcely enough to answer his own purpose."

A new era was ushered into the Civil War on March 9, 1864, when Lincoln presented General Ulysses S. Grant with the rank of Lieutenant-General of the Army of the United States. After Grant took over command of the Federal forces he pressed the war on all fronts, and disregarding casualties moved toward the Confederate capital.

Grant sent Benjamin Butler from Fort Monroe up the James River with a force of 40,000. He gained control of the railroad between Richmond and Petersburg. Then he was met by a brother Mason, John Gregg, in command of the brigade that once belonged to Hood. Although Gregg's men were outnumbered they drove the Federal force back through a misunderstanding in the orders. The brigade standard of the Confederate troops accidentally moved— so did the Southern troops.

Gregg was killed on October 7, 1864 while in command of an advance force near Richmond. John Reagan, the Masonic Postmaster General of the Confederacy, wrote of his friend: "There was no more sincere and truthful man than Gregg."

From the Wilderness to Spottsylvania Court House Grant led his men through a hail of bullets and with a tremendous loss of life. Then to Cold Harbor where it was no different.

During a brief lull in the Battle of Cold Harbor the cries of Federal wounded directly in front of the troops of General Robert Hoke were plainly audible. Many of his men, unable to stand the pleas for water and do nothing, rushed out of their trenches with canteens. They were met by a shower of bullets from the Union line. Hoke was so infuriated he ordered his men to cease assisting their enemy.

Some time later, two men who had been on patrol approached the general. They told him they had found a wounded Union soldier who was a Mason and had begged for help. Hoke pondered, then told them if they wanted to risk their lives to bring the soldier into the Confederate lines he would not object. The two Masons rushed out, picked up their brother and returned to the trenches without receiving a scratch, although lead had been whistling all around them.

Clinton F. Paige, the Grand Master of New York, told his members on June 7th: "Truly, the record of the year is written in blood. Yet, above the din of battle and the wail of the dying, from the prison and the hospital, the 'still small voice' of Masonry is heard attesting the truth and power of Masonic love. The baser passions, inflamed by deadly strife, have vanished at the remembrance of former vows, and the firm grasp of the uplifted steel, given place to the warm grip of brotherly love. Thousands of our brethren who have been participants in these tragic scenes, bear testimony to many beautiful exemplifications of the noble tenets of our profession ... that though civil strife may sever all national, political, and religious ties and associations, yet the mystic tie unites men of very country, sect, and opinion, in one common bond of allegiance which death alone can sever."

Three days later, John Grim of the 7th Ohio Independent Battery was taken prisoner. While he was riding beside "a handsome lieutenant in the Confederate gray" he noticed the Masonic square and compasses on his captor's watch chain. So Grim let him know he was a Mason—an act that freed him, for a short time later his friend helped him cross over to the Federal lines.

Grant pulled his troops away from the Cold Harbor stalemate and headed for Petersburg. All that stood between him and Richmond were two Confederate Masons, Beauregard and Henry Wise, and their two thousand men armed with discarded weapons. For three days they did hold back the over-whelming Federal forces; then Lee arrived to ease the pressure.

The Master of Putnam Army Lodge, No. 8, under a Massachusetts warrant, wrote a letter on July 9th from Petersburg which stated that "Masonic obligations are recognized by our enemies." One of his members, Lt. Isaac D. Paull, fell mortally wounded at Spottsylvania. His body was carried behind the Confederate lines and buried with Masonic honors. Another, Corporal Simpson, was wounded during the same battle and recognized as a Mason "by a rebel officer, who directed his men to fill his canteen, and placed him in a comfortable position ... from which position, a few hours afterwards, we recovered him."

Davis said he hoped the number was complete, but it was not, for three days after writing the letter he was killed. His body was sent to Cambridge, Massachusetts, where his funeral was held on July 19th.

Lee sent Jubal Early and the Masonic general, John C. Breckinridge to attack the Federal capital. Only the intervention of another Mason General Lew Wallace, who fought against heavy odds until reinforcements arrived, kept Breckinridge from keeping his promise to visit the White House.

Two weeks later, on July 30th, the town of Chambersburg, Pennsylvania was burned. But a kind act stood out during the affair—a Confederate officer recognized the Masonic Temple in the town. He placed guards about it and rode away. It was the only building left standing in that part of Chambersburg.

Although the South was in dire straights as the summer of 1864 drew to a close, the Democratic party in the North declared the war a dismal failure. It demanded an immediate cessation of hostilities and nominated a Mason, George B. McClellan, to oppose the incumbent Abraham Lincoln for the Presidency of the United States.

A Mason, who later became a judge in Rhode Island, was involved in a "minor" skirmish at Waynesboro, Virginia, on September 28th. Federal cavalry attempted to destroy a railroad bridge. They were almost successful, but the Confederates caught them and proceeded to drive them back to the city. The Rhode Islander, in an attempt to turn the tide, mounted a horse and led his provost guards into the fight. In the battle he became separated from his command and found himself riding alone into the Black Horse Troop of the 4th Virginia Cavalry.

The Federal rider, with his sword waving frantically, sabered men right and left and "might possibly have escaped, but a shot fired by a Confederate brought his horse down and he fell with it." His life would have ended then but for the timely intervention of Captain Henry C. Lee who recognized the fallen man as a Brother Mason.

"The hero of this affair, which sounds like a romance, turned out to be Captain George N. Bliss, of the First Rhode Island Cavalry."

The whole story of Masonry during the Civil War "sounds like a romance." For all through the struggle Brother aided Brother—and wives and daughters of Brothers.

Because of a piece of cloth shaped into a small apron, many homes were saved from looting and burning. Because of a peculiar wave of a hand, lives were saved and wounded men made as comfortable as possible. Because of a small specially shaped piece of metal the last earthly remains of many men were consigned to the earth with dignity.

But the story of Freemasonry in times of strife is more than a romance—it proves conclusively that there is beauty in the love of a man for a man.

## The Beginning of the End

California was far removed from the scenes of war, but the hearts of many of the members of the Grand Lodge were close to the result of the strife. Grand Master William C. Belcher, on October 11, 1864. told why: "We know that the homes of our childhood have been made desolate, and are filled with sorrow and mourning, for their young men have gone forth in beauty and strength. and they come not back again … with most intense anxiety do we watch the progress of events. As citizens, we feel deeply, and perhaps sometimes bitterly; but I am happy indeed to say that, as Masons, we have continued to gather around our altars; that no sound of confusion or strife has there been heard: and that our brethren appear to have remembered the ancient Charges, and have sedulously excluded from the Lodges all disputes and controversies about politics and political matters."

In Boston, Massachusetts, three thousand miles away, the Grand Lodge held a special Communication three days later to lay the cornerstone of a new Temple. The old one had been destroyed by fire on April 6, 1863. The spirits of those in attendance were not dampened by the war; it took two hours for a parade moving at quick step to pass over the parade route, after which "choice and tempting viands" were enjoyed by 700 guests at Faneuil Hall.

Thomas Sadler, Grand Master of Kentucky, told his Grand Lodge: "It is to be much lamented that our once happy country has been engaged in a war in which brother is arrayed against brother, father against son, and son against father, in deadly conflict, causing a wide separation between the best and warmest of friends—a state of things, which as a Mason I deeply regret, and hope and pray for a speedy reunion of true fellowship among all, but more particularly among brother Masons.

"During the past year many of our friends have fallen in various battles that have been fought in our and sister States. I say sister States. for I am unwilling to give up a single one of them."

The Grand Lodge of Kansas was unable to hold its scheduled annual communication because the "state was threatened with invasion, and contending armies struggled on the border." Although the Grand Master was present the number of members in attendance was so small he postponed the communication until December.

The citizens of a small town hundreds of miles from the nearest battle were completely surprised to find they had been invaded by Confederate soldiers. Even the Royal Arch Chapter in town was disrupted. causing the Secretary to write: "… Being about to confer the degree of Past Master, upon Brother Wilcox, when Satan, the Prince of Devils, commenced a raid upon the banks of St. Albans, (Money being the root of all evil.) and robbed them of many thousand dollars. About twenty of the infernal imps of the lower regions cut and covered with impunity, killed Mr. Marrison, a worthy citizen, which created a great excitement in our quiet village for a half hour, until the troops of his Satanic majesty had departed.…"

For slightly less than thirty minutes on October 19, 1864, the town of St. Albans, Vermont, was "in the possession of the Confederate States of America." Before the Confederates made their hasty retreat, hotly pursued by a posse, they uncharitably threw Greek fire all over the water closet of the American Hotel causing it to burn for a full day.

A Mason named "Shupe" and a friend paid a visit to the armies of the "Potomac and the James." They were highly impressed by the number of Masonic pins they saw on the breasts of the soldiers, particularly among the surgeons. Shupe went on to write: "A person who has never been in the army would find it difficult to understand how the finer and social feelings of the men are disregarded in necessary discipline—how completely machine-like, one of a large lot of the same sort, a soldier becomes and is. No antecedent relations of officer to privates is permitted to work disrespect of discipline; there is no bond of sympathy, no level upon which shoulder-straps and stoga-shoes meet, save one, and that one is not disregarded. The Masonic tent is where men, without distinction of rank, 'meet upon the level and part upon the square.'

An army nurse gave this account of an act that involved Masons: "In a charge made on the enemy during the great battle of Spottsylvania C.H., May 8th, 1864, our men were repulsed and compelled to leave their dead and wounded on the field. Among the sufferers lay one young Sergeant scarcely able to move, his life-blood flowing rapidly from three severe wounds in thigh, breast and ankle, while the rebels came dashing over the prostrate forms in pursuit of flying troops. Expecting death at any moment, he exerted himself to the utmost, and by means of the mystic sign was so fortunate as to succeed in attracting the attention of the Lieut. Col. commanding the rebel Regiment. The Col. at once ordered a man from the ranks to take him carefully to the rear and treat him kindly."

The Confederate colonel did not stop there. After the furious fighting had eased, he sought out the Federal soldier and gave him a letter to take to a Masonic surgeon. No "treatment more skilful or tender" could have been desired during his fourteen days stay in the Division Hospital of Longstreet's Corps.

The nurse was so impressed by the act, she stated, evidently overlooking the fact that most Masons are Christians, "I can only say that Masons act more like Christians toward their brethren under difficult circumstances than Christians themselves do."

Once again Abraham Lincoln defeated a Mason for the Presidency of the United States. George B. McClellan received only 21 electoral votes out of 233. But the election of the Mason Andrew Johnson as Vice-President was to go a long way toward eventually reuniting the ununited states.

During the annual communication of the Grand Lodge of Virginia a letter was read which informed the members that several items belonging to Centreville Lodge No. 80, Virginia, were in the possession of a Federal surgeon. They were soon to be on their way to Richmond.

Savannah, Georgia, fell to overwhelming Federal forces on December 21, 1864, after a siege of eleven days. Solomon's Lodge No. 1, was placed in danger from the mobs who began plundering the city as soon as the Confederate troops left. But the Lodge was saved. General John W. Geary, when informed of the prevailing conditions, placed a strong guard at the disposal of the Worshipful Master. The mob was dispersed before any material damage could be done.

The members of the Lodge were so appreciative of the kindness of General Geary they adopted the following resolution:

Resolved: That Solomon's No. 1, AFM remembers with deep gratitude this truly Masonic act of kindness on the part of Gen. Geary also other favors which he extended to it while comd'g officer of this post, and would assure him that his treatment of our fraternity, and the citizens of this place, in general, in those trying times gave relief to many anxious hearts, and will always be appreciated by them; and therefore be it further Resolved:

That the thanks of this Lodge be and the same we hereby tender to P.G.H.P. Jno. W. Geary of Penn.

Eighteen months later, while Governor of Pennsylvania, Geary received a copy of the resolution. (The copy mailed earlier had been lost. ) In a letter to the Lodge he stated:

In the performance of those duties, I was actuated by no motives, but which were in every respect compatible with those of a soldier dictated by the true principles of charity and humanity. For the spirit and action thus manifested, I am entitled to no extraordinary credit or praise; for they should pervade the human heart in every circumstance of life and should be particularly prominent in every action of those connected with Freemasonry. Since then the rude scenes of war have passed away and fratricidal strife has ceased, and peace again spreads her genial influences over common country. God grant we may ever rejoice under one Flag, and one destiny.

We have reason to be thankful that our lives and health have been spared amid the chances and changes of the stormy period it has been our lot to witness, and for the generally increasing harmony and prosperity which seems to prevail throughout the nation. And here I feel again justified in referring to our beloved institution, by saying that to Freemasonry the people of the country are indebted for many mitigations of the sufferings caused by the direful passions of war.

One of the most difficult problems Masons had to face throughout the war was finding Lodge Communications they could attend. The fall of Savannah solved that problem for Isaac H. Boyle of Walker's Missouri Light Battery (Federal), according to a letter he wrote to a brother Mason:

… But once within the last year have I beheld the "Great Light" or heard the sound of the Master's gaval calling the Craftsman to labor, and that once was last night January 5, 1865. In company with Bro. Curtis, of Illinois, I sought admission into Solomon's Lodge, No. 1, and after patiently waiting until some hundred or so officers of the army (and some privates, too,) had passed through the hands of the examining committee, I was ushered into the most beautiful Lodge room it has ever been my privilege to enter, just in time to see the closing scene in the raising of a Brother to the sublime degree of a Master Mason. The chair (or rather, "throne",) was filled by the Master of the Lodge, Rich Turner, Esq., a venerable, intelligent and worthy Mason. The room was crowded to a degree of uncomfortableness, by citizens and soldiers, (Generals, Colonels, Majors, Captains and Privates, mingling together as if such a thing as rank existed not in the service). The work was beautifully executed, and everything seemed to conspire to render the evening one of pleasure and of profit. By my side sat a rebel prisoner, who had got permission to visit the Lodge without a guard, the word of a Master Mason being sufficient guarantee that he would return promptly to his quarters when the Lodge should close. Rebels and Union men mingled in that throng as if no war was going on, and I doubt not each one prayed that the clangor of arms might soon cease. Oh! Masonry, thy influence over the human soul is truly wonderful! A little incident occurred worthy of record. An officer of the Federal Army brought into the Lodge a "collar and apron," both very beautiful, for the purpose of having them restored to the rightful owner. It seems that a party of our soldiers were pillaging the house of a rebel, carrying off, not eatables, (a soldier's lawful prize) but everything else that struck their fancy. The lady at the sight of the devastation of her household, exclaimed, "Is there a Freemason here who will protect me?" The words ran like an electric spark through the nerves of Capt. …, who instantly commenced an indiscriminate booting of the mob from the premises. Pursuing his way with the column, he was informed a soldier had carried off from the house alluded to, some articles pertaining to Masonry. The soldier was forced to give up his spoils, (of what use to him?) and the gallant and true Brother carried them safely to Savannah, and at the meeting last night placed them in hands that will convey them to the rightful owner. This incident affected me more than anything that has ever come to my notice in our noble institution. God bless Freemasonry.

Early in the beginning of the year 1865, James A. Seddon, Jefferson Davis' Secretary of War, resigned. The Confederate President reluctantly accepted his resignation and called General John C. Breckinridge, a Mason, to Richmond to become the sixth, and last, Secretary of War for the Confederate States of America. He was to play an important part in the last days of his government.

Almost four years of war found the South in a deplorable condition. Food was practically non-existent; clothing was so scarce curtains and drapes, when they could be found, were being made into wearing apparel; shoes, where found, were a makeshift affair. Most of the South was in the possession of the Federal government. All that was saving the Confederacy was a group of half-starved, half-clothed, bedraggled, but valiant men in the trenches at Petersburg

## The Shooting War Ends

The Civil War brought an increase in the membership of Freemasonry. The increase and the type of men the Lodges were accepting alarmed many Grand Masters.

Thomas Hayward, Grand Master of Masons in Florida, expressed his concern: "But few of our Lodges have had the opportunity to assemble as heretofore, but some have been engaged more than usual and have done much which I fear will not redound to advantage. Some have initiated members residing in other jurisdictions. Soldiers have been admitted, emergency declared jurisdiction waived and degrees conferred without sufficient evidence of character. All of this is calculated to create dissatisfaction and disturb the harmony among our sister Lodges."

The Grand Master of Michigan, Lovell Moore, on January 11, 1865, proved the universality of Masonry when he took to task the Northern Grand Lodge of the District of Columbia for invading the jurisdiction of the Southern Grand Lodge of Virginia. He also found fault with another Northern Grand Lodge, Indiana, for "unjustifiable infringement upon the prerogatives of the Grand Lodge of Mississippi." Consequently, he refused to recognize Masons who had received their degrees in a Military Lodge working under dispensation from the Grand Lodge of Indiana while it was on the soil of Mississippi.

On the same day the Grand Lodge of Vermont met. Its Grand Master, Leverett B. Englesby, also had kind words to say about Southern Masons: "Of many kindnesses conferred, courtesies extended, even while bitter feelings would seem to be most violently engendered and aroused, it may not, perhaps, be well to speak, lest we seem to magnify ourselves. It is pleasant, however, to know, that while in no particulars have duties been neglected or failed to be discharged to the uttermost that have been or could be required, Masonic vows have not lost their force; and brethren. when it was proper for them so to do have not failed with kind words and kindlier acts to respond to the claims of Brotherhood."

The Confederate Soldiers in the trenches at Petersburg were being starved into submission. The Confederate Congress had been informed. in a secret session, that there was not enough meat in the South for the armies in the field. What meat there was had to be obtained from abroad. Not only meat was scarce, so were all of the necessities of life.

Sherman, following Grant's orders, marched through the Carolinas leaving a trail of devastation behind. Roads were covered with butchered hogs, cattle, mules, and furniture.

Columbia, South Carolina, surrendered on February 17th, but it was not spared. Even the Catholic convent, presided over by a nun who had educated Sherman's daughter, was burned, despite the pleas of the Mother Superior. Eighty-four squares of buildings were destroyed, including "the capitol building, six churches 11 banking establishments, the schools of learning, the shops of art and trade, of invention and manufacture, shrines equally of religion, benevolence, and industry."

Four days earlier, the Grand Secretary of Louisiana, Samuel M. Todd, reported he had received a letter from a Mason who was a prisoner of war on Johnson's Island in Ohio. Because many of the prisoners were Masons, the Grand Master of Louisiana had permitted a letter appealing for funds for them to be circulated to all his Lodges. The results were so good another letter was sent from the prison camp requesting no further aid be sent. Their appeal had been sent to Northern Lodges also, and they had received from Louisiana $600, "from the Masons of St. Louis. $165., of Nashville $165., of New York $20., and in Boston they had on hand, subject to our order! several hundred dollars."

Sheridan's cavalry began raiding almost at will in Virginia toward the end of February. His raiders arrived early one morning in March at the home of Mrs. Meriweather Anderson in Ivy, some five miles from Charlottesville. The Federal troopers pointed their pistols at the heads of the women and ordered them to give up everything in their possession. While the raiders were inside the house, Mrs. Meriweather took a small Masonic apron from a bureau drawer, ran with it to the porch and jumped on a bench. Holding the apron high, she cried, "Is there no one here who can protect the widow of a Mason?"

The response was instant! A soldier leaped from his horse, ran into the house and booted every soldier out. And for the next three days, although the troops encamped beside the house, not a soldier set foot inside the yard.

It was during one of Sheridan's raids on Waynesboro that the Grand Master of Virginia, General William Harman, was mortally wounded. Twenty months later, the Grand Lodge of Virginia took an unprecedented action when it adopted a resolution permitting Mrs. Harman to use the name "Masonic Female Seminary of Staunton" for her school. It went a step further by requesting all Masons to "aid and assist this enterprise as far as they can consistently with their duties as Masons."

The morning of March 4th, 1865, found a heavy rain falling in the District of Columbia, but by noon the sun had broken through the black clouds. Much damage had been done as the inaugural parade was hampered by mud making the streets almost impassable. Even so, the display was "exceeding beautiful." Thousands of people lined the streets and "among the benevolent societies present were Lodges of Odd Fellows and Masons, including a colored Lodge of the latter fraternity.!'

The Vice-President elect, Andrew Johnson, a Mason, was escorted into the Senate Chamber at 11:45 by Vice-President Hamlin. Johnson, before taking the oath of office, made a short speech in which he extolled the virtues of the Constitution of the United States. He turned to each group present—Supreme Court Justices, Senators, members of the Cabinet—and told them their power was derived from the people and only the people.

Mr. Lincoln took the oath as President for the second time. During his address he claimed: "All knew this interest (slavery) was somehow the cause of the war." He stated no group "expected for the war the magnitude or the duration which it has already attained."

Lincoln closed his address with the now famous phrase "With malice toward none, with charity for all...." Something that has been practiced by Masons since time immemorial.

At Five Forks on April 1st, Sheridan attacked the Masonic general, George Pickett, with an overwhelming force and drove him from his entrenchments with a heavy loss in lives and prisoners. The following day Grant assaulted the whole Confederate line about Petersburg and A.P. Hill was killed. On the second day of April. 1865. Petersburg and Richmond were evacuated.

By nightfall of the second, the mobs were running rampant through the streets of Richmond. The four principal tobacco warehouses were set on fire; the bridges across the James River were destroyed, and the ships Richmond and Virginia, were blown up. The next day Federal troops under the command of the Mason, General Godfrey Weitzel, entered Richmond and endeavored to put out the fires.

Masons Hall, the home of the Grand Lodge of Virginia, was saved from destruction by a Federal Provost Marshal, A.H. Stevens, who was a member of the Putnam Lodge in Massachusetts. He placed a guard about the Temple and the homes of several members of the Fraternity.

The North wildly celebrated the downfall of the Confederate capitol while Jefferson Davis and his cabinet were escaping. Lee fought his way to Amelia Court House where he expected to find large quantities of supplies for his starving and ill-clothed men. But they were not there. The train carrying them had not bothered to stop: it had hurried on to Richmond. So the dispirited Confederate troops staggered on to Appomattox Court House.

General Grant had been suffering from a severe headache. But on Sunday, April 9th, it left him suddenly, for with all hope gone, General Lee sent the Federal Commander a note agreeing to discuss terms of surrender.

In the village of Appomattox Court House was the home of Wilmer McLean. He had owned a home near Manassas which became the scene of the first major battle of the Civil War when Beauregard had used it for his headquarters. To avoid further war activity McLean had moved to quieter surroundings, only to find himself in the midst of more soldiers than he had ever before seen. In his home Lee waited for Grant.

The opposing generals were extremely friendly with each other. For some time they talked in generalities. until Lee reminded his counterpart about the reason they were together. The solemn discussion that followed was finally settled agreeably to both. then Ely Parker, a Mason and full-blooded Indian, was given the task of writing the final draft. "His handwriting presented a better appearance than that of anyone else on the staff."

General Lee bid his command a sorrowful farewell the following day and left for his home in Richmond. Grant, taking most of his staff, left for Washington. The Masonic general, Joshua L. Chamberlain, was left to accept the surrender.

On April 12th the soldiers of the Army of Northern Virginia walked up the hill from the tiny mouth-formed waters of the Appomattox River. The remnants of the Old Stonewall Brigade, hating to lay down their arms, were in the lead. Then Chamberlain, whom even Southerners years later termed "a great Yankee general," ordered his men to give the surrendering Confederates a full military salute!

The complexion changed. Instead of a humiliating "walk up the hill," the Confederates regained their pride, snapped to smart military routine, and responded to Chamberlain's dignified honor. Later that day the last arms were stacked.

On the fourteenth "Old Glory" was raised once again over Fort Sumter. General Robert Anderson, the Mason, aided by Peter Hart, the Mason, attached to the halyards the same battle-scarred flag they had removed exactly four years earlier and amidst thunderous applause raised it to the top of the pole. "Six thunderous cheers were given for the old flag replaced upon Sumter; and three times three for President Lincoln, General Robert Anderson, and the soldiers and sailors."

That night, while the celebration was at its height, President Lincoln was mortally wounded.

The New York Times, on April 15th, 1865, used heavy black lines to mark the columns on the front page. Its headlines read: "AWFUL EVENT. President Lincoln Shot by an Assassin. The Deed Done at Ford's Theatre Last Night."

The whole nation mourned the loss of Lincoln. For the first time since his political career commenced, his critics were silent. An assassin had accomplished what nothing else could.

Although Lincoln was not a Mason, Lodges and Grand Lodges throughout the country took note of his death. George C. Whiting, Grand Master of the Grand Lodge in the nation's capital, stated: "As members of a loyal and order-loving association, … are called to share in the deep and universal sorrow, it is meet that we should recognize that amiable and virtuous conduct, and the inflexible fidelity to his trust, which so marked him as the fit successor to our illustrious brother—the great and good Washington—and in some appropriate form give expression to our sense of the loss our country has sustained." The Grand Lodge was ordered in mourning for a period of six months.

Typical of the expressions of all Masons was the one made by John F. Houston, Grand Master of Missouri:" 'A great man has fallen in Israel.' The Chief Magistrate of this mighty nation has fallen—not upon the battlefield, amid the thunder of hostile cannon, the clashing of the sword and bayonet, and the discharge of death-dealing musketry, but by the hand of an assassin—his work unfinished, and his kind and genial nature extinguished forever."

Edwin Booth, the brother of the man who mortally wounded Lincoln, was an innocent victim of what had transpired. His Lodge, New York, No. 330, wrote a reassuring letter to Edwin, the man who would rather confer the Master Mason's Degree than "receive the plaudits of the people in the theatres of the world." They endorsed him as "a good man, a true friend, a loyal citizen and a faithful brother."

The President of the Confederate States went from Richmond to Danville, Virginia, taking his Cabinet with him. After the surrender of Lee he moved his government to Charlotte, North Carolina, and finally Washington, Georgia. In the meantime it appears that General Sherman had asked President Lincoln whether to capture Davis or let him escape. Lincoln answered him by reciting an anecdote about a temperance lecturer in Illinois. The lecturer arrived at a wayside inn wet and cold. The landlord asked if he would have a glass of brandy. "No, I am a temperance lecturer and do not drink." But after a pause he went on, "I shall be obliged to you for a drink of water, and if you should put a little brandy in it unbeknownst to me, it will be all right."

But Davis was captured at a small creek near Irwinsville, Georgia, by Federal cavalry, on May 10th. The Confederate States of America had come to an end and with it an era also ended.

Freemasonry had played an important part in the Civil War. After its failure to prevent a catastrophe, it did all in its power to mitigate the harshness, bitterness, and cruelty of war. Its success was tremendous. But its greatest role was to be played in the days and years that followed. A country had been divided. Words had been spoken that left marks which were never to heal. Freemasonry had to step into the breach.

The shooting war ended in May, 1865. But another war-of-words started before the firing had stopped. Politically the verbal war still exists. Masonically the opposite has been and is true! Masonry—a house that was never divided, remains a house undivided !

*– So Mote It Be –*

# THE LEWIS MASON

## Norman C. Dutt, FPS

*1962 Certificate of Literature*

THE LEWIS is an instrument used in operative Masonry, and consists of an iron cramp usually made in three sections. This is inserted into a cavity prepared for that purpose in any large stone. It forms an attachment for blocks and tackles, (system of pulleys), whereby a stone may be raised or lowered to a designated position, swung into position and deposited upon the site chosen.

The contrivance is old and was known to the Romans, and some recovered from old ruins are on display in various European museums, the Vatican has quite a number in assorted sizes. In England many old stones have been discovered with excavation for the insertion of a Lewis. The word is most probably derived from the old French levis, any contrivance for lifting. The modern French call the instrument a louse.

In speculative Freemasonry and the English system in particular, the Lewis is found on the Tracing Board of the Entered Apprentice, where it is used as a symbol of Strength, because, by its assistance, an Operative Mason is enabled to lift the heaviest stones with a comparatively minimum exertion of physical power.

The age of a Lewis is eighteen years and is permitted by England, Scotland, Ireland, Germany, Netherlands, all the Australian

Constitutions, New Zealand, some of the Canadian Grand Lodges and a few of our Latin American Brethren. It is practically unknown throughout the U.S.A. with the exception of Pennsylvania. A surprise to many Crafts[men is that various Prince Hall Grand Lodges in the U.S. permit the Lewis.

The three French Grand Lodges allow the Lewis and the qualifications are stringent. The French call the two wedge shaped pieces 'Louveteaux' or little wolves. The Grand Orient and Grand Lodge of France are not recognized by most of the Masonic world but the National Grand Lodge enjoys this privilege and closely follows the English system.

There also exists in France an organization known as the compagnonage that is similar to Freemasonry. The pattern being so great the arch traitor Bernard Fay recommended to Hitler that it be destroyed, and it was nearly accomplished. A remarkable feature of this organization is the Sons of Solomon calling themselves "Loups" or wolves, which corresponds to the English Lewis.

The son of a Freemason in England is called a Lewis, because it is his duty to support the sinking powers and aid the failing strength of his father; or to bear the burden and heat of the day, that his parents may rest in peace and happiness. From an eighteenth century catechism comes the following:-

Q. What do we call the son of a Freemason ?
A. A Lewis.
Q. What does it denote?
A. Strength.
Q. How is a Lewis depicted in Mason's lodge?
A. As a cramp of metal (etc).
Q. What is the duty of a Lewis ... to his aged parents?
A. To bear the heavy burden ... so as to render the close of their days happy and comfortable.
Q. His privilege for so doing?

A. To be made a Mason before any other person, however dignified by birth, rank, or riches, unless he, through complaisance,
waives this privilege.

It is sometimes stated that the son of a prominent Mason is entitled
to this honor, such is not the case. It is only granted after an enquiry
by the Grand Master in the form of a dispensation to so confer.

In light of the institution of Lewis, Freemasonry apparently enter-
tains, the principle that good blood and excellent bringing up can
be relied on up to a certain limit. The ordinary aspirant must be of
the full age of twenty-one years. In some of the Hispanic-American
Lodges the age is twenty-five years and the Grand Master may grant
a dispensation for those twenty-one to twenty-five years of age in
special cases. The son of a Master Mason in good standing or repute
may, if the Grand Master wishes to issue a dispensation in his favor,
be initiated at the age of eighteen years. Many do not regard this in
any way a reward for his father's faithful service: the rules for admission are directed toward just, upright worthy men, and these alone,
and it appears to be a reasonable supposition that the mere fact of
being the son of a Master Mason in good standing may be thought
by the Craft to have benefited in character from that circumstance.
It is to be carefully noted that there is no right to a dispensation; it
is discretionary and it must be issued by the Grand Master: it is, in
fact, a privilege which is granted sparingly and after enquiry. This
has been particularly true in the United Grand Lodge of Germany
as one would be led to believe, that in its effort to recover and grow,
there would be considerable leeway in the Lewis.

In the afore-mentioned countries the brethren are told in the first
degree tracing board lecture that it is a privilege which carries with
it certain appropriate duties. The man who is received into the Society early because his father is a member of it, is expected to support
and aid his father. He gives the Craft the benefit of highly desirable
family continuity. and just as members of various trades are elated
when sons follow in their father's footsteps, so are we pleased when
we see father and son sitting together in a Masonic Lodge

There is greatness in association of tradition, and there is added strength in ties that bind several members of a family. The accepted Lewis is expected to pay, and pay willingly, for the fact of being rewarded as an adult into a mature Society as it were on his father's guarantee. He is obliged to prove his fitness in the discharge of his obligation

The ritual has never directly referred to wives and mothers. We must never attend Lodge or visit without detriment to our connections, which actually refers to our families. The Lewis's obligation is similarly to his parents: the word is not father and the words are equally definite: … to bear the burden and heat of the day, from which they, by reason of their age, ought to be exempt; to assist them in time of need, and thereby render the close of their days happy and comfortable. It is no more than the duty of any child towards its parent; but it is seen as an obligation which carries additional weight in the case of a Lewis.

The symbolism of units of metal dovetailed into a stone cavity is apt, for it carries and expresses the idea of support: to raise great weights and fix them on their proper bases. If a son is prepared to support his parents, then by that very fact he establishes an early claim to be received into an adult society: it is a mature responsibility that he has assumed.

Regulations for the admission of a Lewis no doubt vary in every jurisdiction. Actually all that is stated is in the Tracing Board charge, as distinct from the *Book of Constitutions*, is that a Lewis is the son of a Master Mason and that his privilege for accepting the duties and obligations of a Lewis is "that of being made a Freemason before any other person, however dignified." This in practice, is usually taken to mean that a Lewis under the age of twenty-one years is the first candidate to be taken in the working of a double first degree. The *Book of Constitutions* fails to define a Lewis, although it uses the term, in the heading under the appropriate rule. From the wording it appears that a Lewis is the only person who can be initiated under the age of twenty-one years: it leaves the path open to construe the word Lewis as probably it should be construed, to include the sons of Freemasons who are not under that age.

New South Wales Constitution, (Australia), Regulation 151 (d), *Book of Constitutions*:- "No person shall be made a Master Mason (d) unless he is the son of a Master Mason and of the full age of eighteen years, and the written consent of his father or guardian and a dispensation from the Grand Master has been obtained." This regulation is indeed under the word Lewis. Up to date it has not been satisfactorily explained. These along with many other regulations were taken verbatim from the English *Book of Constitutions*. Likewise most of the other Grand Lodges in Australia follow the English system.

The sons of Master Masons under the Scottish Constitution may be entered at eighteen years of age and upwards. No dispensation is required. This rule was in effect when George Washington was made a Freemason in Fredericksburg Lodge. It is only necessary for the Master Mason to have attained that degree at any time during the life time of his son, the Candidate, and not before his birth.

There is a seventeenth century manuscript in the archives of the Grand Lodge of Scotland that states: "You shall not make any mold, square or rule for any that is but a Lewis; a Lewis is such a one as hath served as apprentice to a Mason, but is not admitted afterwards according to this custom and manner of Making Masons."

Ireland, and on the subject the history of the Grand Lodge of Ireland, means more to American Freemasonry than the great majority of American Freemasons could ever guess and for reasons which are both interesting and solid. Those reasons are too many and complex for the scope of this paper, but will bear earnest investigation by all those who desire more light on this subject.

Irish Constitution: Rule 133—A Lodge shall not initiate any person until he shall have attained the age of twenty-one years, unless by Dispensation from the Grand Master or the Deputy Grand Master, in the Dominions or the Colonies from the Provincial Grand

Master or his Deputy, or in India or elsewhere overseas where there is one, from the Grand Inspector.

A number of explanations have been advanced as to the meaning of the word itself, and this is primarily of academic interest. The fact remains that it is common Masonic practice, outside of the U.S.A. and some Latin-American Lodges, for the son of a Master Mason to be admitted in proper circumstances before he comes of age. That practice is to be solemnly regarded, as a distinct privilege, and for the Freemason who enjoys it, to accept, and usually to discharge a particular obligation which in itself, but helps to confirm the strength of his character.

It is the perfect ashlar into which the Lewis is usually represented as being dovetailed. This represents not merely the parent, but the one who can look back in retrospect of life in piety and virtue, is the parent who is most worthy of support, and for his son to have the privilege of early admission he must in fact be able to establish that he is a Master Mason of good repute and standing. It is a most important privilege and signal honor, and nothing to repine about if chance has not brought it to us, and a highly prized distinction to those who have been fortunate to have been the recipient of the Lewis.

# RECOMMENDED MASONIC READING

## Alphonse Cerza, FPS

*1965 Certificate of Literature*

IN THE YEAR 1963 there was published *Education and Masonry in Texas to 1846* by the Committee on Masonic Education and Service for the Grand Lodge of Texas. Just off the press is the second volume on this subject. Written by Brother James David Carter, formerly of Texas, but presently the Librarian of the House of the Temple, Washington, D.C., the book is entitled *Education and Masonry in Texas, 1846 to 1861*.

This volume of 753 pages represents the highest type of research and writing by one skilled in the art of finding the pertinent facts and presenting them in a clear and interesting manner. This volume does not only tell the story of how the Craft and its members helped in establishing the educational system of public schools in Texas but is a veritable sourcebook of biographical sketches, organization of schools, legislative action taken in this field, and the active part taken by the Masons of the period. A large part of the book is devoted to a discussion of all schools operating in Texas during the period covered. An adequate bibliography and a long index make this a workable tool for scholars researching this subject.

Copies are available from Brother Harvey C. Byrd, Grand Secretary, P.O. Box 446, Waco, Texas, at $6.50 a volume.

The November, 1964 issue of the *Masonic Journal of South Africa* presents a lecture delivered by Brother L. Dickman, before Semper Vigilans Lodge No. 7362, entitled *The History Behind the V.S.L.* This article contains some interesting items about the Holy Bible and is a very good condensed history of the various editions of the Great Light. Our readers interested in this subject are urged to secure a copy of this issue of this magazine.

This issue also has two other articles of interest. One is entitled *Why Freemasonry Lives* in which it is demonstrated that the exemplary conduct of each Master Mason has kept up our good reputation in the world and that our teachings have helped make this a better world in which to live. The other article is entitled *Do's and Don'ts For the Young Mason* giving some good sound advice: his duty to vote on candidates for the degree, discretion in recommending new members, upright conduct at all times, and other bits of good advice that all of us could heed with profit.

Interested readers should communicate with: Z.E. Conradie, 406—408 Empire Building, 52, Kruis Street, Johannesburg, South Africa.

Available from the Superintendent of Documents is a booklet entitled *Representative Speeches of General of the Army Douglas MacArthur.* It reproduced most of his famous speeches and displays his fundamental beliefs in a style so characteristic of our illustrious Brother.

Last month there was reviewed in this column Alex Mellor *Our Separated Brethren: The Freemasons.* Since the publication of our last issue word has been received that copies of his volume can be secured with dispatch by sending 30 shillings (approximately $4.25) to the Secretary, Quatuor Coronati Lodge, 27 Great Queen Street, London, W.C. 2, England.

# FREEMASONRY IN NEW ZEALAND

## Dr. Ross Hepburn, FPS

*1966 Certificate of Literature*

## PART I.—CRAFT MASONRY

### Early Freemasonry in New Zealand

IT SHOULD be stated at the outset that Freemasonry in New Zealand is controlled by the Grand Lodge of New Zealand, which is a sovereign Grand Lodge recognised by and in fraternal relations with the various Grand Lodges in U.S.A. and Canada. New Zealand does not have the Doctrine of Exclusive Territorial Jurisdiction as it is known in U.S.A. The reason for this is a matter of history; and there are still English, Irish and Scottish Lodges working in New Zealand under the jurisdiction of their respective Grand Lodges in Britain; but no new Lodges will in future be chartered in New Zealand by any of the three British Grand Lodges.

New Zealand is a Dominion, similar in status to Canada and Australia, but it has only the one Parliament and central Government, and does not have any division of powers between a Federal, and Provincial or State Government. Similarly it has only one Grand Lodge, and not several as in Canada and Australia.

When New Zealand was settled in the 1840's and 1850's, the immigrants from Britain brought their Freemasonry with them, and it was not long before Lodges in New Zealand were chartered by the Grand Lodges of England, Ireland and Scotland. As soon as a sufficient number of Lodges of any one Constitution were established in any District, the Brethren applied to their own Grand Lodge in Britain for the establishment of a Provincial Grand Lodge (now called a District Grand Lodge). At the head of each District Grand Lodge, was a local Brother who was the direct representative of the Grand Master in the District, and had very wide powers to deal with day to day problems of administration that arose in his District. Some of these District Grand Masters became very autocratic and dictatorial. As a consequence, before long there was a confused patchwork of District Grand Lodges throughout New Zealand, with concurrent Jurisdiction in particular areas, each in control of their own Lodges. The result was chaos, as each District Grand Master was supreme in his District and there was no higher Masonic authority in New Zealand; and any questions that could not be dealt with locally had to be referred to Britain by mail—which in the days of sailing ships was very slow—and later by cable when this method was possible, which was very expensive and generally unsatisfactory.

**Formation of the Grand Lodge of New Zealand**
The logical conclusion was the formation of the Grand Lodge of New Zealand, and a meeting was called in 1876 to consider this. However owing to the extreme opposition of several English District Grand Masters, the matter was shelved in the meantime, but it was subsequently revived in 1884. Later a Masonic Union was formed with a view of promoting a Grand Lodge of New Zealand. Eventually, after many meetings, much correspondence and many circulars (for and against) this movement was successful, in spite of the bitter and unrelenting opposition of two English and one Scottish District Grand Master who even went to the length of forbidding their Lodges to discuss or even mention the question of the new Grand Lodge.

The formation of Grand Lodges in several Australian States in the meantime, provided a precedent, and the cause of the promoters of the Grand Lodge of New Zealand was assisted considerably.

The Grand Lodge of New Zealand was formed by 41 Lodges with a total membership of 1236. It had been hoped to have more foundation Lodges but this was not possible, owing to the opposition already mentioned.

Until the formation of the Grand Lodge of New Zealand in 1890, New Zealand was Masonically unoccupied territory. After 1890 it became Masonically occupied territory, and the new Grand Lodge claimed that henceforth no overseas Grand Lodge could charter any Lodge therein. For nearly ten years, Lodges under the Grand Lodge of New Zealand, must have been rather isolated, as it was a considerable time before recognition of the new Grand Lodge could be obtained from the Grand Lodges of England, Ireland and Scotland. This was refused, nominally on the ground of lack of information, but largely owing to disputes regarding the retention of the British Charters by the Lodges which had gone over to the Grand Lodge of New Zealand.

Recognition was first obtained from a number of American and Australian Grand Lodges. After the formation of the Grand Lodge of New Zealand, there was a good deal of confusion locally between Regularity and Recognition. This was largely caused by hostile circulars issued by the local District and Provincial Grand Masters of the British Constitutions.

Eventually M.W.Bro. Sir Francis Bell (Grand Master 1894 and 1895) visited England in 1896 and had a personal interview with His Royal Highness the Prince of Wales, Grand Master of England (afterwards Edward VII) and as a result, the Grand Lodge of England passed the necessary resolutions to enable recognition to be effected in 1898–99. Recognition was granted by the Grand Lodge of Ireland in 1898 and by Scotland in 1899. A dispute with the Grand Lodge of Scotland regarding the creation of new Lodges by it in New Zealand was finally settled in 1913. The

above piece of Masonic history is in strong contrast with the ami-
cable manner in which the three British Grand Lodges co-oper-
ated and assisted in the formation of the Grand Lodge of Indiana
a few years ago.

### The Present State of the Craft

As at 30th September 1965, the Grand Lodge of New Zealand
had 436 Lodges with a total membership of 46,760. This, even by
American standards, is quite a large Grand Lodge; and our Grand
Lodge in 1965 celebrated its 75th Anniversary. Its Lodges comprise 427 Craft Lodges and eight Lodges of Research in New Zealand, and one Craft Lodge (Calliope No. 252) in Western Samoa. At
present the Lodges of other Constitutions working in New Zealand
comprise: Ireland 3, Scotland 7 and England, a number exceeding
30, but exact figures are not available to the author at present.

### Administration

The Office of the Grand Secretary is located permanently in Wellington (the capital city) and this is the Office of Grand Lodge.

The Deputy Grand Master and Grand Wardens are appointed by
the Grand Master and are each chosen from a different Division,
not being the Division to which the Grand Master is allocated.

If the Governor-General of New Zealand is Grand Master
(which has occurred on a number of occasions) an additional officer called the Pro Grand Master is elected. He is a local Brother,
and the one who would otherwise have been Grand Master. On
completion of his term of office he is given the rank of Past Grand
Master Honoris Causa, unless of course he is elected Grand Master
in his own right.

### Masonic Districts

New Zealand is divided into 13 Masonic Districts with a Provincial
Grand Master at the head of each. The Provincial Grand Master (or
one of his Assistant Provincial Grand Masters) normally conducts

the Installation of the Master in each of the Craft Lodges in his District. He is not quite the equivalent of the American District Deputy Grand Master, as the latter is, I understand, in charge of a group of Lodges rather than a territorial district.

The Canterbury Masonic Province (in which I reside) is the only one in New Zealand which has a Provincial Grand Lodge and it is therefore termed a Province rather than a District. The Provincial Grand Master of Canterbury is elected by the Lodges in the Province and holds office for three years, whereas the Provincial Grand Masters of the other Districts are appointed annually by the Grand Master, and usually reappointed and hold office for a total of three or four years and sometimes longer.

The Grand Lecturers differ from those in U.S.A. It is their duty to prepare and deliver Lecturers in Craft Lodges on the ethics, symbolism and history of Freemasonry. They are in no way concerned with the teaching of ritual (as in U.S.A.), and have no authority over or powers of supervision of Lodges; and they may not in any way interfere with matters of ritual or etiquette. Grand Lecturers normally take an active part in the work of Lodges of Research and in Masonic Education generally.

## Official Ritual

The Grand Lodge of New Zealand has had a printed official Ritual for over sixty years. The Book of Constitution provides that this must be used by all Lodges. This rule however does not apply to any Lodge to which a Charter was issued by the Grand Master on or before 16th May 1912, or to any Lodge of another Constitution transferring its allegiance to the Grand Lodge of New Zealand, so long as the previous customary Ritual is adhered to. The Official Ritual is largely based on English working with traces of Irish and Scottish working due to its historical origin. There is an alternative Third Degree provided which can be adopted by resolution of the Lodge. This is usually known as the "Scotch Third."

## Masonic Halls

Suburban and country halls are usually owned by the individual Lodges and city Masonic Halls by a Masonic Hall Company in which the various Lodges (and some individual Brethren) hold shares. Masonic Hall Companies are frequently in financial difficulties and have periodically to increase their rents to meet rising costs.

## Masonic Benevolence

This is a big subject which can be dealt with only briefly here. Masonic Benevolence is dispensed to elderly Brethren and widows of Brethren in poor circumstances; and in certain cases by way of scholarships to the children of Brethren for higher education. In the case of children of Royal Arch Masons the cost of the scholarship is shared with Grand Chapter.

Assistance is chiefly by way of:

(a) Annuities

(b) Grants for repairs and painting

(c) Taking over existing Mortgages and allowing them to run on free of interest during the lifetime of the beneficiary. If the Brother or widow being assisted, owns a house, Grand Lodge takes a Mortgage to secure the amount advanced (e.g. for annuity, repairs or painting) and this is repayable at the death of the Brother or widow, or if the house is previously sold. This enables the financial assistance to be given for the personal use and benefit of the Brother or widow, and not for that of the children or others who may inherit the property, and who might otherwise profit financially by the assistance given. The money advanced thus comes back to Grand Lodge and can be used again to assist other Brethren and widows.

Advances by way of annuity are limited to what is permitted by the New Zealand Social Security (Pension) laws—that is, so as not to reduce the amount of Social Security Benefit payable by the State.

**Masonic Institutions**
In addition, Grand Lodge gives financial assistance to two Masonic Institutions, not under its direct control, namely The Kirkpatrick Masonic Institute at Nelson, a Home for girls of school age who are the daughters of Freemasons, when illness, the death of a parent or other circumstances mean that the girl will benefit from a new home; and also to the Roskill Masonic Village, a home for elderly Freemasons and wives and widows of Freemasons, established at Auckland.

Grand Lodge also makes grants to the various Masonic Almoners' Associations and to the Masonic Charitable Trusts, and the money is thankfully received and faithfully applied.


# PART II.—ROYAL ARCH MASONRY

**Early Royal Arch Masonry In New Zealand**
ROYAL ARCH MASONRY in New Zealand is controlled by the Supreme Grand Royal Arch Chapter of New Zealand which is a sovereign body and is recognised by and in fraternal relations with the various Grand Chapters in U.S.A. and Canada.

As in Craft Masonry, New Zealand does not have the Doctrine of Exclusive Territorial Jurisdiction as known in U.S.A. The reasons are the same as in Craft Masonry, and there are still English, Irish and Scottish Royal Arch Chapters and English Mark Lodges working in New Zealand.

**The Formation of the Grand Chapter of New Zealand**
The history of the formation of the Grand Chapter of New Zealand runs on parallel lines to that of the Grand Lodge of New Zealand with certain differences. First the formation of the Grand Lodge of New Zealand gave the impetus to the formation of our Grand Chapter; and secondly there does not appear to have been any active opposition from the British Constitutions working in New Zealand.

The primary cause of the formation of Grand Chapter was due to the unique system adopted by English Royal Arch Masonry, by which each Chapter is attached to a Craft Lodge and bears the same number but not necessarily the same name. When the Grand Lodge of New Zealand was formed, a number of the English Lodges working in New Zealand had Royal Arch Chapters attached to them; and when the Lodges concerned, went over to the New Zealand Constitution, the Chapters were left in an anomalous position, like colonies without a mother country. The logical solution was the formation of the Grand Chapter of New Zealand, and this took place in 1892. The prime mover was M.E. Companion E.T. Gillon of Wellington, a Scottish Royal Arch Mason who had also been one of the principal Brethren active in the formation of the Grand Lodge of New Zealand. Grand Chapter was formed by seven Chapters—five English and two Scottish—and M.E. Companion E.T. Gillon was elected and installed as First Grand Principal.

It was agreed that all the degrees as recognised and practised in Scottish Royal Arch Masonry be included in the Constitution of the Grand Chapter of New Zealand. These degrees include the Mark Master, Excellent Master, Royal Arch, Ark Mariner and Red Cross Knights (Red Cross of Babylon). It was also decided that until otherwise ordered, and so far as they are applicable, the Laws and Regulations of the Supreme Grand Royal Arch Chapter of Scotland should be the Constitution of the Grand Chapter of New Zealand.

The Scottish form of ritual was also adopted, though of course both the Book of Constitution and the Ritual have been subject to alterations in detail over the intervening years. It is interesting to notice that M.E. Companion H. Thompson, the first Grand Master of the Grand Lodge of New Zealand, became First Grand Principal of Grand Chapter in 1894; while M.E. Companion E. T. Gillon received the rank of Past Grand Master (Honoris Causa) in Grand Lodge in the same year.

The Cryptic degrees of Royal Master, Select Master and Super Excellent Master were adopted by Grand Chapter in 1937, first as side degrees. Later the Constitution was altered to provide for the Councils to be separately chartered and each Council to be attached to a Royal Arch Chapter as is the practice under the Grand Chapter of Scotland. This alteration was made owing to objections to our procedure from the General Grand Council of U.S.A.

## The Growth of Grand Chapter

Grand Chapter has grown from seven Chapters in 1892 to 104 in 1966 (with 99 active Chapters). Most Chapters have several Lodges to support them. There are 8012 Royal Arch Masons under Grand Chapter as at 30th September 1965 as compared with 46,760 Craft Masons under Grand Lodge at the same date. We have no figures for the three British Constitutions operating in New Zealand but the proportion will probably be about the same.

## Offices in Grand Chapter

The principal offices in Grand Chapter are as follows (with the American equivalents in parentheses):
- First Grand Principal (Grand High Priest).
- Depute Grand Principal (Deputy Grand High Priest).
- Second Grand Principal (Grand King).
- Third Grand Principal (Grand Scribe).
- The New Zealand Grand Scribe Ezra is equivalent to the American Grand Secretary of Grand Chapter.

## Grand Chapter Ranks

The First Grand Principal and Pro First Grand Principal (present and Past) are Most Excellent. The Depute Grand Principal and Second and Third Grand Principals, Grand Superintendents and Executive Officers namely Chairman of Supreme Committee, Grand Scribe E Grand Treasurer and Grand Registrar, and also the Grand Lecturers (present and Past) are Right Excellent. Others are Very Excellent. For convenience the First Grand Principal is often referred to as the Grand Z. an abbreviation for Grand Zerubbabel.

Originally—following Scottish procedure—all present and Past Principals of Chapters were Most Excellent. Eventually it was decided to make a distinction, and it was decided that only First Grand Principals (present and Past) should be Most Excellent. Other Grand Principals were Right Excellent. Alterations in the list were made with the introduction of additional officers such as Pro Grand Z (Most Excellent), Grand Superintendents, Executive Officers and Grand Lecturers (Right Excellent).

The Pro Grand Z is elected if the Governor General is First Grand Principal, and in the event there is no Depute Grand Z. The Pro Grand Z receives Honoris Causa rank as Past Grand Z after his term of office, unless he is elected Grand Z in his own right.

**Supreme Committee**
Supreme Committee is located for two-year periods in each of six different principal cities and the Executive Officers (other than the Grand Scribe E) are chosen from that District. The Grand Scribe E is a permanent officer and at present resides in Auckland and attends the meetings of Supreme Committee in the various centres as required.

**Districts and Divisions**
For the purpose of the allocation of offices, New Zealand is divided into three Divisions and each Division consists of several Districts. The offices are allocated to the three Divisions for one year each in rotation. Normally each officer holds office for only one year, except the Executive officers (usually two years) and the Grand Superintendents of Districts, generally for two or three years.

There are twelve Districts, each in charge of a Grand Superintendent who conducts the Installations in the Chapters in his District with the assistance of local Grand Chapter Officers. There are no Provincial or District Grand Chapters. The Grand Superintendent is the head of his District, although in fact he usually has among his Grand Chapter Officers, Companions of higher rank than himself (e.g. Past or present Grand Principals) but these assist him in the local work of his District.

## Recognition

As in the case of the Grand Lodge of New Zealand, there was considerable delay in obtaining recognition by the Grand Chapters of England, Ireland and Scotland. Grand Chapter was fortunate in having a very able and persistent Grand Scribe E in the person of Most Excellent Companion H. J. Williams, P.G.Z., who held that office from 1892 until his death in 1922.

## Visits by First Grand Principal Excellent Master Degree

The First Grand Principal is expected nowadays, as part of his duties, to pay an official visit, at least once during his term of office, to each of the twelve Districts in the territory. The Visit usually includes attendance at a Combined Meeting of Chapters in the District, details of which are arranged by the local Grand Superintendent after correspondence with the First Grand Principal. Usually a degree is worked (unless it is an Installation meeting) and subsequently the Toast of the First Grand Principal is proposed in the Refectory after supper, and the First Grand Principal gives a suitable address of an informative or inspirational nature and meets as many of the Companions as practical and convenient. The meeting is usually held in the principal town or city in the District.

## Installation of Principals of Chapters

The Installation of Principals of Chapters is conducted by the Grand Superintendent of the District with the assistance of present and Past Grand Chapter Officers. The office of Grand Superintendent is therefore a fairly onerous one, as he has extensive correspondence and this requires his personal attention, since he has no Secretary.

At one time—before 1908 when Grand Superintendents were first appointed—the Installations were conducted either by one of the Grand Principals resident in the District or by some Grand

Chapter officer, present or Past, who was willing to undertake the work. For a long time Grand Chapter rejected the idea of electing Grand Superintendents on the ground of expense, namely the cost of their travelling expenses; but their introduction has proved a great success and they have often been described as the "key men" of Grand Chapter. They rank immediately below the Third Grand Principal and are frequently promoted to be Grand Principals some years after vacating office.

**Grand Lecturers**
Three Grand Lecturers are appointed each year—one in each Division. Their duties are similar to those of the Grand Lecturers in Grand Lodge. They are concerned with Masonic Education and the delivery of lectures, and not with the teaching of ritual.

**Excellent Master Degree**
The Excellent Master is different from the American Degree of Most Excellent Master. The latter is not accepted by the Grand Chapter of New Zealand as equivalent to our Excellent degree. If an American Royal Arch Mason wished to witness the Excellent degree, he must first affiliate with a Chapter under the Grand Chapter of New Zealand and take the Excellent degree himself as a candidate and thus be duly obligated and receive the secrets of the degree. This information may be of interest to American Royal Arch Masons visiting New Zealand. Similarly an American Royal Arch Mason could not affiliate with our Chapter of Research in Auckland unless he has first taken the Excellent degree.

**Past Master Degree**
We do not have the Degree of Past Master as worked in American Royal Arch Chapters. There is no need for it as it is not necessary to be a Past Master before becoming a Royal Arch Mason. The secrets of an Installed Master are conferred on the Master-Elect in a Board of Installed Masters held within his own Craft Lodge.

## Annual Convocation of Grand Chapter

The Annual Convocation of Grand Chapter is held in turn in the four principal cities, Auckland, Wellington, Christchurch and Dunedin and in Provincial cities such as Napier, Rotorua, and Invercargill, which have sufficient hotel accommodation. The city chosen usually the principal city in the District from which the incoming First Grand Principal is selected, so that if possible he can be installed in his home District. Failing sufficient hotel accommodation in the home District the Convocation is held in a large city in an adjoining District in the same Division.

## Grand Scribe E

Grand Chapter is not large enough to maintain a full-time Grand Scribe E and office staff; and Grand Lodge refuses to permit their Grand Secretary to act as Grand Scribe E. The present Grand Scribe E is a Public Accountant practising in Auckland, and provides his own office and staff; and he fits in the work of Grand Chapter with his accountancy practice. This arrangement is most satisfactory and I hope that it will long continue.

# PART III.—OTHER MASONIC GROUPS

## Rose Croix, or Antient and Accepted Rite

THIS IS similar to the American Scottish Rite, though I understand that the ritual is somewhat different. There are 35 Chapters in the control of the Supreme Council of England and Wales; and 19 Chapters and 3 Sovereign Councils under the Supreme Council of Scotland.

It should be stated here that under the Supreme Council of New Zealand under England, it is not as easy to obtain either the 32d or the 33d as in U.S.A. where both are given freely. The 30d, 31d and 32d are conferred only on Past Sovereigns and the number of 33d is limited to members of the Supreme Council, Inspectors General of Districts and a very few Honorary Ranks. Consequently it is not possible in New Zealand for the average Brother to attain the 32d much less the 33d. Under the Supreme Council of England there are only five 33d Brethren in New Zealand at present, namely the three Inspectors General and two Past Inspectors General. The 33d is the highest rank to which the average Brother can aspire. This is granted on the recommendation of the Chapter supported by that of the Inspector General. The 32d and 33d are granted only on the recommendation of the Inspector General. The position appears to be much the same under the Grand Chapter of Scotland but no details are available to the author.

The 4th to the 17th Degrees are conferred by name and the 18th or Rose Croix Degree is worked in full, the candidate being first given the Secrets of the 17th Degree. The 30d and higher are granted by Patent but the 30d is worked occasionally in full when a minimum of three present or past Inspectors General 33d must be present. Candidates for the Rose Croix Degree must be Master Masons who profess the Christian Faith and are of high moral character. The requirement of the Christian Faith excludes Jewish Brethren from going beyond the 17th. A candidate must have received the three Degrees of Craft Masonry in a Lodge or Lodges recognised by the Grand Lodge of England and must (unless a Dispensation is granted by the Supreme Council) have been at least three years a Master Mason. Brethren belonging to Lodges under the Grand Lodge of New Zealand are qualified under this provision.

Though there is no specific rule about it, candidates at one time were usually expected to take the Royal Arch Degree before being invited to join a Rose Croix Chapter. Personally I favour this practice and regard the Royal Arch as a suitable preparation for the Rose Croix. Brethren who join the Rose Croix first are generally satisfied with it and fail to join the Royal Arch at all. There is of course a close personal connection in New Zealand between the Rose Croix Chapters and the Knight Templar Preceptories due to the same Brethren belonging to both. The latter Degree requires the Royal Arch as a qualification.

## Knights Templar

There are 9 English Preceptories (equivalent to the American Commanderies) and 18 or 19 Scottish Preceptories in New Zealand. The Scottish Knights were earlier in the field and were more active.

The Knight Templar Preceptories work the Degree of Knight Templar and also occasionally the Side Degree of Knight of Malta. The Red Cross of Babylon is not worked by the Preceptories but is part of the Royal Arch system in New Zealand and is conferred as a Side Degree in a Red Cross Council within a Royal Arch Chapter.

## Royal Order of Scotland

The Provincial Grand Lodge of New Zealand was formed in 1919 and the headquarters were located successively in Christchurch, Dunedin and Wellington. The Order later became semi-dormant and in 1954 the Provincial Grand Master, R.W. Bro. George Russell resigned; and the Order was then divided into two Provincial Grand Lodges, one for New Zealand North and the other for New Zealand South. Following the division, the Order has flourished in both Provincial Grand Lodges with more local interest and more frequent meetings. The Provincial Grand Lodge of New Zealand North is located in Auckland and that of New Zealand South has alternated between Dunedin and Christchurch and is at present located in Christchurch. The author was Provincial Grand Master from 1958 to 1963.

## Secret Monitor

The Allied Degrees are not worked in New Zealand but the Secret Monitor is worked as a separate Degree under the Grand Conclave of England. There are 16 Conclaves in New Zealand. The Grand Master, Sir George Boag has visited New Zealand twice within recent years.

**Red Cross of Constantine**
This is worked under the Grand Imperial Conclave of England. There are four Conclaves in New Zealand.

**Royal Arch Knight Templar Priest**
This Degree is worked under the Grand College of England. There are two Tabernacles in New Zealand. The Grand High Priest Bro. G.W. Bourn visited New Zealand several years ago and many of our local Brethren were privileged to meet him in various capacities. The author does not belong to this Degree or to the Secret Monitor or the Red Cross of Constantine.

**Societas Rosicruciana In Anglia**
This corresponds to the American S.R.I.C.F.A. We have one College in New Zealand, the Christchurch College, meeting at Christchurch. It was chartered in 1906 and after working for several years became dormant. The author received the Zelator Grade in the Metropolitan College, London in 1929 and had a considerable part in the revival of the Christchurch College in 1935. The College is now active and has an enthusiastic membership.

**General**
Freemasonry in New Zealand has, of late, suffered the same troubles and problems as our Brethren overseas (including U.S.A.) namely poor attendance, loss of interest, shortage of candidates and falling membership. It is one of the tests of the ability of a Master (or other presiding officer) if he can hold together his Lodge or Chapter under adverse conditions, by the use of lectures, Demonstrations of Proving, Catechetical Lectures and other forms of Masonic instruction.

The author has done a good deal of lecturing in his own Masonic Province during the past two years; and he is very pleased to note that the attendance at meetings where a lecture is given, is nowadays quite good and the Brethren are inclined to ask questions of the lecturer at the end of the meeting. At one time attendance fell heavily when a lecture was being given, as compared with the normal attendance at a meeting with Degree work.

It would be fitting to conclude by saying how much the author appreciates the very great kindness, assistance and co-operation of his many Masonic correspondents in U.S.A. including M.W. Bro. H.W. Bundy, R.W. Bro. Ward St. Clair, Wor. Bro. H. V. B. Voorhis, Wor. Bro.J.B. Vrooman and the late M.W. Bros. Ray V. Denslow, Dr. William Moseley Brown and C. C. Hunt.

# TWO THEORIES TO LOOK INTO

## Harold V. B. Voorhis, FPS

*1968 Certificate of Literature*

I ONCE wrote (in *The Story of the Scottish Rite of Freemasonry*— 1965) "I hesitate to enter into a controversy but I have ventured in nebulous fields before and have been pushed to the 'river's edge' more than once, and have survived numerous jostlings without permanent scars—so one more excursion will not make or break me, historically."

The present undertaking, however, is not presented in the nature of a controversy, as what will follow is just a partial recording of what I have found relating to the subjects I have chosen. The comments which I make are mostly to give the reasons why I bring these things to the attention of Masonic historians. I admit, in the first place, that the "sources" of what will follow are nothing more than the figments of imagination of the authors for the most part, but I enter into "their worlds" purely as an exercise in theoretical thinking. This may stimulate others to look into the subjects, if possible, to a much greater extent—especially the Operative Masonry part.

These are fascinating pictures, if nothing else, and also subjects which have not only been ignored by Masonic historians, but when mentioned at all, have been without documentation.

When an historian in the United States writes upon matters in the British Isles, especially upon Masonic subjects, his output is looked upon by disdain, even though the sources and data have been secured with the kind help of British Brethren. I am in that difficult position again now, but as this is not a history, per se, I have no qualms along the line of disdainfulness.

It is the historical void between the time of Operative and Speculative Masonry, which many Masonic historians have said, or intimated, will never be filled, which prompted me to bring these two theories to the attention of Freemasons. I am not putting forth any thesis about the subjects, but just making some of the material available for the "thinking Mason" in one place.

### John Cleland and the Druids

To begin, I must say a few words about an individual whose name would probably be in the realms of oblivion had he not written a book now called *Fanny Hill*, circa 1749. In fact, although thousands of people know about the book, very few probably know the name of the author. He wrote a dozen or so books, pamphlets and dramas, in addition to Fanny Hill. He was an authority on the ancient Celtic language. A thumb-nail sketch of his life will suffice here.

In the Introduction of Memoirs of Fanny Hill, privately printed in 1907—The Kamashastra Society—Paris and Benares, called *A Genuine Reprint of the Rare Edition of 1749*, 250 copies (of which the one at hand is No. 30), it says that John Cleland was born in 1707. Biographies say "about 1710." It also states that "his father, Colonel Cleland, was the original of 'Will Honeycomb' of Addison and Steele." Lt. Col. William Cleland (1660–1689), killed in the Battle of Dunkeld, whose poems were published in 1697, could not have been the father of John Cleland. He was more than likely a son of William Cleland (1674–1741), of Scotland, who lived in Westminster, where the author of Fanny Hill went to school.

He was Consul at Smyrna and following some misunderstandings with his superiors, left the service and went to Bombay, where he worked for the East India Company. Next, he travelled about the Orient and Europe and finally returned to England, where he was imprisoned for debt. He wrote some articles for the public prints, including the *Public Advertiser*. While in jail, one of his publishers (Griffiths) offered him 20 guineas for any MS. which might sell. Fanny Hill—originally called *Memoirs Of A Woman Of Pleasure* was the result—being published in two parts. Some of the wording was changed to make it more "sensational."

Cleland was hauled into court after it was published but released on a promise not to write such material again. Lord Granville, who he had befriended, sought and secured a pension of a hundred pounds a year for him from the government. He then wrote several works, including dramas, some of which are:

1751 – *Memoirs of a Coxcomb*

1755 – *Titus Vespasian*

1755 – *The Ladies' Subscription*

1758 – *Timbo-Chiqui or the American Savage*

1765 – *Surprises of Love*

1765 – *The Man of Honour*

1766 – *The Way to Things by Words and to Words by Things*

1767 – *Specimen of a Etimological Vocabulary or Essay by Means of the Anilitic Method to Retrieve the Ancient Celtic.*

He wrote some pamphlets also—two of which are *Origin of Musical Waifs at Christmas* and *The Origin of Freemasons*. They were printed along with other works and appear to have been written in 1766. He also wrote an *Essay on the Real Secret of the Free-Masons* in 1767.

He died on January 23, 1789 at a place called Petty, France, which has not been identified.

The Celtic language essay, the Musical Waif essay, and the Masonic essay appeared together, the latter on pages 108–123. The first two paragraphs of the latter are of interest:

"There is hardly any thing that can be more unlikely, than that of an Oath of Secrecy, of so tremendous a nature, as that of the Free Masons at their admission, is by themselves acknowledged to be, should originally have had no foundation, but in so arbitrary and improbable a fiction, as that of the Masonry, either of the Temple of Jerusalem, or of that of any other remote country or age; or, worse yet, no foundation at all; for surely there can be none, or less than none, in the humor of swearing a sacred, inviolable oath, merely for the sake of swearing it; since nothing can be more clearly presumable, than that the Institutes of that society, such as it exists at present, are not only perfectly innocent, but even laudable.

"The inventors then of that oath, must have unpardonable trifled with the awful solemnity of such an engagement, if, at the time of its first institution, there had not existed a cause for that oath, proportionate, at least in some measure, to its precautions against violation. And of this cause it is, that I now propose to offer the result of my attempt at an investigation, a cause which will at once acquit the first authors of the original institution of so heavy a charge as that of making light of the imposition of a sacred oath, and open a view into the shades of the remotest antiquity, with which this institution has an immediate connexion, though it did not come into existence 'till after the Roman invasion of Britain, and most probably, since the commencement of Christianity in it."

He then gives a long drawn out commentary from the time that the Romans invaded England, delineated from various sources and covering the nature of the Druids, who were on the Island when the Romans arrived. He traces the downfall of the Sect, which, he says, was reduced to an "unhappy remnant of the Druidical votaries to the last extremities of ruin and dispair." He says that among the names by which they were known was "MAY'S-SONS." He notes that the Maypole was the real symbol of the Druids and that they celebrated their feast in May. Also, that the symbol was used by them "as the Cross was in Christianity." He writes at length upon this subject and concludes that the present Masonic Society lost sight of the origin when it took up the Hiramic Theory to cover up the real origin of Masonry. He ends by saying that far from entertaining any disrespect of the present Society of Free Masons it has the "spirit of social instinct, and of universal charity and benevolence to mankind."

Now what do we learn from Cleland's theory? In a word (no pun intended) that Freemasonry came from The Druids and that the name as *May's sons*. An interesting theory, and not exactly unplausible, either. So much for that.

Now let us come into a period many centuries later—just prior to the formation of the Grand Lodge at London—say 1710–1723. This is the period of which Masonic historians say so little. They often excuse their lack of information by offering their own reasons why we have such a dearth of documented material of this period.

I realize that many of the statements made about the period are the conclusions of the writers, but they show a trend of being copied from one another, with some tricky word changing. Even in the list of papers presented in A.Q.C. we find only a few references to the Druids, and not much or often is much said about the happenings of James Anderson, who compiled (so he said) the 1723 and 1738 *Constitutions* of The Grand Lodge of England.

From *Guild Masonry in the Making* by Dr. Charles H. Merz of Ohio, U.S.A., 1918, 478 pages, we find many and sundry statements, quotations, and some documentary evidence (which I use in toto, without checking) upon which he advances a plausible theory of what happened just before the formation of the Grand Lodge at London. If it could be documented by records, which he says are said to be extant but mostly unavailable, it would become a most interesting piece of history. The sum and substance of the theory amounts to the following:

Quoting from a statement by a Brother S. Stewart Stitt, P.M.—"In the early part of the 18th Century, a Judas (according to the Operatives) arose in the person of one Rev. James Anderson, a Presbyterian Minister, who was Chaplain of St. Paul's Operative Lodge

(1st. January to September 1715).... It is certain that he was mainly responsible for the modern Speculative System. He was expelled from the Worshipful Society of Free Masons for his disloyalty."

Brother Merz admits that facts about Dr. Anderson's career as an Operative Lodge Chaplain "are very difficult to state satisfactorily." He was told that records are in possession of the present Operative Guild but are not available for public inspection. They purport to show that Dr. Anderson was Chaplain of a Scottish Operative Lodge in 1709, and that he came to London the following year, where he became Chaplain to the St. Paul's Operative Lodge, which was then thirty-five years old, having been formed to build the new St. Paul's with stones prepared at Portland.

The rules of the Operative Lodges appear to exempt Doctors and Chaplains from passing through the customary ceremonies and time limits for advancement. Instead they took an oath regarding the first six Grades—the final, or Seventh Grade, only being held by three Masters.

It is claimed that Anderson, in 1714, began to make non-Operative members at a charge of five guineas (about $25). In that year, so the claim goes, he made seven such members:

1 – Anthony Sayer—an employee in the drawing office under Sir Christopher Wren.
2 – George Payne—chief secretary to the Commissioner of Taxes
3 – Rev. John Theophilus Desaguliers
4 – John, 2nd. Duke of Montagu
5 – Johnson—a Doctor who received fees for medical examination of Apprentices
6 – Stuart—a lawyer who prepared contracts
7 – Entick—gentleman, not otherwise identified

Regarding the first four, who became the first four Grand Masters of the London Speculative Grand Lodge, we find that they belonged to Lodges which might have been selected or even formed by Anderson himself, meeting in the following Taverns:

1 – Apple-Tree
2 – Horn
3 – Horn; Rummer & Grapes; and Bear and Harrow;
4 – Bear and Harrow

The Engraved List of 1729 notes that The Goose and Gridiron Lodge was formed in 1691. The Crown, according to this same list, was formed in 1712. How much truth there is in these records is questionable.

In Anderson's account of 1738, he says that in 1716 the four Lodges that met were:

Goose and Gridiron, Crown, Apple-Tree, and Rummer and Grapes, and that they and some old Brothers met at the said Apple-Tree. No individuals are mentioned. On June 24, 1717, they met at the Goose and Gridiron and formed a Grand Lodge and elected Antony (sic) Sayer, Gentleman, Grand Master. On June 24, 1718 they elected George Payne, Esqr. Grand Master. On June 24, 1719 they elected The Reverend Brother John Theophilus Desaguliers, L.L.D. and F.R.S. Grand Master. On June 24, 1720, George Payne was again elected Grand Master. And, on June 24, 1721, John Montagu, Duke of Montagu, was elected Grand Master. Sayer belonged to Apple-Tree; Payne to Horn; Desaguliers to Horn and Rummer & Grapes; while Montagu to Bear and Harrow. Thus two additional Lodges came to view since the 1716 meeting—Horn in 1718 and Bear and Harrow in 1721.

An anonymous work, published forty-six years after the event—*The Complete Freemason or Multa Paucis for Lovers of Secrets*, says that six Lodges met at the Apple-Tree Tavern. If we use the four of 1716 and two of 1717, we do have six. Henry W. Coil, in his Encyclopedia (page 276) succinctly says that "there is no documentary or eye witness evidence at all that any one of them existed prior to the formation of the Grand Lodge."

During the month of September 1715, the Operative Society of the Freemasons of the City of London, with Sir Christopher Wren being Grand Master and Thomas Strong in the Second Chair, expelled Anderson and his seven "gentlemen" from the Society, runs the claim. Then in 1716, because the members of the four Lodges enumerated found themselves neglected by Wren – they decided to form themselves into a Grand Lodge and "chuse a Grand Master from among themselves."

The statement made by Anderson, about Sir Christopher Wren cannot be construed to mean anything else but that he was a Grand Master. As, after several years of investigations, no evidence has come to light that he was a Speculative Mason, it seems rather obvious that he was then the Grand Master of the Operatives.

Anderson, it appears, was Imperator of the Speculative Grand Lodge of 1717. He is the only one who has left us any record of it. In working out the system he made use of the Operative or Gothic ritual, so far as he could, never having been received into the Operative VII Grade or Degree, Mackey's opinion reflects the general view of those who have studied the subject:

"The modes of recognition, the methods of government, the legends and much of the ceremonial of initiation were in existence among Operative Masons of the middle ages, and were transmitted to the Speculative Masons of the eighteenth century. The work of Anderson, Desaguliers, and their contemporaries, was to improve (?) and to enlarge, but not to invent."

Dr. Merz thinks that "any effort upon the part of the Operative Society to bring Dr. Anderson's work into notice meets with the disapproval of Speculative writers." Brother Morcombe, editor of "The American Freemason" in the May 1913 issue, remarked concerning this same theme that "a very effective veil has been drawn and of intention rather than accident."

Masonic writers who have commented on the Anderson matters, pooh-pooh the whole theme mentioned above by saying "show us the evidence." What about the other side? There are no minutes of the Grand Lodge 1716–1722! There are no minutes of Anderson's Lodge of Antiquity 1715–1723 which have never been seen, nor any of the other five Lodges mentioned above. The Grand Lodge of England, in 1911, in a circular letter, said that "the ritual of Freemasonry, so far as the first and second degrees are concerned, is, in part, no doubt, derived from the ceremonies of the Operative Guilds."

I submit that the Operative Theme, so far as it relates to Anderson's expulsion from the Operative Society, together with the seven "gentlemen"—and their forming a Grand Lodge, is undocumented. However, it does have the elements of a believable story. That is more than can be said about the contentions of writers who bring forth the formation of the Grand Lodge in 1717 "out of thin air" more or less. Their only reason seems to be the statement made by Anderson that Sir Christopher Wren was "neglecting" the Lodges. The Lodges referred' to as being neglected by Wren had finished their operative work and disbanded. I have never noticed any references to the Speculative Lodges mentioned by Anderson before the Grand Lodge was erected. I don't think we will find any contemporary references if Anderson erected them.

I am not proposing that the "Operative Theme" be accepted, but I do suggest some work be done toward examining any evidence which may be produced by the present Lodges supposed to have been involved in the formation of the Grand Lodge, circa 1715–1722. And, in contra-distinction that the Operative bodies come up with some documentary evidence, to support their theme. Surely some Masonic historians in England, many of whom are exceedingly qualified to make the investigations needed, could be a particular service to those of us not "on the spot" and have no entree to the Places of deposit of documents.

# THE SOUL OF FREEMASONRY

## Franklin J. Anderson, FPS

### *1970 Certificate of Literature*

WHEN A MAN desires to become a member of the Masonic Fraternity he signs a petition for the degrees stating that he freely and voluntarily offers himself for the mysteries of Freemasonry. After the Lodge receives the petition, and the proper procedures have been followed, the hour for balloting arrives, and the Master announces that the Lodge is about to ballot on the petition of Mr. John Jones to receive the mysteries of Freemasonry. The ballot being favorable, due record is made that Mr. Jones was elected to receive the mysteries of Freemasonry. On the eve of initiation before any move may be made toward entering the Lodge, the candidate must again assert that he is offering himself for the mysteries of Freemasonry.

Through each of the degrees, either in thoughts expressed or implied, the idea of mystery is conveyed to the candidate.

Scholars, historians, authorities dispute about the age of Freemasonry. At times the disagreement is caused by a lack of understanding of terminology. Freemasonry is over 250 years old if by that term is meant that society which created the first Grand Lodge. If Freemasonry's earliest document, the Regius Manuscript is correctly dated, Freemasonry is nearly 600 years old. If belief in the early date mentioned in that manuscript is sustainable and

Freemasons met in the City of York A.D. 926 then Freemasonry is more than 1,000 years old. If by Freemasonry is meant an organization which employs symbols and religious practices which come from the dawn of civilization, then Freemasonry is as old as civilization itself.

Whatever age we may assume Freemasonry has attained, many generations of human life are represented. In all phases of human endeavor, social, political, civic, and in the fields of science, art, and culture vast changes have taken place. Our mode of life has transformed from bare existence to luxurious living; transportation from foot to ox-cart to horse to steam to air; communication from tom-tom to electronics; kingdoms have waxed and waned; the entire world has become much different.

Through all these changes Freemasonry has retained the same ideals, taught the same principles and maintained the Ancient Landmarks of the Fraternity. Through all these ages and changes, to each one who has entered the portals of Freemasonry, the hint of mystery, the desire to know what Freemasonry really is, has ever been present.

The principles and beliefs of the Fraternity, many of the practices, the exoteric work, is published for any to read who care to do so. But there is an indefinable something more, something which we can not explain. A Brother when asked to explain Freemasonry replied, "I know what it is until you ask, but when you ask I cannot explain." Freemasonry is an emotion deep within us, a mystery which we propose to call the Soul of Freemasonry.

In the unabridged dictionary there are several definitions of soul, four of which we find applicable to use in defining Freemasonry.

**1. Soul—A person who leads or inspires.**
How true this is of the Fraternity as well as of individual Masons. All the good works of the Fraternity must be done—not as an organization—but by Masons as individuals, yet it has been the result of the associations formed within the confines of the Lodge room,

the result of inspiration gained from the teachings of Freemasonry, that these beneficial works came to fruition.

Consider the role that Freemasonry has assumed through its votaries in framing the Declaration of Independence, the Constitution of these United States and many other important landmarks in our country's history. Consider the part that Freemasonry has played, through its members, in every forward movement of education, civic associations and government on every level. Someone has said that every movement for good in every field has had as its prime movers or most ardent supporters those who were members of the Fraternity. Surely, a part of the mystery, a part of the Soul of Freemasonry is its capacity to inspire and to provide leadership.

## 2. Soul—The necessary or central part of anything, that part which gives vigor and character.

Consideration of this definition of soul immediately brings to mind the ritual and the laws of Freemasonry as the central and necessary parts of our system which impart vigor and give character when properly used and consciously interpreted.

No composition is more beautiful, more majestic and more satisfying to the peace of mind than our ritual. We love it, we never tire of hearing it, and each hearing brings new meaning to us in each of its words and phrases. Only the Holy Scriptures, divinely inspired excel the ritual in majesty, inspiration and beauty.

The code of Masonic Law, with the Ancient Charges and Constitutions, the basis of all Masonic Laws, the codes of all Grand Jurisdictions give character to Freemasonry.

Each Jurisdiction has its own code or set of laws, yet each lives in harmony with all others. Annually, or oftener, there is an exchange of new laws, a revision of old laws, and an interchange of the activities of each. We need no special dispensation, no passport or visa to visit in sister Jurisdictions, only to be able to prove that we are Brothers. Each Jurisdiction is a law unto itself, the rituals may differ, but we enjoy fellowship one with the other and experience that emotion deep within us which tells us we are Brothers.

H.L. Haywood in one of his articles, commenting on this exchange of ideas between Jurisdictions, gives birth to the idea of nations and religious denominations using a similar system of exchange of ideas and practices. Each becoming more strong, more an entity in itself yet through a free exchange of ideas, laws and freedom, all working harmoniously together. Perhaps here is a field not yet explored that Freemasons could profitably study and promote for the good and eventual benefit of all mankind. Freemasonry does have those qualities which impart vigor and character.

### 3. Soul—The essential part of a person's identity, that part of a man's nature where feeling, ideals and morals center.

Again it is apparent that in our ritual and our laws the ideals and morals of Freemasonry are set forth and described, but it is in the individual Brother that the feelings, ideals and morals center. The Brother who is a Mason in the purest sense of the term, is the center of, and the living Soul of Freemasonry. Each of us has experienced that special, not to be described thrill, that good feeling which comes to us in every Masonic fellowship, with every handclasp and renewal of acquaintance.

We usually think of a soul as something alive, living, immortal. It is my belief that the mystery, the Soul of Freemasonry is constituted of some part of the living immortal soul of every inspired, devoted Brother who has been Freemasonry's progenitors. Those who during their lives left such an imprint on the minds of their associates, that a part of their very selves lives with us still. This thought can be best expressed by a personal incident.

In company with my daughter we visited Abraham Lincoln's home in Springfield, Illinois. We toured the rooms, we viewed the various items on display, we read the placards all in accepted tourist fashion. As we were leaving the last room a placard on the wall read that this was the spot where Mr. Lincoln stood as he was notified of his nomination for the Presidency of the United States. Wishing my daughter to be aware of the historical significance of the place in which we stood I read the placard and told her that here was where history was made. Something in the import of that statement, something in the feeling of the atmosphere filled me with emotion, my voice broke and my daughter was constrained to ask, "Daddy what's the matter?" Now I do not believe in spiritualism or ghosts but I do believe that at that moment, somehow, someway I was moved by the immortal soul of Lincoln. I believe that Freemasons of this day are moved by the immortal souls of Washington, Franklin, Parvin, Ray V. Denslow, Carl H. Claudy and other Masonic stalwarts who labored long and faithfully in the quarries of Freemasonry.

## 4. Soul—That spiritual and immortal part in man which distinguishes him from beasts.

Freemasonry though not a religion is definitely and distinctively religious, the entire philosophy, all its teachings are predicated upon the existence of God, a God in whom we can place our trust, and from whom strength and wisdom flow in response to our prayers. This definite belief in the Supreme Being distinguishes reemasonry from other purely social orders. This is the quality which has preserved the identity of Freemasonry through generations although other organizations have started, flourished for a time but because they had no soul, have perished.

The spiritual in Freemasonry signifies our belief in the Fatherhood of God, the Brotherhood of Man and in the Immortality of the Soul. As an organization we stress more particularly the building of a noble character and moral life yet in every portion of the work we urge a study of and imply a need for the spiritual awareness.

These teachings are most evident in the drama of the Master Mason degree. This is the culmination, the acme of Masonic teaching. Here is set forth the fundamental principles by which man should live with fellowman. Here is the most solemn moment in the life of every candidate in Freemasonry, that moment when he is escorted to the altar and informed that he is to pray alone. Do we always lend to this moment of the degree the dignity and reverence which we should? The drama symbolizes to those of us who are of the Christian faith the crux of the Christian teaching, the promise that if we live according to the Master's precepts we, too, will one day be raised from a dead level to a living perpendicular and Immortal Life. For Brethren of other faiths it dramatically represents their beliefs according to the prophets of old.

Whatever our personal belief, however lax we may be in personal devotions, it seems inconceivable that any Freemason would want to be guilty of irreverence or blasphemy, but if we do not portray this drama with the dignity, the reverence and the majesty it deserves, we are, in a very real sense guilty of these sins.

Freemasonry does have that Spiritual and immortal quality which distinguishes man from beast. It is this—the Soul of Freemasonry—which has enabled our Fraternity to live and serve these 250, 600, 1000 years.

the 16th of October 1646 Elias Ashmole, antiquarian, was received into a Masonic Lodge at Warrington, Lancashire, together with his Roundhead friend and cousin, Henry Manwaring of Carincham, Cheshire. Ashmole's diary gives the time of the event as 4:30 p.m. notes the name of the Lodge's Warden, and the names of six other Masons 'then of the Lodge.' Ashmole's motives for joining were undoubtedly similar to those of the antiquary William Stukeley (1687–1765) who states in his autobiography that, in 1720, 'his curiosity led him to be initiated into the mysterys of Masonry, suspecting it to be the remains of the mysterys of the antients.' It is conceivable that, after acquiring by the study of astrology a taste for the exploration of ancient lore and symbolism, Ashmole not only desired to pain knowledge of such 'Pythagorean' teachings as the Lodges claimed to preserve, but that he was at this particular juncture of his life, also looking for the fellowship of brethren who, if not equally learned, would share his respect for the old and mysterious. Ashmole's note of his Masonic initiation is the earliest known record of speculative Freemasonry in an English Lodge. As has been pointed out by Josten, the note in the diary evidences an advanced stage rather than the beginning of the evolution by which the Craft Lodges were gradually transformed into esoteric societies of gentlemen and members of all professions and trades; for recent research has shown that not only Ashmole and Colonel Henry Manwaring, but all of the seven other Freemasons, whose names are given, were in no way connected with operative Freemasonry.

This brings us to the question of what has enabled Freemasonry to survive the centuries when countless other fraternal and scholarly societies have not. How has Freemasonry survived the anti-Masonry of the 18th century, the 19th century, with its Morgan incident and even the events of the 20th century?

Certainly the organization of Lodges and Grand Lodges, and the fundamental nature of the teachings have played a part. But I cannot help but believe that the most important reason is the very manner in which the great lessons are taught. What magnificent symbolism imparts the spirit of brotherhood in a certain handclasp. What better way to present the means of achieving and the importance of peace and harmony in a Lodge, than to have the candidate so prepared that these lessons are indelibly inscribed on his mind. At the same time he learns a magnificent lesson in charity. There are a great many other lessons imparted in symbolism, the duty of man to man, man to neighbor, man to God, to family and so on and on.

It is fascinating to discover that throughout all the changing periods of history for the last 2,500 years, the same basic valuations have persisted, the same conviction of the superiority of the soul over the body, of the unseen over the seen....

So it is with Freemasonry. We have a practical, realistic means of imparting the greatest of lessons but to, impress them upon the mind requires some physical application and necessitates certain physical qualifications that these lessons may be imparted in an unforgettable manner.

# OF LANDMARKS AND CUSPIDORS

## Dwight L. Smith, FPS

*1973 Certificate of Literature*

WHEN THE brass cuspidors were carried out of the hall of Beaver-dam Lodge in the little town of Mud Creek and stored in the wood-house, it is safe to say that more than one Brother looked askance that the ancient landmarks were being thus tampered with.

I recall an arrangement of "Solemn strikes the fun'ral chime" used many years ago in some of our small rural Lodges. It was a tune so melancholy that it was more of a wail than a melody. Although incredibly depressing, the Brethren liked it, and they accepted the *Pleyel's Hymn* tune grudgingly.

So it was when the wall chart was exchanged for a stereopticon, when the green cracked window blinds were discarded and drap-eries installed, when the pot-bellied stove was moved out and an oil-burning heater moved in.

There is something in the thought of ancient landmarks of Free-masonry that captures the imagination. We are enjoined to pre-serve them and never suffer them to be infringed. The young Junior Deacon in Kipling's delightful poem boasted that his Lodge in India "knew the Ancient Landmarks, an' we kep' 'em to a hair."

So far, so good. Then some brash young Mason inquires what the ancient landmarks are. And there the trouble begins.

The Grand Lodge of England, which should know a thing or two about the ancient landmarks, never has "adopted" landmarks or in any way attempted to define them other than to make casual references to certain practices. To my knowledge, no Grand Lodge of Freemasons outside the United States has ever become concerned about what the landmarks are, or how many there may be.

Not so in the U.S.A. Beginning about the middle of the Nineteenth Century, Grand Lodges started trying to define the landmarks and enumerating them. They literally ran races to see how many ancient landmarks they could "adopt" officially. Some lists became so long and so all-inclusive that it was hardly safe to take aim at the brass cuspidor for fear an ancient landmark would be removed. And the hilarious feature about the various lists of "official" and "unalterable" landmarks is that so many are in total disagreement with their neighbors' lists!

There is a tendency among Masons to get excited over the thought of dispensing with outworn, moss-covered habits and customs that have grown up in our Lodges. Many of those old habits are without official sanction; some are merely tolerated. Extra-ritualistic and superfluous, they have been added from time to time because they looked good at the moment or had an impressive sound. It is doubtful whether they ever served a useful purpose; it is certain they serve no useful purpose now.

But try to get rid of one!

"The ancient landmarks are being removed," someone is sure to say. "There must be no 'innovations in the body of Masonry,' you know." Not one. Everything must remain just as it is right now.

No changes—ever?

To remind the Brethren that there have been changes in the way Freemasonry operates, and that there will be others, is like telling a little boy there is no Santa Claus. As long ago as the Fourth Century B.C. the Greek philosopher Heraclitus was writing, "There is nothing permanent except change." The work, the habits, the customs of Freemasonry; indeed, even the things on which it places emphasis, never have been static, and cannot be so if the Craft is to fulfill its mission in a changing world.

Perhaps it would be well to recall a little historical background at this point. The great Masonic author A.S. MacBride in his book Speculative Masonry lists 16 "innovations" which took place in Freemasonry in England about the time of the formation of the Mother Grand Lodge in 1717. These included such practices as altering the names of Lodge officers and adding some new ones; adopting new tokens and passwords; introducing a new form and mode of obligation; advancing an Apprentice without proof of skill, and many others.

Premier Masonic historian R. F. Gould reminds us that between 1723 and 1738 it is a documented fact that Freemasonry changed from a two degree system to a three-degree system. As early as 1723 three striking "innovations" had been introduced, among which was the abandonment of an established religion and the acceptance of "that religion in which all men agree."

No changes?

What about the adjustments that had to be made because of the anti-Masonic period in the United States, and those that came as a result of the total abstinence agitation of the Nineteenth Century?

What about the innovation that developed when American Lodges were allowed to grow large and impersonal—a condition diametrically opposed to the early and traditional concept?

What about the strictly American innovation that came with the proliferation of other Masonic and related organizations, with the consequent shift of emphasis away from the parent Lodge?

No changes?

Remember when Masonic benevolence was quiet and personal, and there was no such thing as institutional care for the needy, the aged, and the orphan?

Remember when the Doctrine of the Perfect Youth was so rigid as to forbid the admission of a man who had so much as one small slice off the end of his little finger?

Remember when the sponsorship of youth organizations was an activity in which no Lodge would think of engaging?

Yes, and although I am not a veteran Mason by any means, I can think of a sizable number of much needed improvements that have been made in the ritual within my memory. If the Official Work is one of the ancient landmarks, then the poor old landmarks have taken quite a beating just in my time.

* * *

But most of the changes we have been talking about came in years long gone. It is easy enough to look back with a tolerant smile on adjustments that our Masonic ancestors were obliged to make. What happens when there is pressure for change in our today, rather than in someone else's today?

What should be changed and what should not be changed?

Alas, it is at this point that Pandora's box is opened to release the little winged creatures that serve to divert, and annoy, and divide.

Now and then there is a period in which Masons become impatient and "itchy" for change. What the change is doesn't matter too much, just so it is change. That is the way the cycle moves.

When that time comes, those who are concerned with the welfare of Ancient Craft Masonry would do well to remember two points:

First, changes made in remote generations should not be cited as authority for radical innovations in another century. All such changes should be viewed in the light of the times and places in which they were made. It is one thing to introduce three degrees instead of two for a tiny, disorganized group of Lodges in Eighteenth Century England. It is an altogether different thing to consider wholesale remodeling for a tightly organized Craft made up of thousands of Lodges in late Twentieth Century America—a Craft that has operated very well in America, incidentally, for more than two hundred years. To compare the two situations is like comparing watermelons with cucumbers.

Second, although Freemasonry has indeed adopted many changes in its methods in the last two and one-half centuries, each change was a slow, deliberate process. Nothing reckless. No hasty legislation crammed down the throats of reluctant Brethren who had little or no opportunity to voice their convictions. No rush to scramble on board a bandwagon and do what some neighbor has done. No visionary schemes dreamed up by zealots without the careful thought every proposition affecting the Craft deserves.

On the contrary, every change has come about in the normal course of evolution, almost imperceptibly. Masonry changed a little (but only a little) because Masons wanted a change. The ancient landmarks were not removed or infringed at all; they were just applied to new situations.

We are wise if we can avoid the error of identifying as a landmark any practice which may have been helpful a century ago, but long since has ceased to serve us well. Such practices are habits, and nothing more. Many of them belong in the same category as the cuspidor and the pot-bellied stove—worthy of sentiment, but no longer useful.

But let no man tell us that those things we know in our hearts to be fundamental to Freemasonry are like unto cuspidors and pot-bellied stoves.

Let us fight to the last ditch to keep irresponsible Brethren from engaging in indiscriminate tinkering.

Let us take a long, hard look at the motives which prompt every proposal for basic change, asking ourselves whether such remodeling projects are designed to serve Ancient Craft Freemasonry or to serve something else.

And let us be very sure that before any change is made, the Craft is ready for it. What shall it profit us if, in our zeal to establish the Masonry we think ought to be, we splinter and hopelessly divide the Masonry that is?

* * *

In the meantime, lest our temperatures soar above normal at the thought of removing the ancient landmarks, it might help us to gain a sense of perspective by stopping where we are and saying to ourselves, Let's think about this a moment. No Freemason can be certain what the ancient landmarks really are. We can be reasonably sure of only seven. And not one of the old boresome, time-consuming habits we have added from time to time is included among the seven!

The words of a Masonic writer of more than a century ago have always delighted me. "Nobody knows what they (the landmarks) comprise or omit," he says. "They are of no earthly authority, because everything is a landmark when an opponent desires to silence you, but nothing is a landmark if it stands in his way!"

# JOSEPHUS:
# THE GREAT JEWISH HISTORIAN

## John Nocas, FPS

*1974 Certificate of Literature*

THE AVERAGE person probably hasn't the faintest idea who Josephus was. This is not true, however, as to Masons for many will quickly tell you that Josephus was "the great Jewish historian." Beyond that Masonry tells us nothing. What kind of man was he, what about his youth, his manhood, his profession? What made him an authority on Jewish history?

The "believe it or not" about Josephus was that he started out as a priest and later became a soldier. Caught in the web of the Jewish revolt against Rome in the first century he was appointed Governor of Galilee and directed its defense against the Roman Legions. And it was in this capacity that he was known and famous during his lifetime—as a soldier and leader.

Joseph ben Mattityahu ha-Cohen was born in A.D. 37 and is thought to have died about A.D. 100 In his autobiography he says, "I am sprung from a sacerdotal family", and "By my mother, I am of the royal blood. For the children of Asmoneus, from whom that family was derived, had both the offices of the high-priesthood, and the dignity of a king." Judas Maccabaeus, who threw off the Syrian yoke in 165 B.C., was the head of the Asmonean dynasty.

Joseph was a man of high intelligence so he is simply stating facts when he says, "I made great proficiency in the improvements of my learning; and appeared to have both a great memory, and understanding. Moreover, when I was a child, and about fourteen years of age, I was commended by all for the love I had to learning. On which account the high-priests and principal men of the city came frequently to me, in order to know my opinion of the law." He spent his sixteenth through nineteenth years in the serious study of the three religious sects of the Jews; the Pharisees, the Sadducees and the Essenes. His words are, "So I contented myself with hard fare, and underwent great difficulties and went through them all." His choice—the Pharisees!

At the age of twenty-six he was given an important assignment. He was sent to Rome with an embassy to intercede on behalf of some priests who were there in bonds to stand trial before Ceasar. In the rough waters of the Adriatic his ship, with some six-hundred aboard, was lost in a storm. Josephus says "we swam for our lives all the night." Fortunately, he and eighty others were picked up in the morning by a passing ship. At Rome he made the acquaintance of Nero's wife, Poppaea Sabina, and apparently through this friendship with the Empress he was able to obtain the release of the imprisoned priests. Already a diplomat and a leader!

On his return to Jerusalem he found the dark clouds of revolt hovering over the land. He saw immediately the folly of farmers and tradesmen challenging the mighty Roman Empire. He says, "I therefore, endeavored to restrain these tumultuous persons, and persuaded them to change their minds … and laid before their eyes against whom it was they were going to fight. But, I could not persuade them: for the madness of desperate men was too hard for me."

Most of the Jews would have no part in a revolt against Rome and this included the Jewish King Agrippa. He also tried desperately to dissuade the firebrands. There were several groups of these, so determined to have their freedom that no one could reason with them. The boiling point was reached (A.D. 66) when the Masada, the mountain fortress built by Herod the Great, was seized and its Roman garrison slain. Jerusalem was then beseiged and again the Emperor's soldiers slain, although they had laid down their arms under a safe-conduct treaty. This was the point of no return. Savage fighting between the Syrians, who occupied much of the land, and the Jews immediately broke out. Twenty thousand Jews were killed that first day at Caesarea. The Jews retaliated and a bloodbath followed. Josephus says, "So the daytime was spent in shedding blood; and the night in fear."

Cestius Gallus, the Roman Governor of Syria, marched south from Antioch with the Twelfth Roman Legion to put down the revolt. Disaster, however, met him at Jerusalem, where he was repulsed by the savage fervor of the Jewish defenders of the city and forced to retreat. Up to this point the fighting was merely a local revolt to be put down by the nearest Roman Legion. Now, however, Cestius recognized it as a full fledged challenge to the Roman Empire—WAR!

It was the moment of truth, too, for those who opposed the rebellion. Fight with their countrymen? Or, stay neutral and be called a traitor? Josephus talked peace until the last moment, and then, reluctantly, threw in his lot with his brethren. He was, above all, a Jew and a patriot. History, however, proved him right for a million Jews were to die in the ensuing holocaust, and the tiny country to lay devastated for generations to come.

The Sanhedrin met in hurried conference and appointed Generals to defend their small country. Josephus must have been very high in their estimation, for even though he had opposed the revolt, they appointed him Commander of the forces in Galilee. It was the most important post, too, for it would be through Galilee that the Roman Legions would march on their way to Jerusalem. It was up to Josephus to stop them. Josephus was in an impossible situation and he knew it; but courageously he threw all his energies to the task. He raised an army of 100,000 men. They were untrained and he tried desperately to whip them into some kind of a fighting force. It was impossible, however, there was no way in so short a time that they could be trained to stand up to the soldiers of Rome. Since they dare not meet the enemy in open combat there was nothing else to do but fortify their most defensible cities and wait. This Josephus feverously did. Among the cities thus fortified was Jotapada. And Jotapada was the climactic point in the life of Josephus!

Meanwhile, in Rome, Nero turned his attention to Judea. The man he selected to crush the tiny country was Titus Flavius Vespasian, a veteran soldier who had helped conquer Germany and Britain.

Soon Josephus heard the dreaded news. The great Roman General, Vespasian, was marching from Antioch with the Fifth and Tenth Roman Legions. And, worse, his son Titus, with the Fifteenth Legion from Egypt, had joined him. Many cities which had been opposed to the war from the beginning opened their gates to Vespasian as he entered Galilee. Vespasian's immediate goal was Jotapada, a strong bastion in the Jewish defense. The siege of Jotapada was, for the Jews, one of the brightest moments in the wretched war.

The Jotapada defenders fought with almost supernatural fervor and bravery. Josephus describes one sortie by the Jews, "Josephus was then in fear for the city, and leaped out, and all the Jewish multitude with him. These fell together upon the Romans in great numbers, and drove them away from the wall, and performed a great many glorious and bold actions." War was a business with the Romans as we can see from Josephus' next statement, "Vespasian then set the engines for throwing stones and darts around the city. The number of the engines were in all a hundred and sixty ... which made the wall so dangerous that the Jews durst not come upon it."

The end came on the forty-seventh day and Josephus wrote later, "And as for those that were slain at the taking of the city, and in the former fights, they were numbered to be forty thousand. Vespasian gave order that the city should be entirely demolished, and all the fortifications burnt down."

Josephus was not among the forty thousand that died at Jota-pada. He and "forty persons of eminence" hid in a cavern after the city was taken, hoping to escape the city in the darkness. But, all escape routes were blocked by the Romans, and soon their hiding place was discovered. All, except Josephus, were for taking their own lives. To surrender was cowardly, they said, and in any event they would immediately be executed or, even worse, sent to Rome in chains, humiliated in public parade and cruelly killed. Josephus tried to persuade them to surrender, to no avail. One by one they slew each other until only Josephus and one other remained. Josephus then persuaded the other survivor to surrender with him.

When Josephus was brought before Vespasian two of the most remarkable and greatest men of their time faced each other. Josephus faced instant death and he knew it for there no doubt but that Vespasian would eliminate this formidable Jewish leader. Then, like a thunderbolt, came Josephus' dramatic prophecy. Standing before Vespasian he said, "I come to thee as a messenger of great tidings.... Thou, O Vespasian, art Caesar, and emperor; thou, and this thy son. For thou, O Caesar, art not only lord over me, but over the land, and the sea, and all mankind."

There was, as we all know, a prophecy widespread in Judea and throughout the East that the ruler of the world would come forth from Judea—the basis of this belief undoubtedly Messianic. Josephus' bold prediction that Vespasian would become Emperor of the Roman Empire was startling to say the least. Nero was firmly on the throne, with a long life ahead of him. Vespasian was so impressed with this prophecy of Josephus' that he spared his life.

Vespasian soon subdued the Judean cities until only Jerusa-lem remained. He now had an opportunity and pleasure that few Generals have, for the Jews in Jerusalem were engaged in a bitter civil war and he could sit back and watch them kill each other. While he was enjoying this luxury things were happening in Rome. Nero died and after bitter fighting for the throne—during which time three Emperors reigned briefly—Vespasian was proclaimed

Emperor of Rome. Josephus' remarkable prophecy had come true! And, in a way, the Messianic prophecy had come true also, for Vespasian was proclaimed Emperor while still in Judea and thus a mighty King had come forth from Judea.

Vespasian left triumphantly for Rome, leaving the siege of Jerusalem to his son Titus. Josephus was freed from his bonds and he made one last attempt with the defenders of Jerusalem to give up. They refused and the rest is history. Jerusalem fell to Titus in A.D. 70 and the city and temple destroyed.

Because of his many peace-making efforts Josephus had made enemies who now threatened his life. Forced to flee, he went to Rome. In Rome he was warmly greeted by Vespasian and a friendship began that continued until the Emperor's death. Josephus became a Roman citizen and was granted a pension. Josephus says, "And when we were come to Rome I had a great care taken of me by Vespasian. For he gave me an apartment in his own house, which he lived in before he came to the empire." It was here that Josephus settled down and turned historian. The events of the war were still fresh in his mind when he wrote the *Seven Books of the Jewish War*. Later he was to write his *Twenty Books of the Jewish Antiquities*, a history of the Jews.

Josephus was married four times. His third wife bore him three children only one of whom, Hyrcanus, survived. He had two sons by his fourth wife, Justus and Simonides-Agrippa.

It may be said that as regard to literary talent Josephus ranks among the leading writers of world literature. One paragraph in his *Antiquities* has been a center of controversy for centuries—the mention, in Book 18, of Jesus. Some scholars consider it a forgery, inserted long after the original writing. The original was written in Aramaic and lost, so we'll never know the truth. Here is the passage, "Now here was about this time Jesus, a wise man; if it be lawful to call him a man: for he was a doer of wonderful works, and a teacher of such men as receive the truth with pleasure. He drew over to him both many Jews, and many Gentiles. He was the

Christ. And when Pilate, at the suggestion of the principal men among us, had condemned him to the cross, those that loved him at the first did not forsake him: for he appeared to them alive again, the third day: as the divine prophets had foretold these and ten thousand other wonderful things concerning him. And the tribe of Christians, so named from him, is not extinct at this day."

Josephus would have been astonished, to say the least, if he had known that a casual comment he made would in turn make him a household word among the millions of a social fraternity hundreds of years later. It all stemmed from Herod's decision to rebuild the temple in Jerusalem. This second temple had stood for some five hundred years, had been pillaged and desecrated several times, and was in a bad state of disrepair. The repairs that Herod made were so extensive that the result was a new temple, called Herod's Temple. It was much larger than the previous two and rose ninety feet into the air—twice the height of King Solomon's Temple. The work was begun in 19 B.C. and here we'll let Josephus continue as he says, "But the temple itself was built by the priests in a year and six months.... It is also reported, that during the time the temple was building, it did not rain in the day time; but that the showers fell only in the night; so that the work was not hindered." (Book XV, last paragraph, of the *Antiquities*). Notice that Josephus did not say directly that "it did not rain, but that he said "It is reported ... that it did not rain, etc. " It is difficult to see God performing a miracle of any kind for Herod, one of the most wicked men that ever lived, so I think it is safe to say that Josephus was merely reporting a story he had heard and not in any way vouching for its authenticity. (Note: some Masonic rituals in telling of this "miracle", apply it to King Solomon's Temple).

Josephus said that 97,000 Jews were carried off into captivity as slaves and 1,100,000 were killed in the abortive war against Rome. How different the history and future of the Jews might have been if Josephus' advice had been heeded. But it was not and a country was annihilated.

# PRINCE EDWIN, A.D. 926:
# OUR FIRST "SPECULATIVE MASON"

### Alex Horne, FPS

*1975 Certificate of Literature*

OUR FIRST historically-recorded "Speculative Masons" only began coming in mostly at the beginning of the seventeenth century. For example, in June, 1600, John Boswell, the Laird of Auchinleck, (believed to have been an ancestor of the James Boswell who wrote the biography of Dr. Johnson), is found to have signed his name and "made his mark" at a meeting of the Lodge of Edinburgh—the first record of its kind, but probably not the earliest, or there would surely have been more notice taken of the event.

Twenty years later, we found an Account Book noting the names of some non-Operative "Accepted Masons" of the London Masons Company—a Guild of working Masons who nevertheless took in and "accepted" non-Operatives, of whom Elias Ashmole (initiated 1646) is probably the most famous of those later "summoned" to attend one of the London meetings. He was an antiquary, a Rosicrucian and Alchemist, who founded the still-existing Ashmolean Museum in Oxford, the first and probably the finest of its kind, and of which his own collection of antiquities formed the nucleus.

There was Quarter-master General Sir Robert Moray, of Scotland, the first to be initiated in a regular but Scottish Lodge on English soil, at Newcastle, in 1641 (during some military confrontation between the two nations).

There was Randle Holme, III, a Herald and antiquary, Deputy Garter for several counties, a famous writer of antiquarian manuscripts, now in the British Museum. And of course there were others, all of them more or less famous and outstanding in their fields.

Ashmole, for instance, had written *A History of the Noble Order of the Garter*; Moray became the first President of the Royal Society, and is said to lie buried in Westminster Abbey, along with the other "greats."

Sir Christopher Wren was the King's Surveyor and Chief Architect to Charles II, and it was he who rebuilt most of the burned-out city of London after the disastrous Fire of 1666, redesigned and rebuilt St. Paul's Cathedral and numerous other lesser churches (remember your Forever Amber?) He was a self-taught architect of note, a mathematician and inventor of scientific instruments, and Professor of Astronomy—a modern "Leonardo da Vinci" showing excellence in so many varied fields. He is believed to have been Master of the oldest Lodge in England, the still-existing and highly respected Lodge of Antiquity, one of the four old Lodges that created the first Grand Lodge in 1717. And so it goes.

It had probably been their interest in the antiquities and perhaps the symbolism associated with ecclesiastical edifices (especially during the Gothic period) that had prompted these outstanding personalities to join themselves in association with working stonemasons, with the hope of perhaps adding to their knowledge in extraneous intellectual fields. A little later, around the time of the formation of our first Grand Lodge, the Rev. Wm. Stukely, M.D., actually recorded in his diary that "his curiosity led him to be initiated into the mysteries of Masonry, suspecting it to be the remains of the mysterys of the antients." And it is possible, says our "Father of Masonic History," R. F. Gould (author of the five-volume *History of Freemasonry*), that Elias Ashmole—considering his interest in Rosicrucian philosophy—"was influenced by very similar feelings, which he satisfied in the same way."

This illustrates and corroborates much of what Brother Edward M. Selby has demonstrated in his excellent article, "The Word in Masonic Ritual," in the June issue.

But all this is within the modern historical time-frame, when written records of one kind or another were capable of giving us dependable information. But when we begin to delve into the misty region of legend and tradition, we find ourselves pushed as far back as the tenth century A.D., for indications of a purely "speculative" Mason. This was Prince Edwin, half-brother to King Athelstan, who was the first to become the King of all England, at a time when the land was still divided into numerous little kingdoms, fighting among themselves for supremacy.

This Athelstan figures prominently in all our Old Charges of the Operative Masons—those ancient documents that established the written Constitutions of the British Masons, describing the reciprocal relationship between Apprentice and Master, the rules of polite and moral behaviour, the practical requirements and customs of the mason trade, and of good citizenship and religious fidelity, and containing, withal, a traditional "history" of the art of building— which they considered to be synonymous with Geometry—going back to Euclid, the Tower of Babel, and King Solomon's Temple. This may have been legendary and non-historical to some extent, according to our modern conceptions, but it represented the limited and frequently erroneous knowledge of earlier days.

The earliest of these Old Charges is now known as the *Regius MS.*, believed to have been written (in rhyme) about A.D. 1390, but improperly catalogued at one time—and therefore misplaced and overlooked—in the King's Library, and not rediscovered and recognized in its rightful character and importance till 1840—by a non-Masonic antiquary, J. O. Halliwell (and hence called for a time the *Halliwell Poem*), and it now rests in the British Museum. It tells the

story of the art of building, as previously stated, and of the introduction of Operative Freemasonry into England, up to Athelstan's
time. And here begins our story.

In a somewhat later version of these Old Charges—now known
as the *Cooke MS.*, and written about 1410–20, we are introduced
to a "youngest son" of King Athelstan; mistakenly, it turns out, as the
king was never married and had no son, according to our best historians. But in a still later version, the prototype of which may have
appeared about A.D. 1500, this so-called "son" is given a name—
Edwin—and the story now unfolds in all its details, repeated time
and again (with some variations) in all the various versions that
have come down to us.

In the earliest of these versions (the *Cooke MS.*) that makes reference to the "son"—but so far unnamed—the story is told this-
wise, in "modernized" English:

"And after that was a worthy King in England, that was called
Athelstan; and his youngest son loved well the Science of Geometry. And he knew well that [no] hand-craft had the practice of the
Science of Geometry so well as Masons; wherefore he drew him
to counsel [with them], and learned [the] practice of that Science
[in addition] to his speculative, for of speculative he was a Master.
And he loved well Masonry and Masons, and he became a Mason
himself," etc.

This is the first time that we meet with the word "speculative"
in our ancient documents (spelled speculatyf in the original), and
our experts have endeavoured to determine precisely what it was
intended to mean at the time of writing.

Knoop, Jones, and Hamer, in their analysis and commentary on
*The Two Earliest Masonic Manuscripts*, point out that the equivalent Latin speculative "is identical in meaning with contemplative and philosophic, the speculative or contemplative branches
of learning." And Addison, writing in the *Spectator* (1711) draws a
distinction between a purely speculative and an operative member
of a trade or profession, when he tells us that "I have made myself a

speculative statesman, soldier, merchant, and artisan, without ever meddling with any practical part of life." But Edwin, obviously, liked to "meddle" with both.

And Dr. Mackey reminds us, in his *Encyclopedia of Freemasonry*, that "the word Speculative is used by Freemasons in its primary sense as symbolic, or theoretical, when opposed to Operative," and that the Cooke MS. actually "makes use of the word in this technical connection," when it points to Edwin, who was a "Master of speculative," but thought it well to learn the "practice" of Operative Masonry "in addition to his speculative." So that when we say, that "our ancient brethren wrought in Operative as well as in Speculative Masonry" (Iowa Monitor), we are harking back to an ancient tradition, of which Prince Edwin, in the tenth century, was the forerunner.

The story in the *Cooke MS.* now goes on to say that this so-called "son" of Athelstan "purchased a free patent of the King"—a sort of Charter—"that they should make an Assembly when they saw reasonable time," and it is believed that this first Assembly worked up a set of "Charges," consisting of a number of "Articles" and "Points", constituting our first Masonic Constitution.

A somewhat later version, of about A.D. 1500–1550, which now identifies the city of York as having been the locale for this first Assembly, and gives Edwin a name, further elaborates the story to declare that he made proclamation that all who had any knowledge of the writings or customs of the Craft should bring them forth, and some were found to be in French, some in Greek, some in English and other languages, and—in the language of the period—"he did make a booke thereof, and how the science (of Masonry) was founded. And he himself bad and commanded that it should be readd or tould, when that any Mason should be made, for to give him his Charge"—which may probably be the origin for our present practice of delivering a Charge to the Candidate at the end of each Degree.

This, in essence, is the famous *York Legend*, about which so much comment has been made in our Masonic literature during the past one hundred years, revolving around this tenth century Prince Edwin, our traditional first Speculative Mason.

Various versions of these Old Charges came, in subsequent years, to be read to "new Masons," in Operative times, as well as being used to regularize the proceedings of the Lodges who "made" them, in the style of our present-day Warrants or Charters. A large collection of these many versions—some one hundred and fifteen or so—have now come to be known, but many others, once known to have been in existence, have unfortunately been lost, some of them to perhaps recovered prayerfully in time to come. One such—the *Graham MS.*, giving an early version of what later turned into the Hiramic Legend—was actually recovered only as recently as 1936.

These Old Charges finally came to be recast—in what was called "a new and better method"—by the Rev. Dr. James Anderson, by authority of the Duke of Wharton, Grand Master, and was published in 1723 under the prolix title of *The Constitutions ... of the Right Worshipful Fraternity of Accepted Free Masons; collected from their general Records, and their faithful Traditions of many Ages. To be read at the Admission of a New Brother....* This was altered, in the 1738 edition, to *The Constitutions ... of the Free and Accepted Masons....* thus combining the "Freemasons" of the ancient Operative period, with the "Accepted" Masons of the later Speculatives. The figure "926", in the title of this article—for the date of the first Assembly, with Edwin sitting as "Grand Master,"—Anderson himself added, probably out of his own prolific imagination, as it has no historical basis, either for the date, or the alleged Grand-Mastership.

# THE CONFRONTATION OF G.M. ABRAHAM JONAS AND JOHN COOK BENNETT AT NAUVOO

**Mervin B. Hogan, FPS**

*1976 Certificate of Literature*

## PART I

JOHN COOK BENNETT is of no significant consequence in the history of Masonry, Mormonism, or any other known field of human endeavor. The present account is of particular value for its portrayal of some facets of the character of Abraham Jonas, the first Grand Master of the second Grand Lodge of Illinois. Jonas was a self-seeking opportunist, surprisingly skilled in the traditions, history, practices, and jurisprudence of Freemasonry.

Born August 3, 1804 at Fairhaven, Bristol County, Massachusetts, John C. Bennett's age was between that of the older Brigham Young and the younger Joseph Smith. It is abundantly evident that at Nauvoo he held in his grasp the certain and golden opportunity which might well have led to enviable fame and monumental achievement in the church of his choice, as well as his consequent immortalization as one of the distinguished pioneer builders of the west.

Bennett's character, however, was one which did not stand up under the ceaseless and colorless demands of the long haul. As one who had to have spectacular and immediate recognition he was, in this respect, virtually the antithesis of Brigham Young. The latter could patiently and inconspicuously play his part from day to day, carefully and meticulously laying his basic foundation, and then firmly grasp the opportunity the moment it availed itself, and finally-with both ability and stability-drive on indomitably to his ultimate goal.

Bennett's itinerant career is sufficiently obscure and undocumented as to leave any motivated inquirer extremely confused and perplexed. No one has ever learned just what brought him to Fairfield, Illinois or understood what factors caused his almost immediate recognition by the governor of the state with appointment to extremely high and jealously coveted offices. Bennett him self states he came to Illinois from Ohio in June, 1838. On February 20, 1839, Governor Thomas Carlin commissioned him "Brigadier-General of the Invincible Dragoons of the 2d Division of Illinois Militia," and on July 20, 1840 the same authority commissioned him "Quarter-Master General of the Militia of the State of Illinois," at the same rank. His rank was advanced, however, when again the same authority, attested by "S. A. Douglass [sic] , Secretary of State," on February 5, 1841 commissioned him "Major-General of the Nauvoo Legion of the Militia of the State of Illinois."

In the meantime he had moved to Nauvoo in late August or early September, 1840 and was soon baptized a member of the Mormon Church; since he received a patriarchal blessing by Hyrum Smith on September 21, 1840. His spectacular rise in the power structure of Nauvoo is as incredible as it was meteoric. He became Mayor of Nauvoo, February 1, 1841; Chancellor of the University of the City of Nauvoo, May 3, 1841; and on May 6, 1841, "Master in Chancery, in and for the County of Hancock."

As the capstone to all this temporal and secular recognition, he was advancing with equal rapidity to elevation within the ecclesiastical and religious domain. At the General Conference of the Church in Nauvoo, April 7, 1841, he played a prominent role as a speaker on several subjects, and "Gen. J. C. Bennett was presented with the First Presidency as assistant president, until President Ridgon's health should be restored. We thereby see that Bennett had reached a position in the Nauvoo administrative echelon wherein he had few competitors as virtually the second in power and authority to Joseph Smith."

His tenure of this elevated pinnacle was to prove extremely short lived and his decline or fall was to be every bit as precipitate as had been his phenomenal rise. The causes of Bennett's downfall are not really clear. At best, it appears he and Joseph Smith arrived at some unknown and insoluble impasse and, 0nce the question of doubt was raised, Bennett was indefensibly vulnerable.

Probably to avoid unsavory publicity and personal embarrassment, it is clear the Prophet and Bennett reached a private mutual agreement whereby it was attempted to draw successfully a Cover over Bennett's awkward profligacies and philanderings, as well as hopefully to ease the abrupt parting of the ways.

Most unfortunately, however, this was one of those situations which was bound to get out of hand. There were too many people with too many self-interests who got into the act, and salacious, titilating gossip has a far too elemental appeal to be kept in check. Ch a r g e s and countercharges, accusations and refutations, defenses and explanations poured forth and uncontrollable emotions continued to erupt over an ever expanding area. Joseph Smith had the pulpit and the church press as his outlet, while Bennett turned vigorously to the neighboring and surrounding anti-Mormon press, the public lecture platform, and finally gathered together and published a considerable compilation.

This text of Bennett's was published about the first of November, 1842, which means everything relating to it must have been uncommonly rushed in order to make such a surprisingly early date after the time of the first public awareness of this viable controversy. It suggests Bennett had anticipated his coming troubles for some time and had a great deal of work on a planned book —such as collecting letters extolling his character-essentially completed before the open break.

When a man sits down to compile a book and feels impelled to devote 47 of its introductory pages to the "Character of the Author," that man has unwittingly or otherwise revealed the fact he has a genuinely pressing, personal problem. This is the conspicuously displayed situation of Bennett and his ill-chosen compilation, *The History of the Saints; or, An Exposé of Joe Smith and Mormonism*; often referred to as *Mormonism Exposed*. By his poor taste and lack of judgment in his choice of subject matter and his ill-suited manner of expressing himself, he actually succeeded in greatly harming his own reputation. But he did also succeed in directing aroused emotions against Joseph Smith and the Mormons, who were his chosen targets.

While Bennett proved to be one of the highly disruptive and extremely destructive agents directed against the Mormon Church and the related downfall of Nauvoo City, his influence or leadership within Nauvoo Lodge appears to have been negligible or minimal and of no practical significance. The existing record-in the form of the extensive, unpublished, Minutes of Nauvoo Lodge-clearly establishes the continuing leadership and dominant direction of the Lodge by Hyrum Smith from the date of receipt of the Dispensation for the Lodge to that of his murder.

The quoted material which follows is from the official Minutes of Nauvoo Lodge U.D., and is the previously unpublished record given in full as it pertains to the subject-of Bennett's treatment by the Masonic Order of Illinois, when persistent rumor and suspicion forced a demand for action. Bennett served as secretary of the Lodge from the first congregated meeting of the Nauvoo Masons by George Miller in Hyrum Smith's office on December 29, 1841 to the meeting on Friday, May 6, 1842, inclusive. At that time, trouble-which had been continuously stalking him-knocked vigorously at his door, and the stage curtain was about to be rung down on Bennett's halcyon days at Nauvoo.

Thoughtful and discrete action was swift and immediate, as shown by the complete record of the first meeting related to this subject.

Saturday, May 7th, A. L. 5842, A. D., 1842.

5 o'clock A. M. [*sic*]

Special communication' Lodge met pursuant to special notice from the W.M. George Miller. Present, George Miller, W.M.; Hyrum Smith, S.W.; Lucius N. Scovil, J.W.; Newel K. Whitney, Treas.; Willard Richards, Secy. pro tem.; Charles Allen, S.D.; Heber C. Kimball, J.D.; Hiram Clark & Wm. Felshaw, Stewards; Samuel Rolfe, Tyler; Noah Rogers, Brigham Young, Wm. Law, Wilson Law, Stephen Chase, Wm. Marks, Daniel S. Miles, Amassa Lyman, John C. Bennett, S.; members.

A Master Masons lodge was then opened in due form, when a communication was read from Grand Master Jonas, dated Columbus May 4th 1842 & Marked A. After reading the communication the Secretary pro tem. read the Constitution and by laws of the Grand Lodge of Ill's., and the by-laws of this lodge, and compared with the records of the lodge and found to agree, when brother John C. Bennett denied the charge into, and was ready for trial, when it was voted that the W. M. George Miller should reply to the communication, which he did as follows Marked C. A communication from Bodley Lodge No.1, Quincy, Marked B was then read, when it was voted, that the Secretary pro tem. answer the same, which he did as follows Marked D.

No further business appearing, the lodge closed in due form without date.

[*signed*] *Willard Richards,*
Secretary pro tem.

[*signed*] *George Miller*
Master

Although none of the four marked exhibits appears to have survived with the Minute Book, they are really no great or serious loss, as will be seen. It is highly probable Bodley Lodge stated charges to Jonas who, as Grand Master, had no alternative but to act. Bodley

Lodge had always been anti-Mormon and vigorously opposed the
establishment of a Masonic Lodge among the Mormons. Its attitude
and position it had repeatedly made crystal clear to Jonas. In arriving
at such a position and adamantly adhering to it, Bodley Lodge was
simply exercising its intrinsic Masonic prerogative. To its everlasting
credit, it must be distinctly stated that relating to the Mormons there
is no known evidence of any subterfuge, deceit, or questionable
practice at any time on the part of this Lodge. To arrive at an anti-
Mormon position was its right and privilege, and it ever expressed
itself forthrightly, candidly, and without hesitation. Grand Master
Jonas actually assumed a tremendous personal burden and responsibility when he opposed the expressed attitude of every Lodge in
Illinois and granted the Dispensation for Nauvoo Lodge.

At the regular meeting of Thursday, May 19, 1842, convened at
6:00 o'clock P. M. by the Master, George Miller, with Willard Richards as acting Secretary, the subject was again a matter of business.
This portion of the record reads,

> The W. M. then read the following charge preferred against Dr.
> John C. Bennett by Thomas Grover, to wit: "That Dr. John C. Ben-
> nett has palmed himself upon the Masonic Brethren in the organi-
> zation of Nauvoo Lodge U.D. as a regular mason in good standing,
> when I have reason to believe that he is an expelled mason from a
> lodge in Fairfield, Ohio, or from Fairfield Lodge, Ohio.
>
> *[signed] Thomas Grover."*

"On motion, it was resolved that Dr. John C. Bennett be cited
to appear before Nauvoo Lodge U. D. on the first Thursday in June
next at 6 o'clock P.M. to answer to the above charge." At the above
meeting 79 members were present and all the officers were at their
respective stations and places, except the Secretary. Among those
present were Joseph Smith, Hyrum Smith, William Smith, Samuel
H. Smith, Brigham Young, Heber C. Kimball, John Taylor, Wilford
Woodruff, Charles C. Rich, Vinson Knight, Thomas Grover, Eli a s
Higbee, Francis M. Higbee, Wilson Law and William Law. John C.

Bennett was absent. The regu1ar communication of Thursday, June 2, 1842 was called to order at 6:00 o'clock P. M. by Worshipful Master George Miller, with all the officers in their appointed stations and places except the Secretary; which office was filled by Willard Richards, acting. John C. Bennett, Secretary, present. Including officers, there were 111 Master Masons, 2 Fellowcrafts, an Entered Apprentice, and 7 visiting brethren in attendance. Respecting Bennett, the record reads, "The business to be presented before this lodge was the investigation of the charge preferred against Dr. John C. Bennett in a communication from G. M. A. Jonas dated May 4th 1842 (said communication being on file and marked A) but no evidence appearing to substantiate the charge it was

## PART II

"Resolved, that the investigation of the charge preferred against Dr. John C. Bennett be postponed until the next regular communication to take place on Thursday the 16th Inst. and that the Secretary pro tempore, write to Grand Master A. Jonas and inform him of the proceedings of the lodge in reference to this case."

Among those present at this meeting were: Joseph Smith, Hyrum Smith, Brigham Young, Heber C. Kimball, George A. Smith, John Taylor, Elias Higbee, Francis M. Higbee, James Sloan, Newel K. Whitney, Charles C. Rich, Thomas Grover, King Follett, Hiram Kimball, Vinson Knight, Jacob B. Backenstos, and Robert D. Foster.

George Miller, the Master of the Lodge, called the regular communication to order at 6:00 o'clock P. M., Thursday, June 16, 1842. All of the officers were present and Willard Richards served as acting Secretary. There were 112 Master Masons, three Fellowcrafts, three Entered Apprentices and one visiting brother in attendance.

Prominent names present were: Joseph Smith, Hyrum Smith, John Cook Bennett, Wilford Woodruff, George A. Smith, Wilson Law, Charles C. Rich, John P. Greene, James Sloan, Elias Highee,

Hosea Stout, Henry G. Sherwood, William Clayton, and Albert P. Rockwood.

Concerning Bennett, the record states,

> The W.M. then called the Secretary Pro Tem. to read the several communications from G.M.A. Jonas and others relative to the charges preferred against John C. Bennett which was accordingly done. The evidence set forth in those communications satisfied the minds of a majority of the brethren of the reality of his being an expelled Mason; but in consequence of his presenting various documents from men of high standing in Society in the neighborhood of Willoughby, [Ohio], and some from brethren of the Fraternity in the same neighborhood dated about the time Bro. Patterson says he was expelled showing the high estimation in which he was held by those gentlemen; and also referring expressly to a communication from Bro. Patterson to him dated sometime about a year ago, breathing the most friendly feelings, and in the strongest language soliciting the continuance of former friendship, and further in consequence of his still urging that if he had been so expelled he never had been informed of the circumstance until the same was read in a communication from Grand Master A. Jonas dated May 24th [sic], It was
> Resolved, that his case be further postponed until the next regular communication, to take place on the first Thursday in July, giving furtherance for the minutes of the lodge at Pickaway concerning Bennett's expulsion to be obtained, and that the Secretary Pro Tem. shall write to Pickaway lodge requesting a copy of the minutes of their said lodge concerning his expulsion, to be forwarded to Nauvoo as soon as possible and also to write to G.M.A. Jonas stating the proceedings of the lodge in reference to this matter.

On June 24, Nauvoo Lodge celebrated Masonry's traditional Festival of St. John the Baptist. The Lodge membership present consisted of 130 Master Masons, six Fellowcrafts, and three Entered Apprentices; while 18 visiting brethren, including Joseph Kelley of Bodley Lodge No. 1 at neighboring Quincy, were in attendance.

The minutes of the day give the further facts:

At "2 o'clock P.M. Lodge called from refreshment to labor. The W.M. then ordered the Secy. pro tem. to read all the communications touching the case of Dr. John C. Bennett which was accordingly done; after which he called the S.W., Hyrum Smith to the chair...." Among those present were Joseph Smith, Brigham Young, John Taylor, Wilford Woodruff, Heber C. Kimball, Hosea Stout, James Sloan, Wilson Law, and Francis M. Higbee. John C. Bennett was absent. The acting Secretary was Willard Richards.

At the regular meeting of Thursday, July 7, 1842 the subject was again an agenda item. George Miller presided and William Clayton acted as Secretary. No enlightening or explanatory comments are recorded; the Minutes are brief and to the point,

> The W.M. then stated that with regard to the case of John C. Bennett he had not as yet received any communication from Pickaway Lodge but did not judge it necessary to postpone the action of the Lodge in his case any longer. It was therefore,
> Resolved that the Lodge is fully satisfied that John C. Bennett, is an expelled mason, and that his name be stricken from the rolls; and that this lodge regards him as totally unworthy the fellowship, or regard, of all good and honorable men or masons.

The regular communication of Thursday, August 4, 1842 was convened at 4:00 o'clock P.M. with George Miller in the Master's chair and William Clayton acting as Secretary. Grand Master Abraham Jonas now enters the proceedings decisively and authoritatively,

> The W.M. then requested the E.A.s & F.C.s to withdraw, which being done he ordered the Secy. to read a communication from G. M. A. Jonas, setting forth that whether Bennett had previously been expelled or not it was our duty to expell him for his conduct here. The letter was accordingly read but in consequence of our Bye-laws requiring two-thirds of all the members of the Lodge to be present to expell a member; it was resolved that the lodge be convened on Monday next at 4 o'clock P.M. in the Lodge Room to act on this case, and that the Secy. give public notice of the same by posting written notices of the same in various parts of the City.

The special communication called for Monday, August 8, 1842 assembled at 4:00 o'clock P.M. The Minutes of this meeting reveal a great deal of valuable information, by implication primarily. Only two of the regular officers were in attendance and there was not a single officer serving in his titular office. The Junior Warden, Lucius N. Scovil, served as Worshipful Master and Henry G. Sherwood was Secretary, each pro tempore. There were 138 Master Masons and three visiting brethren present. An implied attitude of the Lodge is conveyed by the names of those who are absent. John Cook Bennett, Joseph Smith, George Miller, Hyrum Smith, Brigham Young, John Taylor, Wilford Woodruff, Heber C. Kimball, and all such high ranking members of the Mormon hierarchy and Masons of prominence are absent. Essentially the rank and file membership of the Lodge have been assembled to execute the orders of Grand Master Jonas. The ever loyal, devoted, and dependable Lucius N. Scovil has been called upon to see that the assignment is legally and capably completed.

The record reports,

> The W.M. then called upon the Secy. pro tem. to read the charges preferred against John C. Bennett which was done as follows,

To Nauvoo Lodge U.D.

Dr brethren, I hereby prefer the following charges against John C. Bennett late secretary of this Lodge

1st Seduction. For seducing certain previously respectable females of our city by using Joseph Smith's name as one who sanctioned such conduct.

2nd Adultery. For illicit intercourse with various females frequently.

3rd Lying. In using Joseph Smith's name as before stated, saying that said Smith taught and practiced illicit intercourse with women, he knowing it to be false.

4th Perjury. In swearing that he was under duress when he made a certain affidavit before Esq. Wells, when it is well known he never was under restraint or confinement at all whilst in this city.

5th Embezzlement. For making use of money belonging to the lodge, without either knowledge or consent of said lodge.

6th. For illicit intercourse with a Master Mason's wife.

Satisfactory evidence being set forth before the Lodge in each and every case, the voice of the lodge was taken in each case separately; when it was declared by the Lodge that he is considered guilty of all the above charges without a dissenting voice. Whereupon the following resolution was passed, to Wit;-

Resolved, That John C. Bennett be expelled from this lodge and from all the privileges of Masonry, he being considered one of the most base and infamous adulterers, liars, and a general plunderer of female chastity. And further, that he is dishonest and not worthy to be trusted, that he is perjured and not worthy of credit; and that he has broken his solemn obligation as a Master Mason. And, that the Secy P.T. be authorised immediately to communicate this action of the Lodge to all the Lodges under the jurisdiction of the Grand Lodge of this State.

Possibly due to inexperience on the part of the acting Secretary, the name of whoever preferred the charges is not stated; and then again it may have been an intentional omission.

This long forgotten record will be variously read and interpreted by different people. It is abundantly clear, though, that the Lodge took its own ample time to consider Bennett's case unhurriedly and with due process. It would seem that emotion was at a minimum, and apparently both Christian and Masonic charity of the mind and spirit were graciously extended Bennett by the Lodge. Also, it appears that a rather successful effort was made to keep those matters of the case relating to Freemasonry sharply separate and distinct from Bennett's difficulties with Joseph Smith and the Church.

The real reasons and/or causes why Grand Master Jonas entered the case and insisted on overlooking nothing which could be charged against Bennett, and fully prosecuting him for the same, were most probably not known then and certainly cannot be ascertained now. But the positive and demanding action on the part of Jonas (himself a lawyer) does leave provocative and disturbing queries.

Beyond any doubt, Abraham Jonas insisted on beating the dead horse long after it was dead. That the Lodge was totally unsympathetic and out of harmony with this administrative order is amply demonstrated by the atmosphere in which the last trial was held.

The *Proceedings of the Grand Lodge of Illinois, A.F.&A.M.*, for 1842 present the final, official proclamation,

> Expelled—John C. Bennett, M.M., about 38 years of age, 5 feet 7 or 8 inches high, dark complexion, dark eyes, Roman nose, lost his upper front teeth; quick spoken, good language, by profession a physician, residing in New York; for gross unMasonic conduct; on the 8th day of August, 1842.

Bennett's remaining years reflected much the same pattern he had earlier cast. He followed James Jesse Strang and his splinter group for several years, but again he "fell from grace." He moved to the vicinity of Plymouth, Massachusetts, and resided there for a period of time raising poultry and carrying on in his own way with dentistry and medicine.[1]

He finally left Plymouth under unknown circumstances and moved to Polk County, Iowa. He applied himself to sheep, cattle, and poultry raising, as well as continuing to practice medicine. His talents as a promoter were again demonstrated in 1861 when he became an instigator in the organization of the Tenth Iowa Infantry, in which he served with the rank of major. He became Surgeon in Field and Staff of the Third U.S. Infantry in 1865. His death occurred August 5, 1867, and he is buried in the Polk City Cemetery.[2]

In death as in life, the memory of John Cook Bennett is a deceit and a fraud. Although at the time of his death he was under the sentence of expulsion from the benefits, privileges, and honors of Freemasonry by two Masonic Lodges, his tombstone is embellished with the Masonic insignia of the square and compasses; the emblem of the Order to which he had no right and which he disgraced in every sense.[3]


# NOTES


1. John C. Bennett, *The Poultry Book: A Treatise on Breeding and General Management of Domestic Fowls, with Numerous*

*Original Descriptions, and Portraits from Life*, Phillips, Sampson & Co., Boston, 1854, 320 pp.

2. Ralph V. Chamberlin, *The University of Utah, 1850–1950*; University of Utah Press, 1960, pp. 577–578.

3. Jerry Marsengill, "Grave of John C. Bennett Located;" [Iowa] *Grand Lodge Bulletin*, Vol. 71, No. 9, November, 1970, Cedar Rapids, Iows, pp. 683–684.

# HOW A CATHEDRAL WAS BUILT

## Louis C. King, FPS

### *1978 Certificate of Literature*

THE BISHOP shook his head sadly as he surveyed his aged cathedral. More than three hundred years old, it was decaying beyond repair. Small as it was, it was slowly settling into the soft ground on which it stood. Cracks grew in the walls and the many fires in which the roof had burned off had ruined many of the topmost stones in the walls. A new building was urgently needed.

Not far distant was a rise in the land. Heavily forested, it overlooked the town below, sprawled on the banks of a river. The bishop had often thought of that rise as an ideal spot for a new cathedral. He had even made rough sketches of what it might look like. He was no artist nor was he an architect but he had a good idea of what he wanted. Not too large. He had no need of so large a building as those he had seen at Amiens or Paris. Also, he had insufficient funds for such a project, even for the one he needed but he had a firm faith that God would provide, as He had so often done in the past.

He called the ecclesiastical Chapter of his diocese to discuss the problem. While he was in overall charge the clerics in the Chapter must give their approval. One dissenter was the Treasurer who jealously guarded the cathedral funds. The bishop explained his plan, they all knew the need showed them his sketches and even took them to the place he had chosen. The Treasurer complained of the cost of clearing the trees away but the bishop showed that the timber derived would more than repay that cost in the lumber it could provide for the stagings, forms, shops for the workmen and fuel for their fires and furnaces. Gin poles and derricks for hoisting and the windlasses for them could be made from that wood.

He also pointed out that the ancient quarry from which the old building came was not far away. It supplied an excellent grade of granite which would be necessary for the foundations and other substructures necessary to support the building. For the above-ground structure limestone was to be used. With a beautiful color, it was easy to cut and carve and yet was also strong and weather resistant. No limestone was to be had in their part of France, so arrangements would be made to purchase it from quarries in Normandy. That meant carting the stone over the road for 150 or more miles, a journey that would take an ox-cart two weeks at least.

After much deliberation, the Chapter gave its approval. Now began a search for an architect. In those times communication was slow, no postal system, no newspapers to carry the message. About the best means was in the hands of the troubadors, constantly on the move from town to town, singing and entertaining. While they were entertainers, they often served to carry news as they went. War news, politics, scandal and gossip, all was grist that came to their mills. Likely enough, the bishop informed them of his wants.

In due course, several architects arrived, each eager to persuade the bishop that his were the best, the latest, and most up-to-date designs in this popular new style. One was finally selected and he forthwith sent for his draftsmen and surveyors. With their arrival, they set to work, not to start building but to dig test holes to determine the suitability of the underground to support the weight of the building and also to lay out the trenches where the foundation stones would be laid.

While waiting for the architects to arrive, the bishop had hired woodsmen to remove the trees and prepare them for the carpenters. He also engaged a master quarryman, who hired men to clear the quarries of the centuries-old deposits of earth and overgrowth. Once the architect's crew had found the site suitable, laborers were set to digging the trenches laid out by the surveyors. Two wide trenches went down on both sides, north and south, joined by two similar but semicircular ones at their eastern ends.

The architect had drawn his plans to resemble a long, narrow, round-ended box which stopped short at the western end. The architect had learned from experience that he would be long in his grave before ever the western wall would be built and seldom was that facade built on the original design. His crew of draftsmen had arrived and. for the present, were installed in some unoccupied rooms in the bishop's residence. Their work, for the present, was to determine the dimensions and number of the foundation stones. These figures were sent to the master quarryman who soon had quantities ready for the carters to haul.

At this point, let me interject a thought for modern Freemasons. This is much different from the stories many writers of Masonic history tell, where everything is so simple and easy. In them, the bishop had a desire. A band of traveling masons came in, started work and—presto! A new cathedral appeared! All apparently, the work of this one band of masons. How different it was in real life. The quarrymen were the first masons on the job—but far from the last.

Those trenches were ten feet or wider at the bottom and averaged twenty feet deep. Between the inner trenches and starting just short of the curved portions, and extending about a quarter of the length to the west was an excavation about twelve feet in depth, forming what we would call a basement but which would later be divided into crypts, which would be the cells where the bodies of bishops and other notables would be interred. The foundations for walls and buttresses were vertical on the inner faces but tapered in toward the top. With the arrival of the rough layers, the master mortarman got his boys busy building their kilns. Portland cement, quicklime and plaster did not come in convenient bags and barrels. They had to manufacture their own right on the job from raw rock. No chemists they but they knew how to make them and their products had to be right. Granite blocks of smaller size now followed the footings and the rough masons started laying them up with mortar.

Better than two years had by now elapsed since the first workmen arrived and the foundations would not be ready for several months more. All cement and mortar work shut down with the advent of freezing weather until spring. The work was heaped with straw and the masons took an unpaid vacation until warmer weather. To a good four or five months lost were added the frequent Church holy days when no one worked. So, with the tediously slow work, with nothing but hand tools, is it so surprising that progress was so slow? The marvel of it all is the precision with which it was done, the ingenuity with which the stone parts were fitted together, the work of one man assembled by another to conform exactly to the plans of a third. And most could neither read nor write.

Strongly built carts were moving north over the roads to the limestone quarries and back in an almost unending procession and, by the time foundations were ready for their load, the rough masons were laying a heavy stone floor in the basement. Every so often a pit was dug down deep and foundations for the interior pillars were set in them. Beyond the limits of the basement, toward the western end, a shallower foundation was laid for all the pavement.

When the limestone arrived, a new and much larger group of masons also came. Part of these men were the stone cutters who would take the large slabs of stone and cut them into blocks of the desired size and then trim and dress them exactly as ordered and put marks on them designating their location in the walls. Also, each man put his own personal mark on his work for purposes of pay as they were often paid piece-work rates. None of those marks were letters or numerals. They were small, simple designs, usually lines forming arrows, crosses or angles, but all different. Sometimes a father and son worked together and the son copied his father's mark with an additional line to identify him. It was a simple system but it worked.

The finished stones were taken to the stone setters, those men who performed their work with levels, plumb-lines and plumb-rules. Their tools were the trowel and setting maul. Theirs was the job of setting the stones exactly so in their mortar beds and tried, each one, by plumb-rule and level.

The walls rose slowly but steadily to their planned height of one hundred and thirty feet. Along with their own heavy piers rose their matching buttress piers on the outer row of foundations. This building being of a moderate height would require but one flying buttress per pier so the outer piers were shorter than those inner piers which rose to the roof line. But, down at floor level, a change took place. The outer walls were now being built between the buttress piers, with spaces for windows between. A series of arches, strong, heavy ones, connected the piers some twenty-five feet above the floor, where a floor of stone was laid. Above this floor a series of slender colonettes rose to provide a view of the interior and above them the walls rose to their height at the roof line, with spaces for more windows extending nearly to the roof. A sloping roof was built above this floor, enclosing a walkway that ran the length of the building, interrupted only at the transept on the north and south sides between the nave and the choir. Building the outer shell of the church was indeed a slow, exacting process as indeed every other part was.

While the work on the walls was in progress, work on the inside also went on. Masons laid a heavy layer of granite on the basement to support the main floor above. Then a flooring of thin, smooth slabs was laid on that and rows of arches were erected on which the main floor was supported. The eastern end of the basement was divided into crypts in which the bodies of bishops and priests would be interred in years to come. A circular stair led down to the crypts from a corner of the eastern end of the ambulatory, that space between the inner and outer walls.

With the main floor now complete the carpenters had a place to work and they needed it to, lay out and cut the roof timbers and collar beams. While this went on, strong stagings and forms were being built between the inner and outer piers. It was time for the flying buttresses to be put in place to stiffen the walls against the weight of the roof and ceiling which were soon to come.

The carpenters laid out and fitted each piece of the roof timbers on the floor and then disassembled them until they were finally set in place on the walls. It was no easy task, hauling up those heavy rafters but once a few collar-beams were in place a flooring was rigged and the work moved ahead faster. Then the roof boards went on and the plumbers came in to lay the lead sheeting over all. The roof was on and the building closed in, excepting for the west end which still lacked a wall. The bishop had grown old and was the first to occupy a crypt in the basement. His successor counted the years from the day the work was begun. Forty-eight years! Forty-eight years? Was that too long? No, the time was not excessive. There was that spell, fourteen years back, when the money ran out and for six years no work was done until more money was raised. Then, no work was done in the freezing cold of the season when frost could damage the mortar. So, counting about eight months to every year and the six year layoff, it was more like a third in actual productive years. Changes? Oh yes indeed there were. The old bishop was joined in the crypts by his successor nine years later and the present one was looking toward retirement. The architect had proved his prophecy of the west wall and his son was now in charge, hoping that his son might one day build that western facade. He had sent the boy on a tour of France to get ideas from some of the medium sized cathedrals. The master builder had been killed when a staging collapsed. Now, he had no son to follow him but his replacement was an excellent workman. All the working crews were gone except for a few who had been apprentices twenty years before. Even the people of the town were changed. Half a century is a long time.

Now, with the roof on, it was time to start on the vaulting of the ceiling. Centerings, the forms on which the ribs of the vaults were constructed, were built on the floor and the great keyblocks, six-sided to meet the inner ends of the centerings, were laid out with utmost precision as were the centerings, all of which had to fit their places high above. No mistakes could be tolerated. Much too heavy to be lifted by an ordinary windlass, a great wheel, some fourteen feet in diameter and constructed like a squirrel cage was put together on the floor, dismantled and hoisted piece by piece to the working floor above. There it was assembled on a great axle, longer on one end than on the other and mounted on two upright supports where it could revolve. All assembled, the wheel was attached to a large hawser which reached the floor and when a load was tied on, two large men got inside the wheel and started walking on command. The hawser wrapped around the axle and thus the centerings were slowly raised, seated in place on the piers and the free ends secured by ropes until all six centerings were in place and the key-block set in position. Then all six centerings were slowly lowered until they found their places on the block. With that done all the supporting ropes were removed and the stonework could be started.

Up came the masons, the stones, the mortar. Stone by stone the ribs were formed and the keystone set in its place. Now came the wait until the mortar had reached the critical stage of hardness when the centerings could be cautiously lowered. Too soon, the ribs would collapse. There must be a certain degree of flexibility so that all the parts of all six ribs could adjust to each other. If the mortar set too hard the ribs were unable to make those microscopic adjustments and strains would cause an eventual collapse. More than one ceiling had fallen before the masons learned the cause.

Once the centerings were down, the work floor and the wheel were moved to the next bay and thus would be progress continue until all the ceiling arches were in place. Then the lagging on which the webbing of the ceiling would fill in the spaces between the ribs. This lagging was thin strips of wood, curved to conform to the curvature of the ribs. On these, the lightest stone, cut into very thin slabs were laid and then covered with a layer of concrete to a depth of about four inches poured over the entire area and allowed to set before the lagging was taken down. Of all the hazardous work in the building, the ceiling was the most dangerous. Until stagings were put up to allow work on the under side of the ceiling, all the work was done with nothing beneath them but the stone floor, one-hundred and thirty fee below.

With the floor now clear, drawings the full size of the windows were painted showing the exact size and shape of each stone that went into the upper part of the window frames and the tracery that filled the upper portions. Then, the stone carvers set to work, meticulously following the design, fitting in iron reinforcing bars in places where they were needed. They were then transferred, piece by piece, and cemented into place.

By now, if you have been watching, you will have noticed that there have been several kinds of masons employed; quarrymen, rough cutters, rough layers, cutters and finishers in the stone-yard, the setters on the walls and piers, the extremely skillful cutters and layers on the ribs, the concrete workers on the webs and now, the carvers. Does this assortment of trades sound like the men the story-tellers wrote about? The one gang they'd have you think did it all?

Now a new set of specialists have arrived, to set up furnaces and snug sheds. They have carted in loads of washed sand which they have carefully stowed in bins in the sheds and covered with canvas. Bags of special wood-ash, minerals and metals and long blow-pipes are stowed away, awaiting the furnaces. These are the glass-makers who will supply the glaziers with materials for the windows, clever workmen, the glass-makers. They will brew their mixtures in their furnaces, pick up blobs of it on their blow-pipes, blow them into balloon shapes and then dexterously cut them open to lay out in flat sheets. These, when properly cooled, will be taken by others to tables and cut to match designs drawn on whitewashed tables, color by color and joined by lead strips run in between them until a panel is made, to be fitted into place in the waiting window. Slow, careful work, done to exact dimensions, and held in place by iron reinforcing bars to enable them to resist wind and weather. Years of work lay ahead of them.

Let us see what else went on inside, on the lower levels. The arches that surmounted the bays between the pillars were now being carved with graceful patterns as were the panels between them and the colonettes above. The floor in the curve of the apse had been raised a few feet above the main floor and a marble altar had been built on it, predominating everything in the building. Sculptors were at work carving scenes deep into its surface. It was a thing of beauty and the light from the nearly completed windows of the apse flooded it with glorious light in the morning sun.

Work had begun again on both the north and south transepts. They had been built out far enough to allow the carpenters to put on the roofs but had stopped short of the end walls, awaiting designs for the doorways. Now there were two sets of drawings ready, one for each and the south was to have a small rose window somewhat in imitation of the one the architect's son had seen at Notre Dame at Paris. The northern side was less favored because it was less traveled and therefore less likely to be seen. The transepts were actually vestibules, with ornamental doors but their main reason for being was that they gave the church its cruciform outline when viewed from above, a view few mortals ever hoped to see but was easily visible to the occupants of the celestial regions above and it was they whom it was hoped would be properly and favorably impressed.

The angles of the walls at the transepts were filled with what appeared to be round towers but were really circular stairways, leading from the arcade up to the tribune above and to the roof. One, on the south transept, led down to a tunnel which gave access to the crypts. Those on the extreme ends were the best and safest ways to the walls, as they rose in step with the walls as they went up. Those ancient builders were very practical men in many ways.

They took advantage of many prosaic but necessary things, such as the disposal of the rain water from the roof which, if allowed to run down the walls, would in time have stained them. Deep gutters ran along the tops of the walls emptying into ducts built into the upper parts of the piers, down to just above the point of contact where the flying buttresses met the piers. A similar gutter ran down the tops of the buttresses to their piers where they emptied into vertical ducts and thence to just above the ground. This was one of the latest ideas, picked up by the architect's son on his travels. Notre Dame and some of the other older buildings used the fanciful gargoyles to carry the water out away from the walls to fall where it would. These builders had the advantage of working late in the 14th century, near the end of the period when this style was at its fashionable peak, and used the best methods.

Those flying buttresses, which I have not thus far mentioned, were put in place at about the time the roof was to go up. The building, being only of a moderate size, was nowhere as tall as the great old cathedrals and was to have but one set of arches to support the walls. Unlike the ceiling arches, which were erected from above by the use of the great wheel, had to be built from below, on stagings. Accidents occurred occasionally by collapsing stagings but, of course, the work went on with much the same methods as the interior arches were, supported on centerings. The same meticulous skill went into them as in any other part and the walls never showed defects from their placement.

The stonework was just about at an end now, except that the western end still stood open to the elements as it had for all these years. The carpenters and wood carvers had taken over in the choir and were building the benches and partitions for the singers. There was the bishop's throne and other furniture to be made, wooden statues to be carved and painted. The ceilings and walls were to be painted and in some places plastered to cover defects that had appeared. Still, the western wall was wide open like the end of a Zeppelin hanger of the 1920s.

The old architect's grandson was now the architect in charge and his years of travel as a youth were now about to pay off. His designs were a combination of the best features of several he had studied and admired. Three portals, two square towers, one enclosing a peal of bells, the gift of the merchants of the town, which, over the years had grown up the slope almost to the cathedral.

Once again the call had gone out for laborers to excavate, the quarrymen to reopen the quarry and cut foundation stones. The old stone-wagons were refitted for the roads and arrangements made with the limestone quarries to furnish more stone. Carpenters were hired to make ready the stagings, derricks and all the other woodwork, much of which had deteriorated.

The foundations, not so extensive as before, were to be much heavier than before as the load on them would be greater and more concentrated. This new wall was not to be a simple wall. Rooms and stairways were to occupy a part of it. The towers, modified versions of a pair of Norman towers the architect liked, were to rise to a height of two-hundred feet. The new bishop had wanted spires built on them but was dissuaded when the Chapter warned him that funds were again running low. The wall between the towers had to be deepened considerably to accommodate the vestibules of the portals. The center one was to consist of seven concentric, pointed arches, diminishing in height and width to conform to the width of the large, double-leaved doors. The flanking portals were smaller and less ornate. The rear, or inner, wall was to rise to the peak of the roof but, midway between the peak and the flat roof of the frontal extension, was a large, pointed arch built into the facade, to serve as a frame in the center of which was to be a rose window over twenty feet in diameter. The greater part of the towers was finished several years before the intricate tracery of the rose was carved and installed.

The concentric arches of the portals had been taken over by the carvers who spent years patiently carving the complex designs planned for them. The bells were hung in the north tower and a platform was installed for the bell-ringers to work on. The massive oak doors were hung on the ornamental hinges, the pride of the master smith who also made the locks, latches, and handles at his forge.

The glaziers at long last completed the rose and all the other windows. A gilded cross was mounted at the peak of the roof over the rose and little by little, the stagings were coming down. The last work was done by the paviors, the men who laid the beautiful mosaic flooring all through the interior. Outside, they laid a flagstoned parvis, as wide as the building and extending a hundred feet away, to meet with the cobblestones of the town's main street. One by one the huts and shanties that had housed generations of workmen were torn down until none remained except the Carpenters' Hall. Large and beautifully constructed by the joint efforts of the masons and carpenters, it served as an office building for both trades and also held living quarters for the elite groups of both, the men who would permanently remain as a maintenance force. Three sculptors lived there who carved the marble statues that would adorn the cathedral.

The cathedral was completed! And in only ninety-four years, setting a record of sorts for a building of its size! The last halt in the work was only for two years as the town had been enjoying a period of prosperity and the people ascribed it to the virgin to whom the edifice was soon to be dedicated, as a sign of her impatience to see the work finished that would glorify her name. A total of ninety-four years seems long but as I once mentioned, with an average working year of eight months and the time out while funds were being raised, that it was built in that time was indeed a record.

Bishops came, lived a time and then were laid beside the one who had started the work. The latest arrival from Rome, the fifth since it was started, consecrated the edifice with pomp and ceremony. A procession was formed on the parvis, of all the clergy, the townspeople falling in on the cobbles below and, as the bishop recited the old Hebrew Introit, "Introibo ad Altare Deo", he entered, to the Altar of his God. The building was blessed and duly dedicated to the virgin and great joy filled the congregation. And then the new bishop withdrew to his apartments to contemplate certain changes he had in mind.

Such was the way with cathedrals. Constantly being altered, redesigned, modified, changed. But, for now, the work was complete. The procession that had filled the street and cathedral was but the visible part of a much larger, invisible parade. Bishops had come and gone. The grandson of the first architect had finished the work and was about to turn over the business to his son and retire. The Chapter who authorized the project were now but names to the present Chapter. Master builders had come and departed without count. The masters of the gans and lodges were almost countless and of all the myriad workers who had had a part, however humble, only a guess could be made. Two thousand? Three thousand? Hundreds of tons of stone, a small forest, had been used. The human lives lost or mangled were somehow forgotten. And how many millions of francs were spent?

The cathedral in this story never existed but there were many that did and this is just a representation of how they were built. I have written this story in protest. Too many yarns have I endured written by alleged historians, who plainly had never gone near a real construction site to see how it was done. Instead of honestly portraying the medieval mason as a plain, hard-working man, except for a few, unable to read or write, stolid and patient as an ox but capable of turning out marvels of precision with the crudest of tools. But these starry-eyed writers, in their own ignorance turned out these fairy tales of masons so highly skilled in the arts and architecture that they became companions of kings. True, there were men with these abilities but they were few. There were many, many masons. However laudable their purposes were, they have left us with a heritage of falsehood and error. Personally, I prefer the mason as he was, dumb but human.

I have spent considerable time in the past several years, reading accounts of how those so-called Gothic buildings were put together, not by Masonic authors but by architects, men who knew the work. This story may be overburdened with details but, having become fed up with fantasy, I have endeavored to give others who want to know, a better idea of how our brethren of six centuries ago really worked. And, if this story doesn't line up with your ideas of England, you're right. Remember, I said it was somewhere in France.

# ROB MORRIS AND
# THE CONSERVATORS IN KENTUCKY

## Charles Guthrie, FPS

*1979 Certificate of Literature*

ROB MORRIS, soon after his initiation in Mississippi in 1846, became aware of the great diversity of ritual which he encountered as he visited lodges through out the United States. He determined to bring order out of this chaos. The result, years later in Kentucky, was to cost him his reputation for a time among many Masons. He was accused of trying to profit financially from the sale of rituals, a Conservator Degree which he invented, and attempting to become a Masonic dictator. Apparently, however, he was motivated by the best of intentions.

When Morris first came to Kentucky, he was impressed by the slovenly way the ritual was performed in many lodges. He first visited the Grand Lodge in 1852. In 1853 he had attracted sufficient attention of the Grand Master Thomas Todd to grant him a letter of recommendation to visit lodges and instruct them in the landmarks of Freemasonry. Todd also recommended that the Grand Lodge provide a system of lectures. The committee to which this was referred recommended instead that the work and lectures be exemplified in Grand Lodge.

The next year subordinate lodges were forbidden to hear itinerant lecturers. Some of these, no doubt, were doing a purely commercial work and cared little for the welfare of the lodges they visited. Morris, although he made his living as a teacher of Masonry and publisher of Masonic books and magazines, seems to have had the best interests of Masonry at heart. He wanted it to be as impressive as possible.

Seeking to discover what Thomas Smith Webb's ritual had been, Morris, in 1848, had begun contacting every elderly Mason known to have been a good ritualist in an effort to synthesize their memories into an exact ritual. Eventually he was said to have contacted 50,000 Masons in 2,000 lodges. Probably he had not met this many when he began his Conservator movement in 1860.

Morris was elected Grand Master of the Grand Lodge of Kentucky in 1858. During his year in that office he held three sessions of what he called National Masonic Schools of Instruction at which he lectured and taught different phases of Masonry, including ritual. When the Grand Lodge met in October, 1859, Morris reported that he had engaged four brothers (John Augustus Williams, E. D. Cooke, S. D. McCullough, and Grand Senior Warden Lewis Landrum) to lecture in the lodges.

A resolution recommending the Webb work as taught in the Schools of Instruction was not passed. The Grand Lodge did recommend a speedy return to the work and lectures of Webb. Perhaps this gives one a clue to why the Grand Lodge and individual lodges were unwilling to adopt Morris's ritual. Each lodge and each member probably felt that the ritual it used was the pure Webb work and were unwilling to charge. This was an affront to Morris and a precursor of worse to come.

In 1860 Morris launched the Conservators, an organization with members throughout the United States. He hoped to introduce his ritual into each Grand Lodge. The conservator organization began June 24, 1860. It was to end June 24, 1865. The plan of organization was secretive. Morris was Chief Conservator and had one Conservator and two deputies in each lodge. These were to work secretly for the adoption of Morris's work in each lodge and ultimately in each Grand Lodge. Morris invited the men he desired as Conservators to receive a degree he had invented. This degree, based on Nehemiah 2:12 and succeeding verses, and *Mnemonics*, his printed ritual, cost each recipient $10. This amount was necessary to pay for the costs of printing and other expenses. It was seized upon by some as evidence that Morris was enriching himself from the work.

*Mnemonics* was unintelligible to anyone without its key. The majority of Masons seemed to regard it as a violation of one of the first teachings of an Entered Apprentice. This was another weapon for Morris's enemies. Some were no doubt jealous of his intellect, ability, and other activities The stage was set for the explosion that soon came in the Grand Lodge.

In 1862 Hiram Bassett, a Conservator, was Grand Master. In his opening address he deplored the lack of uniformity in ritual. He asked that a plan to right this condition be devised. That same year Thomas Sadler, Grand Senior Warden, introduced a resolution, which the Grand Lodge adopted, to investigate the Conservators. A committee of Past Grand Masters, Wilson and Swigert and Grand Treasurer Albert G. Hodges were appointed for this purpose. Swigert and Wilson had served in the Grand Line with Morris, and Hodges had published Morris's *The History of Freemasonry in Kentucky* in 1859. The next year Past Grand Masters J. M. S. McCorkle and Thomas Todd and Grand Master Thomas Sadler were added to the committee. At that time it offered a resolution forbidding all persons to work or lecture on the Conservator ritual and forbidding all Masons under the Grand Lodge of Kentucky to hear such lectures or work, to receive Conservator books, or to join the Conservators.

After this report was adopted, Bassett and Grand Master Cooke asked the committee to meet with them and Morris in Louisville November 18, 1863, where they might be heard in explanation. Previous to this meeting, the committee received a letter from Mor-

ris stating that the sole purpose of the conservators was to establish
uniformity of work by prudent, and lawful means, and that there
were 2,900 members, including twenty-eight grand masters. He
asked that the committee publish his letter as a part of their report,
which they did. Morris was in New York at the time of the November meeting in Louisville, but sent another letter stating essentially
the same position.

When the committee reported to the 1864 session of the Grand
Lodge, it reviewed the history and publications of the Conservators
and concluded that the Conservator ritual was not the unadulter-
ated Webb ritual, but represented a version of it as revised by Morris according to his ideas. This position was bolstered by approximately thirteen pages of quotations of well-informed Masons of
other jurisdictions.

The committee next noted that complete uniformity of work
could not be attained. The principal object to be sought was preservation of the main outline and symbolism. No attempt should
be made to secure minute details of verbiage. It thoroughly condemned the use of ciphers, keys, and notes. It noted that the
whole Conservator movement was worthy of "a disciple of Ignatius
Loyola," and branded it as unmasonic and liable to abuse in the
hands of a Chief Conservator. This, of course, was true, but seems
highly unlikely in Morris's hands, especially since the movement
was to expire eight months later anyway.

The Committee reported seventy members of the Conservators
in Kentucky as of May 1, 1862, but does not give their names. A list
compiled by Ray V. Denslow in 1931 lists seventy-seven, including Morris, Grand Master Bassett, Elisha D. Cooke, John Augustus
Williams (Grand Senior Warden in 1861–62), Fred Webber, 33d
(Treasurer General of the Scottish Rite, Southern Jurisdiction), W.C.
Munger (Grand Commander of the Grand Consistory of Kentucky),
and M.J. Williams, who would become Grand Master in 1865.

The Grand Lodge adopted a resolution forbidding the use of the
Conservator ritual or any other written or cipher work of the eso-

teric portions of the degrees, and ordered any Kentucky Masons owning *Mnemonics* or other Conservator ritualistic material to deliver it promptly to the Grand Secretary who would hold it subject to the Grand Lodge's order.

Upon the adoption of this resolution, Past Grand Master Thomas Todd presented a communication dated October 24 [sic] and signed by Past Grand Master Bassett and nine others saying that they had voluntarily withdrawn from the Conservators since the organization which they had hoped would promote the peace and harmony of the Craft had actually disturbed it. They did not admit that the organization was clandestine. On the other hand, they said that they had the right to consider the Conservator ritual good and true work because it explained so fully everything in the degrees and was the only work that most of them had ever seen exemplified in the Grand Lodge.

After some complaints about the use of and possession of *Mnemonics* over the next few years, a motion was brought before the Grand Lodge in 1884 recommending that the Grand Lodge recognize and recommend to the subordinate lodges the Webb work as promulgated by Past Grand Masters Rob Morris and Hiram Bassett. This was tabled and the controversy was allowed to die.

After Morris's death in 1888, the Grand Lodge bought the remaining copies of *Mnemonics* and the plates from which they were printed. These were stored until 1914 when the Grand Lodge adopted a resolution ordering Grand Master George B. Winslow and Grand Secretary Dave Jackson to destroy them. They carried out this order September 18, 1915, and destroyed the books. The plates could not be located.

Although Morris was not successful with the conservators in Kentucky, his work seems to have become the basis of the present Indiana ritual. The nationwide uniformity Morris hoped for did not result and probably never will. Although the Civil War interfered with his hopes, perhaps the major reason for Morris's failure with the Conservator ritual lay in the fact that individuals, lodges, and Grand Lodges were hostile to his plans because each thought he—or it—had the genuine Webb ritual, not realizing that anything transmitted orally is certainly changed in the process. Others felt that it was dangerous to have so much power in the hands of one man as appeared to lie in Morris's as Chief Conservator. The secret degree of Conservator and the fact that some who might have desired it were not invited to receive it alienated still others. There may have been some who wanted it to fail because of jealousy of Morris and his other accomplishments.

At any rate Morris passed into the bad graces of the Grand Lodge of Kentucky and did not emerge until some years later. Complicating matters was the fact that he became indebted to the Grand Lodge for over $1,000 in 1859 and could not repay it. This resulted in legal action being taken. It was not until 1878 that he seems to have regained the full confidence of the Grand Lodge and again became prominent in its activities. In 1884 he was made Poet-Laureate of Freemasonry. He died at LaGrange in 1888 and was buried with full Masonic honors with Past Grand Master Hiram Bassett presiding,

Despite the allegations of his detractors, Morris does not seem to have made more than a living from his various Masonic activities, and was said to have had no more than $75.00 besides his house and library at the time of his death. A movement begun in his home lodge, Fortitude No. 47 of LaGrange, culminated in contributions from many Masons to erect a thirty-one foot monument of Barre Granite at his grave in LaGrange, where his house is, now maintained by the Order of the Eastern Star. Thus, despite the conservator uproar, Morris today is recognized as perhaps the most outstanding Mason ever to be a member of a Kentucky lodge.

# REFERENCES

Collins, Lewis and Richard H. *History of Kentucky*. Frankfort. Richard H. Collins, 1874 Rept. Kentucky Historical Society, 1966

Denslow, William R. *10,000 Famous Freemasons*. Trenton, Missouri, William R. Denslow, 1957–61

Denslow, Ray V. *The Masonic Conservators*. St. Louis Grand Lodge A.F. & A.M. of Missouri 1931

Grant, H. B. *Doings of the Grand Lodge of Kentucky, 1800–1900*. Louisville Masonic Home Book and Job Office 1900

Kenaston, Jean McKee. *History of the Order of the Eastern Star*. Cedar Rapids: The Torch Press 1917

Morris Robert, *Freemasonry In the Holy Land*. New York Masonic Publishing Company, 1872

Morris Robert, *The History of Freemasonry in Kentucky*. Louisville. Rob Morris, 1859

Morris Robert, *The Poetry of Freemasonry*. Biography written by His Son, Chicago: The Werner Company, 1895

*Proceedings at the Coronation of Rob Morris as Poet Laureate of Freemasonry*. Chicago: Knight and Leonard, 1885

*Proceedings of the Grand Lodge of Kentucky, F.&A.M.* Louisville, Grand Lodge of Kentucky, 1852–1888

Rule, Lucien V. *Pioneering in Masonry, The Life and Times of Rob Morris*. Louisville, Lucien V. Rule, 1922

Smith, Dwight L. *Goodly Heritage*. Indianapolis: Grand Lodge F.&A.M. of Indiana. 1968

*The Supreme Council 33d Washington*. The Supreme Council AASR, 1931

Voorhis, Harold Van Buren. *The Eastern Star. The Evolution From a Rite to an Order*. Richmond, Macoy, 1976

# THE LODGE AS PRIMARY COMMUNITY

## John Mauk Hilliard, FPS

*1980 Certificate of Literature*

PICTURE, IF YOU WILL, a venerable urban lodge with a small membership slowly declining in numbers, and advancing in age. Picture also, a time in the mid-seventies which finds a group of young Masons, in their late twenties and early thirties, children of the Sixties, the Age of Confrontation, Politics, of War and Protest, men who grew up in a time of Social Activism and Change, drifting to a great Eastern city from the far-flung states where they grew up and were educated, pulled to the great metropolis by the force of education or careers; picture these men finding their way by accident and coincidence into this staid, nearly dormant old lodge, and there confronting a handful of old men, Children of Depression and World War, and of an earlier America; old men led by a Lodge Secretary who had, virtually single-handedly, kept the lodge alive in the fierce decade of the sixties, with a little help from a couple of retired Past Masters, a lodge with the usual sprinkling of semi-comatose sideliners, drowsing through dreary meetings.

Picture a lodge with a few vigorous Grand Lodge magnates who long since left it in spirit if not actuality, for more fertile Masonic lives grazing the lush purple pastures of the Most Worshipful Grand Lodge, men for whom the lodge represents an embarrassment, an uncomfortable reminder of the days when they were part of the common herd.

And all this in a city in turmoil, a society faced with a shortage of space, money, energy, options, and an abundance of dirt, noise, deviance, and irresponsible behavior springing from the poverty, greed, and indifference of its populace.

Bitter old men dreaming of a richer, more fulsome past for City and Lodge, and ardent young men filled with the excitement and stimulation of urban living and fresh hope-filled careers: A volatile mix, set for one grand Masonic explosion. For the first time in seventy-five years, the sidelines and lower chairs of office filled with men wearing beards! Extraordinary conflict results, a clash of values in which the young, seeking an image of a Freemasonry vital in the tradition of Washington, Franklin, Voltaire, Mozart, Burns, Goethe, and Kipling, find instead the hostility of rigid old minds set in a siege mentality conceiving themselves the last survivors of the good fight, striving to hold back the barbarian hordes at the last gate of freedom, as the bulwarks of civilization give way all around.

However, the setting maul of time and death now begins to work, as it inevitably does, in favor of the young. The old tire, die or leave. The young inherit. But inherit what?

A shrinking, and much left visible craft. An aging, demoralized institution, in some sense as much afflicted by the structures of its traditions as sustained by them, an institution slow to confront the change and diffusion of cultural and social attitudes following World War II.

It is true that numbers are not necessarily measures of vitality. But in the face of declining numbers, comes more and more public indifference to the Craft, and with the lessening of a wide public consciousness of our nature, aims, and mission, there is bound to follow a diminution of public appreciation and good will, and with it a diminished opportunity for men who are "Masons at Heart and by Nature" to seek us out simply by reason of this lessened visibility and lower public esteem.

Many Masons proudly and bravely assert: "We're not getting smaller, we're getting better." We are no longer a mass movement as we were in the 1880s, 90s and after World War I and II; I do not say that we should be a mass movement again, but I cannot escape the notion that as a mass movement, Freemasonry touched thousands more lives in a profoundly significant, productive and fruitful way that would not have been possible had we restricted ourselves to the elitism and esoteric, deeply private approach of our European brethren. Mass movements are not in and of themselves bad; witness Christianity, and the other great religions. If indeed we have been losing the chaff and retaining the fertile grain of the Order, then we should be witnessing, in the intimacy of smaller more compact lodges, a renewed bond of commitment to the Craft and its grand principles, a revitalized community capable of sustaining its members in the wild and often vicious throes of an unpredictable world and inconstant fate. Do we see such renewed bonding? Do we see men growing mentally hale and spiritually strong in fresh unity of association and spirit in our lodges throughout the land? I think, Brothers, if we answer honestly, the answer, the sad answer, is "No."

What then, is likely to happen? We must face the inevitable fact of shrinkage and contraction for our Gentle Craft. We must be prepared to see the dissolution of many Masonic institutions especially the concordant bodies, and such institutions as our masonic homes (which, ironically enough, have an existence predicated on endowments and sustaining populations garnered by American Freemasonry in its guise of a Mass Movement). The recent action of the Shrine in permitting members to retain good standing in the Shrine, even though they may have been dropped from other Masonic bodies represents in my opinion an opening salvo of eventual independence and an attempt to cut away a vital organ from a gangrenous body.

Perhaps the question is "Should Freemasonry survive?" I have within my current acquaintance plenty of Masons who would answer that question in the negative, convinced that none in current or future generations is worthy of this jeweled institution of great worth; men who would see it die a quick death and be interred with them in forgotten tombs.

But for myself, I say "Yes," as I am sure most Masons would.... I am convinced in times of rapid, intolerant change, that jettisoning institutions that have proved helpful over a range of ages, continents, cultures, and seasons of man may prove dangerous to the survival of our race. We humans can never tell when some forgotten, musty concept in the mind's spiritual attic will prove newly adaptable as a tool of survival, nay even as a tool for the enchancement of our lives. So it is with Freemasonry. Human beings need Landmarks … landmarks to chart the course of turbulent lives, to anchor one's hope and dreams, to govern one's frantic progress. Now, more than ever, modern man needs a sense of identity, and more importantly, a sense of community. And what is Masonry in its greatest and happiest aspect but a school of human relations; in its most sublime attribute, but an extended family? I believe that it is the greatest fraternal complex ever devised by the mind of man, and perhaps still in its infancy, the exaggerations of its antiquity by many of its addled and more dotty historians, notwithstanding. Two hundred years of Grand Lodge Freemasonry is but a short time relative to the life of institutions like the Church and the nuclear family. And so, if the Shriners stitch the cockade of independence on their jaunty fezzes, how should the remnant of us who are left in the Craft proceed?

We must return to the Basic nature of the institution so as to emphasize the Gentle Craft's greatest strengths. If you'll pardon the pun, we must prepare our lodges as crafts: small, self-contained, compact, well-balanced, highly responsive communal units which can sweep like great ships thru the buffets of time and storms that shroud the future; they must be fitted like space ships to probe the deep space of history that lies ahead of us.

I have a few strategies to suggest:

We must reaffirm the inherent spirituality of our ritual. All Masons acknowledge that it is central to our Gentle Craft. It is no overstatement to say that it is the very foundation and fabric of Masonic institution. It is the vessel which contains and transmits from one generation of craftsmen to another the essential message and fundamental spirit of Freemasonry. And like any institutional element of such paramount importance, it has been and is, subject to corruption. A traditional notion would hold that the greatest abuse of the ritual is the tendency for lodges to neglect its proper exemplification by permitting sloppy or inadequate memorization and floor work, or reference to ciphered ritual books or monitors. Certainly, the accurate and expressive recitation of ritual, when done with conviction coupled with smooth floor work, is much to be desired in order to make the Masonic experience complete for candidates and Brothers alike. When done properly ritual can proceed at a stately, yet efficient pace, and can powerfully inspire and motivate.

I submit, however, that the greatest corruption of Masonic ritual is not sloppiness or inefficiency (as unpleasant and unattractive as those things may seem) but rather a failure of conviction and will and focus on the part of many Masons, both ritualists and side-liners alike. The persistent notion that a Brother's worth to a lodge should be measured by how much ritual he can commit to memory and rattle off at a moment's notice is a distortion and perversion of the fundamental task of ritual. Ritual exists to focus the powers of the heart and mind on the deep and hidden realities that we humans might otherwise miss or ignore in the pedestrian familiarities of daily life.

To know ritual perfectly and recite it faultlessly will be to no avail if he who speaks, and he who hears are deaf to its revelations. The hearts of the ritualist and his listener must quicken in the presence of the mystery; ritual and mystery are one, and anything less, even though it be word-perfect, rock-bound, and copper sheathed in rote memory, is futile and deadening to exemplar and beholder alike.

If we cannot take each step toward death with the Master Craftsman as he himself takes it, if we cannot sense with him the approach of the fearful end which awaits him as the implacable price of fidelity, if we cannot feel with him the agony of leaving a sacred and beloved task unfinished, if we cannot mourn with Kings who have lost a friend, and Craftsmen who have lost a teacher, and above all, if we cannot yearn with all our hearts for that which is forever lost, then truly the foundations of the Ancient Craft will crumble though perfect its ritual be.

At the same time we must drop the insistence that every man do as much ritual as he can pound into his tired brain. As one of my clergy friends who is also a Mason so aptly puts it, "Masonry is the only institution I know where we insist that every member of our congregation be a clergyman."

We must build into the lodge structure the concept of Gifts. If I may paraphrase our socialist friends, "From each according to his gifts, to each according to his need." We must establish a "socialism of fraternity" … by using people for what they do best. We must broaden, somewhat, the concept of lodge leadership by opening an avenue to the Warden's and Master's chairs through service other than that of learning reams of ritual. To try our leaders by the measure of whether a man can learn and deliver the Middle Chamber lecture gives no scope to men of great talent and ability who would make superb leaders in the Craft. I propose that we broaden the concept of the chair system to include Ritual, Education and Membership Committees and choose our future lodge wardens from men who excel at one or several of these functions. I do not wish to jetison the Chair System completely as it serves the function in healthy lodges of differentiating competition and conflict among a number of ambitious and aggressive men who aspire to leadership. It guarantees that everyone will eventually arrive at the Oriental Chair, and thereby lessens the inevitable jockeying for advantage and position.

The role of lodge governance of the Past Masters and Secretary must be reduced, probably by involving the PM actively in the committee system, and in the life and administration of the Lodge. The Buzzard's Roost in the SE corner of the Lodge comes into being and its denizens flock there, and squawk, wail, and dirty the floor, because of the anxiety and unease brought on by retirement from the Oriental Chair. "From the ranks you came, and to the ranks you must surely return...." Some PMs cannot forgive the Lodge for giving and then retaking the greatest gift in its power. Reincorporation in the life of the Lodge is necessary by giving them responsibility. Otherwise, they fight hard to maintain the illusion of an all-wise elite.

About secretaries, little good can be said. Since they so often have to compensate for the gross inadequacies of the many wounded birds who all too often reach the Master's Chairs in our Lodges, they inevitably fall prey to the occupational hazard of meglomania that appears to infect all the secretaries' race. They begin to fancy themselves indispensable as they pick up the pieces for the incompetents and they end by completely identifying the Lodge with their own, by then, quite warped egos. It is therefore necessary for the Lodge to remain actively conscious of the need to regard the Secretary as being in a purely clerical and administrative role as a support person for masters and wardens, and to constantly readjust administrative duties and priorities to prevent or discourage secretaries from assuming too much responsibility. Bylaw provisions limiting secretaries terms to no more than five years might prove helpful.

We should consider lessening the role of the Grand Lodge and dispersing or reorganizing to some extent, the welter of appendant and concordant bodies. Grand Lodges were Anderson's greatest innovation on and in the Body of the Craft. Originally intended to serve as administrative tools for coordinating mutual relations and efforts among Lodges and also to serve as the instruments for propagation of the Craft, they have become, in many Grand Jurisdictions, massive Masonic bureaucracies girded round with legions of men hungry for the purple of Craft.

Overlaying its administrative function and to some extent warp-
ing it, the Masonic Grand Honors Syndrome, with hordes of District Deputies, and masses of purple-and gold-sheathed magnates
of the Grand Line, has succeeded in siphoning off enormous talent
and energy from the primary community, the symbolic lodge.

Originally perhaps this Honors System served like the Chair System internally in Lodges, to differentiate conflict and competition
by drawing away the more ambitious and potentially troublesome
Past Masters into the giddy heights of the Grand Celestial Sphere
of the Grand Lodge. The Symbolic Lodge can no longer afford the
loss of talent. Even the terminology is askew: the term "Constituent" lodges is a travesty—Grand Lodge itself should be subordinate. I would eliminate all Grand Rank although not the Grand
Lodge itself. The overwhelming, smothering presence of Grand
Lodge must be alleviated. I am not suggesting its dissolution, however. We still need a grand structure, even if reduced, to adjudicate
disputes, for consistent record keeping, to organize and marshall
the resources of all lodges to serve the needs of each, and most
importantly, to maintain a visible profile for the institution above
the bland plane and horizon of the rest of society. This is necessary
simply to attract the attention and interest of potential members.

The appendant bodies also draw off too much precious energy
from the primary community. I would recommend the reincorporation of these bodies within the structure of the symbolic lodge
(we may not want to keep all of them) much in the manner of the
Scandinavian and Continental Systems in which lodges work several degrees. This would tend to refocus interest in the primary
community.

At the same time the institution must be more open in and
with society. This is not to say that we should give up the canon of
secrecy which is a major landmark.

We Freemasons consider our ritual a highly private, and intensely
personal matter, and anything that smacks of intrusion or invasion of
this, for us, very special system of allegory and symbol is rather upset-

ting. We should always be happy to discuss the general essence and aspects of the order with any human being who inquires in good faith, but the specific form of and detail of allegory and symbol is an intimate matter which, I think, should honorably lie beyond the range of a general curiosity on the part of the uninitiated.

This is not to say that we can preserve the secrets of the Craft from prying eyes. Anyone who has access to a major public library can find expose after expose of our ritual. Films like the recent Murder by Decree reveal much to the public. But we Masons value secrecy because it too is a symbol. It is a symbol of the bond among us. The process of maintaining a quiet and dignified silence on the forms or our liturgy constitutes a mental discipline that constantly reminds us of our obligations to each other and reinforces them. So, if the world finds out, it matters not a whit. It matter only that we keep the faith of secrecy with one another. Secrecy's primary function is intended to be an internal bond, not an external veil.

In this context, I must say that I favor the practice of asking men to join the Fraternity. In my opinion the proscription against this practice is no landmark. I do not approve of arm-twisting, fraternity rushing, or proselytizing techniques, but if I encounter a decent, God-fearing man whom I believe would help and be helped by the Craft, I first will make him aware of it, then when he shows genuine interest, apprise him of the procedures for joining; if he continues to evince interest, I will invite him to join, and offer to be his proposer.

Let us make a clear distinction between what is secret about our institution and what is not: the forms we may jealously guard; but the substance and essence and consciousness that give rise to the forms, we should be willing to share with the world—at least with those of our friends and neighbors who have a genuine interest and not an idle curiosity. There is nothing of substance about Freemasonry that we cannot and should not share with those who have a legitimate interest of scholarship, or personal search.

I would lower the age of membership to 18. We all know that eighteen year aids are not terribly mature, but what better way to be exposed to maturity than in the body of the Craft? Indeed, the concept of education in the Craft must be reinforced.

A Lodge should be a place where one is exposed to exciting ideas, both Masonically and in terms of the general culture. It should be a place of civilizing discourse and enlightening deliberation. The Grand Lodge of California is sponsoring Adult Continuing Education and Self-Development Courses for its brethren. This extends Masonry's mission. This, I believe, is an extraordinarily valuable notion: The recitation of ritual should be not an end in itself, but a starting point and blueprint for a sweeping educational investigation of the many principles it embodies.

Who will transmit to the young the role models for productive fraternal communities if not the Ancient Craft? Our commitment to DeMolay, Jobs Daughters, and Rainbow extends the mission of the Craft into the World of the Young.

I propose that lodges should be permitted to open on and do business in the Entered Apprentice Degree (as is done in Great Britain) in order to establish a full sense of immediate Brotherhood between new candidates and lodge brothers. What better way to begin to educate and incorporate a man within the body of a community than to immediately insist on his sharing and exercising those responsibilities and obligations of membership and participation from his first exposure to that community.

We Masons dare not neglect our pastorial mission to minister to the needs of individual brothers. Here I speak not of the sick in body, but rather of those forgotten, dim figures that every Lodge loses sight of through reticence or neglect. To lavish attention upon the lonely in our ranks, to visit and succor the afflicted in body and spirit, to turn the light of blessed, genuine interest upon those brothers whose presence in the Craft has, from neglect or indifference to them, begun to fade, is and could be a major tool for our survival. To restore to the community the forgotten men in our ranks will bestow a fresh apprehension and sense of that potent bond that exists between all Masons, not only to the forgotten brothers who formerly languished in the twilight of the Lodge's ranks, but also to those brothers who seek them out anew.

We should constantly seek a variety of experience, background, and condition among our members. One of our most powerful Masonic concepts is that of the Traveler, the Sojourner, he who works and receives Master's Wages in a strange coin in faraway lands, the stranger who finds comfort and succor among those whom are met as strangers and parted as brothers. There are many ways and places where Masons may work and receive Master's wages, and the Craft needs to be there in all of them in order to offer the bonds of unity to the sojourner. To this end, we should broaden the concept of multiple memberships on the English model to enable brothers to involve themselves with as many lodges as they feel comfortable in supporting. We must form lodges at Colleges or Universities, and revive the practice for the military, and imbed The Craft as a living force in institutions like seminaries, space and sea colonies, and stations.

We cannot neglect the women's movement. I believe that single sex institutions are perfectly acceptable, in a truly liberated society. Men may enjoy the sole company of their sex, and women theirs, as indeed the feminists now discover with their "consciousness raising groups." But we dare not forget the androgynous tradition in Masonry which stretches from the 18th Century French "Lodges of Adoption" to modern co-Masonry and our own Rob Morris' Order of the Eastern Star. Please be open to this issue. The real power of the human race may indeed reside in the women. They can help us be open to the feminine, nurturent side and dimension of our own being.

More democracy in Grand Lodge structures would tend to make the Craft more responsive to the demands of change. We are the only institution I know which is so totally dominated by the "Old Boy System"—a Masonic oligarchy made up of Past Grand Masters, Past District Grand Masters, and a few other be-purpled figures dominates the life of Grand Lodges and their constituent districts. It is even worse in the appendant bodies. It has been so long since any Grand or Supreme Institutions in Masonry had a genuine franchise for their rank and file that democracy is virtually unknown on that level of the Craft. The problem does not really exist in the primary community, the Lodge itself, because the very immediate and intimate nature of the communal bonding makes for more immediate feedback and response when Masters or cliques attempt to abuse power. The immediacy of the Lodge situation makes for a more natural mechanism of check and balance in human relations.

The basic emphasis must be upon the Lodge, the primary community. Many will not agree with the changes or shifts in emphasis which I propose herein. I do not expect agreement, but I would welcome an acknowledgment that the concept of change is not alien to Freemasonry, but is indeed a major building stone in the structure of the Gentle Craft. Each generation has redefined the Craft to suit its own changing cultural context.

In the final analysis of our motif, the Builders must be as aware of the process of creation as they are of the act of completion, if indeed they are to do true work, and square work. The notion of man as imperfect and incomplete is the foundation of Freemasonry. The poet tells us "no man is an island, entire of himself." Man must change for it is only through change that past and future may be reconciled. Through the ages great men, from the Tao and Zen Masters of old, to St. Paul in his blinding vision, have realized that their kingdoms are not come, that continual adjustment, searching, discovery, loss and rediscovery is necessary to realize the human self. The house not made with hands requires all the craft and power and skill of the builder, if it is to withstand the rigor of time, space, and the human soul.

The ancient notion of oneness, of becoming complete by incorporating the worlds around us, both human, natural, and divine, is the true calling of our Ancient Craft. We are the Children of Hiram who search for that which is lost, that part of ourselves obscured by greed, lust, weakness, intolerance, power, or indifference; we search the bright corners of life and the dark shadows of the grave for the link with the infinite that makes whole our fragile, broken selves.

The Japanese Orientalist Kakuzo Okakura, at the turn of the century, once mentioned that in Japan there was an old saying that: "… a woman cannot love a man who is truly vain, for there is no crevice in his heart for love to enter and fill up." This is a powerful image, and tells much about the nature of love.

My brothers, there are in our hearts crevices aplenty, for so we are taught in the Sublime Tale of Hiram Abiff. Do we seek that which is lost? It is lost from our hearts. Let us pray to the Great Architect and to the memory of our Masters of Old, that together we may fill the crevices, the gaps, the emptiness of one another's hearts with all the potent tools of our ancient calling: Peace and Harmony, Love, Relief and Truth.

# PHYSICISTS, THE ROYAL SOCIETY, AND FREEMASONRY

## by Richard H. Sands, FPS

*1981 Certificate of Literature*

THIS ESSAY[1] is about an event in history which later had an enormous impact upon this country in its formative years, yet one about which the average American knows little.

The period in question is the last half of the seventeenth and the first half of the eighteenth century, with particular emphasis on the period from 1714 through 1738. The event in question was the establishment of what has been called "Speculative Freemasonry."

Before discussing the circumstances surrounding this event I would like to begin with an anecdote that illustrates both how I became interested in the topic of this essay, and what few credentials I may have for speaking upon it. In 1964 I was a young Associate Professor of Physics, and already feeling the social confinement of the Ivory Tower, where professionals talk incessantly—even at parties and dinners—about their own narrow fields of expertise. I decided to get back to the real world by broadening my social contacts in the community. I had tried the church but largely because the membership was dominated still by university professionals, the relationships I found there remained super-

ficial and unsatisfying. I remembered that my father had been a
Free and Accepted Mason and clearly held his associations with
chat fraternity in high regard. I had learned as a child to recognize
Masons, and as the years rolled by I discovered that "nine times
out of ten" when I met someone in the community whom I considered worthy of respect I found out later that he was a Mason.
Surely this was not coincidence! I also knew that one had to ask to
be made a Mason: the members of the fraternity are forbidden to
solicit or recruit. Thus it was that I sought Freemasonry via one of
the men of my church for whom I held particular respect. I knew
little about the fraternity except that it numbered many good men
among its membership.

Upon entering the lodgeroom for the first time I was impressed.
Among the first words I heard were those of a ninety-year-old man
reciting a verse from the Old Testament. (I was blindfolded and
therefore acutely aware of voices.) The impression was that of listening truly to "the wisdom of the ages." As the ritual unfolded, I
became increasingly fascinated by the form and content of the
largely symbolic presentation. I was the recipient of moral instruction presented in the most meaningful and palatable manner possible; namely, by symbols and by allegory. In due course I witnessed
a play Shakespeare himself would have been proud to compose. It
was an allegorical lesson portrayed by some twenty members of
the community, ham actors every one. just for my benefit. Lest the
allusion to Shakespeare seem overstated, let me quote one of the
world's great actors, Edwin Booth, on the same subject:

> In all my research and study. in all my close analysis of the
> masterpieces of Shakespeare, in my earnest determination to
> make those plays appear real on the mimic stage, I have never and
> nowhere met tragedy so real, so sublime, so magnificent as the leg-
> end of Hiram. It is substance without shadow—the manifest des-
> tiny of life which requires no picture and scarcely a word to make
> a lasting impression upon all who can understand. To be a Wor-
> shipful Master. and to throw my whole soul into that work, with
> the candidate for my audience and the Lodge for my stage, would

be a greater personal distinction than to receive the plaudits of the people in the theatres of the world.[2]

Clearly, someone of great intellectual achievement had drafted this system of moral instruction and written this allegorical play, but who? What did it mean? Where could I read about it? I found some fifteen books in the library on the subject of Freemasonry but nothing in them to excite a young man and a practicing physicist. And so I abandoned the search.

Fourteen years later a chance clue aroused my curiosity anew. I had become Chairman of the Department of Physics and as such I received a telephone call from Warren Pierce, who has a talk show on radio station WJR in Detroit. He wanted me to call him at 7:00 p.m. that evening and tell his listeners "what would happen if you were to throw a penny off the Empire State Building in New York." It was early afternoon so I had a few hours to research the question. Now, one doesn't just sit down and calculate the effect of air friction on a penny. A penny falls erratically: it sails and then tumbles, like a dropped playing-card. When I investigated this matter I discovered that the laws of air friction were first delineated in detail by two men, Sir Isaac Newton and Join Desaguliers' who for some three years (1715–1719) dropped objects off a tower in London, timing their fall, and from those measurements deduced the Laws of Air Friction. As it happens, I had learned earlier that Desaguliers was reputed to be the "Father of Freemasonry." Here was the added motivation I needed to begin research in earnest: a fellow physicist had played a major role in starting Freemasonry in its present form! Could it be that this was why I was so attracted by the format of its ritual? A sense of spiritual kinship caused me to continue my study of Desagulier's life long after the question of the falling penny was dispatched.

Jean Theophile des Aguliers[3] was born in La Rocheile, France, on March 1, 1683, the son of the pastor of the Protestant congregation at Aitre. Following the revocation in 1685 of the Edict of Nanres, which had bestowed civil and religious freedom on the French Protestants, many of the most enlightened citizens of France emigrated, carrying with them the arts and skills of a highly educated culture. England, in particular, benefited enormously from Louis XIV's permitted Catholic persecution of families like the des Aguliers. Legend has it that the young boy's father concealed him in a barrel when they fled France (the Huguenots being forbidden to take their children out of the country). They made their way first to the island of Guernsey and then to England. The Reverend des Aguliers was admitted subsequently to the Church of England and ordained a Deacon and Priest on the same day to the French Chapel in Swallow Street, London. The more aristocratic portion of the refugees worshipped at this chapel. Later the elder des Aguliers surrendered this ministry and began a school in Islington, where this son (now John Theophilus Desaguliers) was educated until the father's death. In 1705, John entered Christ Church, Oxford; he obtained his B.A. in 1710 and was admitted to orders by the same Bishop Henry Compton who ordained his father. The same year he became lecturer in Experimental Philosophy at Hart Hall, Oxford, until 1713.

In 1712 he began to give public lectures, for which he charged a fee, in the subject of "Natural Philosophy." He was evidently the first person to make a living as a public lecturer, and he was a popular one because his lectures were illustrated by experimental demonstrations. He invented a form of the planetarium, for example, to introduce his audience to some fundamental Newtonian principles. On July 29, 1714, he became a Fellow of the Royal Society upon the recommendation of Newton, who was impressed sufficiently by Desagulier's ability to make him one of the two curators of experiments for the Royal Society. In 1718 he obtained a Bachelor and Doctor of Laws at Oxford. His publications and experiments were extensive, the former a record of the latter. (He also published a long allegorical poem, The Newtonian System.) In addition to the experiments from which the laws of air friction were deduced, he devised a smokeless fireplace and designed the heating and ventilating system of the House of Commons in 1723. He was considered an expert in air circulation and public water

works. When old Westminister Bridge was built (1738–9) his opinion on the structure was often sought. He first introduced the term
"conductor" into the literature of electricity, and his monograph A
Dissertation Concerning Electricity had profound influence in the
eighteenth century. He earned the Copley Gold Medal from the
Royal Society in 1741, an honor shared with later scientists such as
Franklin, Priestly, Herschel, Volta, Pavlov, Einstein, and Bohr.

Desaguliers is purported to have been initiated in 1712 into
the Lodge Antiquity, the oldest of the few lodges of operative Freemasonry existing in London: however, there is no concrete evidence that he was involved with the craft prior to 1719. He was
impressed by the religious toleration he found in that community
of informed citizens, and impressed even more with the opportuni-
ties it afforded to build a new orderly social structure. I use architectural metaphors deliberately. Freemasonry in its present form
grew out of the craft of architects, sculptors, metal workers, artists
and stoneworkers who built the great cathedrals in Europe and
England during the middle ages. The founders of modern Speculative Freemasonry saw in this professional background a foundation, and a spirit of creative enterprise informed by traditional
skills, upon which to construct a new social destiny. Freemasonry,
contrary to the popular conception of it as arcane or occult, originated during the Enlightenment as a problem-solving public interest group. This explains the attraction it exerted upon talented men
like Desaguliers.

Being the capital of England, London was especially sensitive
to political changes, and most of these were traumatic at this time.
Queen Anne, the sister of exiled James II and the last Protestant
member of the Stuart family, died in 1714. In order to assure a Protestant succession George I, a great-grandson of James, came from
his native Hanover to assume the throne. A leader who didn't even
speak English, he ushered in a governmental spoils system of noto-
rious degeneracy, preserved for us in the satires of Pope, Gay, Swift
and other London wits. The mood of the populace became one of

cynicism, rebellion, and intense fear of encroaching chaos. Problems of inadequate social control—"crime, turbulence, and hard-living"—characterized London life, not to mention widespread poverty. Two social institutions traditionally appointed to preserve order, the church and the family, were no longer adequate to the task. The clergy were discouraged from social technics lest the church itself suffer from the spirit of reform. Nor did the family seem an anchor for the ship of state. Economic individualism in an era of nascent capitalism led to the disintegration of the family structure, as we see it most of the fiction of the period, beginning with Robinson Crusoe. London appeared to many of its inhabitants a jungle-city, in need of new modes of authority and new associations devoted to the forging of legitimate paradigms of social cohesion. From this background two organizations emerged which made such claims, The Royal Society and Freemasonry, the former first.

## II

The Royal Society of London for Imparting Natural Knowledge is the oldest scientific society in Great Britain and one of the oldest in Europe. It grew out of an informal "club" in the sense that as early as 1645 weekly meetings were held in London of "divers worthy persons, inquisitive into natural philosophy and other parts of human learning, and particularly of what hath been called the New Philosophy or Experimental Philosophy." On November 28, 1660, after a lecture by Christopher Wren, the Society got its formal start. A "memorandum" in the first journal book of the Society records the occasion:

> "Memorandum that November 28, 1660, these persons following, according to the usuall custom of most of them mett together at Gresham Colledge to heare Mr. Wren's lecture. viz., The Lord Broucker, Mr. Boyle, Mr. Bruce, Sir Robert Moray, Mr. Paul Neile, Dr. Wilkins. Dr. Goddard, Dr. Petty, Mr. Ball, Mr. Rooke, Mr. Wren,

> Mr. Hill. And after the lecture was ended, they did, according to the usuall manner, withdrawn for mutuall converse. Where amongst other matters that were discoursed of, something was offered about a designe of founding a Colledge for the promoting of Physico-Mathematical Experimentall Learning."

On the following Wednesday, Sir Robert Moray brought word that the king (Charles II) approved the design and purpose of the meetings and a form of obligation was originated which was signed by all the persons listed in the above memorandum and by seventy-three others. On December 12, fifty-five was fixed as the number of the society with persons of the degree of Baron, Fellows of the College of Physicians, and public professors of mathematics, physics and natural philosophy of both Gresham College and Oxford being supernumeraries. Gresham College was appointed to be the regular meeting place of the society.

Sir Robert Moray was chosen president on March 6, 1661, and served until the society was incorporated, when Lord Brouncker was appointed the first president under the charter. In October 1661, the king offered to be entered one of the society and the next year. July 15, 1662, the society was incorporated under its present title. A second charter in 1663 conferred further privileges. that charter announced that the business and design of the Royal Society is ... to examine all systems, theories, principles, hypotheses, elements, histories, and experiments of things natural, mathematical, and mechanical ... in order to the compiling of a complete system of solid philosophy for explicating all phenomena produced by nature or art, and recording a rational account of the causes of things

At this early stage, the "correspondence" actively maintained with continental philosophers formed an important part of the society's labors. Selections from this correspondence furnished the beginnings of the *Philosophical Transactions*, a publication now of worldwide celebrity. The Society also published additional treatises, among them Isaac Newton's *Philosophae naturalis principia mathematica*, the fountainhead of all subsequent work in physics and astronomy.

From the beginning, one of the most important functions of the society was the performance of experiments before the members, and much of the early meetings were occupied by the discussion of such experiments. At the time Desaguliers joined the Society, experimentation itself had been exposed to a generation of ridicule, which makes his devotion, and that of his colleagues, the more admirable. The anti-hero of Thomas Shadwell's play, *The Virtuoso*, Sir Nicholas Gimrack, had become the prototype of the mad researcher into useless knowledge. Later satires by Samuel Butler, Alexander Pope, Joseph Addison, and—most severe—Jonathan Swift in the third book of *Gulliver's Travels*, further established the research scientist as an object of derision.

Like his Fellows, Desaguliers remained steadfast. In *A System of Experimental Philosophy Prov'd by Mechanics* (1719), a work disavowed by Desaguliers but consistent with his beliefs, this statement precedes a lengthy set of experiments and conclusions:

> That we may not be deceived by false notions which we have embraced without examining, or that we have received upon the authority of others, we ought to call in question all such things as have an appearance of falsehood, that by a new examen we may be led to the truth. (pp 1–2)

"By a new examen we may be led to the truth." The Royal Society remained committed to the construction of a new philosophy that would serve a chaotic society by offering systems not subject to mockery or doubt, and thereby consolate what seemed in danger of collapse.

Totally independent of these developments, a similar evolution occurred in the fraternity of Free and Accepted Masons.[4] On December 27, 1716, four lodges in Westminister, London, consisting mostly of "accepted masons" decided to "cement under a Grand Master as the Center of Union and Harmony" and form a

Grand Lodge. The four lodges were described by the names of the taverns or ale house" where they met:

1. At the Goose and Gridiron Ale-house in St. Pauls Church-yard
2. At the Crown Ale-house in Parker's Lane near Drury Lane
3. At the Apple-Tree Tavern in Charles Street Convent Garden
4. At the Rummer and Grapes Tavern in Channel Row, Westminister

These clubmen made contact with some "old Brothers" who knew even more about the history and customs of the old guilds, and assembled them in the Appletree Tavern on June 24, 1717. They "put into the Chair the oldest Master Mason and constituted themselves a Grand Lodge pro Tempore in due Form and forthwith revived the Quarterly Communications of the Officers of the Lodges (called the Grand Lodge)." The assembly chose a Grand Master from among their number until "they should have the Honour of a Noble Brother at their Head" as was customary for the guilds. The precedent for their "revival" is not clear, but the purpose of the Grand Lodge was very attractive; namely, to "hold the annual Assembly and Feast" for Saint John the Baptist, one of the patron Saints of Masons, in proper (and well lubricated) style.

There followed the eventual transformation of the guild "club" into a new form of fraternal association: Speculative Freemasonry. The first Grand Master, Anthony Sayre, was simply referred to as "Gentleman," and we know little else about him; however, in 1718, Sayre's successor as Grand Master was George Payne an "accepted mason" who wished to enrich the club life of the guild by recovering its heritage. Payne's hobby was antiquarianism and he led a group within the membership that appreciated the historical aspects of masonic membership during his year 'several old Copies of one Gothic Constitutions were produced and collated". Perhaps most important the Reverend Dr. John Desaguliers, a physicist and teacher of great energy and high reputation in London's scien-

tific circles, became intrigued with the idea of teaching morality by
use of the same methods of "scientific" education which he used
to teach mathematics and physics. He found in the old Gothic
Constitutions an excellent basis on which to build such a system
of moral instruction. Desaguliers was regarded as a superb teacher
and he had developed a method of graded instruction in all of the
sciences "from the easiest truths to those more complex." Perhaps
he saw similarities in the system of graded skills from Apprentice
to Master described in the old Constitution. Desaguliers was most
probably the mayor force in the incorporation of a system of moral
instruction into the convivial aspects of the new speculative Freemasonry. Unfortunately. the minutes of the first six years were lost,
so we can only imagine the conflicts and interplay between the
"educators" and the "clubmen" which followed.

The active involvement of Dr. Desaguliers, LLD and FRS with
Freemasonry was a social coup of which the members apparently
were quite aware; they elected him Grand Master in 1719. Probably
because of his prominence, during that year "several old Brothers"
who had neglected the Craft previously visited the Lodges, some
Noblemen were made Brothers and several new Lodges were constituted. One of these old brothers was Reverend James Anderson;
Anderson moved in the same social and scientific circles as Desa-
guiliers, was a F.R.S. and interested in science, history and geneal-
ogy. He "put all of these interests in the service" of Freemasonry
and played an import tent part in its development.

In 1723, Anderson and Desaguliers co-authored The Constitution of the Free-Masons, containing the History of that Fraternity. It
is of interest to note that a reprint of this was the first book about
Freemasonry published in the United States, in 1734.[5] The young
publisher, not a Mason at the time but later to become the Grand
Master of Masons in Philadelphia, was Benjamin Franklin, America's first renowned physicist.

Together, Anderson and Desaguliers succeeded in attracting
and enlisting the aid of up to forty-five percent of the Fellows of

the Royal Society in the years 1723–1730. Signature books of the Masonic lodges and the Royal Society permit positive identification of individuals enrolled in both organizations.

A few are shown here

## Grand Masters Who Were Also Fellows of the Royal Society

| Date of Appt | | Date of F.R.S. |
|---|---|---|
| 1719 | Desaguliers | 1714 |
| 1721 | 2nd Duke of Montagu | 1718 |
| 1723 | 2nd Duke of Buccleuch | 1724 |
| 1724 | 2nd Duke of Richmond | 1724 |
| 1725 | 7th Earl of Abercorn | 1715 |
| 1727 | 3rd Lord Coleraine | 1735 |
| 1731 | Earl ol Leichester | 1729 |
| 1733 | 7th Earl of Strathmore | 1732 |
| 1734 | 20th Earl of Crawford | 1732 |
| 1736 | 4th Earl of Loudon | 1738 |
| 1737 | 2nd Earl of Darnley | 1738 |
| 1739 | 2nd Lord Raymond | 1740 |
| 1741 | 14th Earl of Morton | 1733 |
| 1757 | 15th Earl of Morton | 1754 |
| 1762 | 5th Earl Ferrers | 1761 |
| 1772 | 9th Lord Petre | 1780 |
| 1782 | H.R.H. Duke of Cumberland | 1789 |
| 1790 | H.R.H. Prince of Wales | 1820 |
| 1813 | H.R.H. Duke of Sussex | 1828 |
| 1790 | Acting Gr. Master, Lord Moira | 1787 |
| 1775 | Antient Gr. Master, 4th Duke of Atholl | 1780 |

## Deputy Gr. Masters Who Were Also Fellows of the Royal Society

| | | |
|---|---|---|
| 1721 | John Beale | 1721 |
| 1722 | J. T. Desaguliers | 1714 |
| 1724 | Marlin Folkes | 1714 |

| 1726 | J.T. Desaguliers      | 1714 |
| 1739 | William Graeme        | 1730 |
| 1741 | Martin Clare          | 1735 |
| 1745 | Edward Hody           | 1733 |
| 1766 | 12th Viscount Dillon  | 1767 |
| 1812 | H.R.H. Duke of Sussex | 1828 |

## Senior Gr. Wardens Who Were Also Fellows of the Royal Society

| 1729 | Sir James Thornhill    | 1723 |
| 1750 | 2nd Lord Carpenter     | 1729 |
| 1731 | George Douglas         | 1732 |
| 1742 | Edward Hody            | 1735 |
| 1744 | William Graeme         | 1730 |
| 1767 | 12th Viscount Dillon   | 1767 |
| 1771 | Sir Watkin W. Wynne    | 1773 |
| 1778 | Henry Dagge            | 1779 |
| 1782 | Sir Herbert Mackworth  | 1777 |
| 1790 | H. Crathorne           | 1795 |
| 1792 | J. Day (Past Rank)     | 1793 |
| 1793 | J. Dent                | 1811 |
| 1799 | 4th Earl of Pomfret    | 1805 |

## Junior Gr. Wardens Who Were Also Fellows of the Royal Society

| 1723 | John Senex          | 1728 |
| 1735 | Martin Clare        | 1735 |
| 1756 | William Graeme      | 1730 |
| 1770 | Sir Watkin W Wynne  | 1773 |
| 1775 | Henry Dagge         | 1779 |
| 1784 | James Meyrick       | 1800 |
| 1797 | J. Hunter           | 1785 |
| 1804 | J. Crooke           | 1821 |
| 1808 | William Camac       | 1821 |
| 1813 | S. McGillivray      | 1838 |

## Alphabetical List of Early Freemasons
## Who Were Also Fellows of the Royal Society

Aberdour, James Lord (14th Earl of Morton) – 1733 – GM 1741

Andrews, Joseph – 1726 – Rummer, Henrietta St.

Arbuthnot, John – 1704 – Bedford's Head, Covent Garden

Bacon, John – 1750 – University Lodge

Bates, Thomas – 1718 – Dolphin, Tower Street

Beale, John – 1721 – Crown & Anchor, St. Clements – DGM 1721

Beckett, William – 1718 – Swan, Ludgate St.

Bedford, Duke of  – 1741 – Queen's Head, Bath

Bradley, James – 1718 – Three Kings, Spittlefields

Bridges, John – 1708 – Bear & Harrow, Buthcer Row

Bristow, William – 1742 – Queen's Head, Bath

Campbell, George – 1730 – Old Devill, Temple Bar

Carpenter (2nd Lord Carpenter) – 1729 – Horn Tavern, Westminster
     – SGW 1730

Chambers, Ephraim – 1729 – Richmond Lodge

Clare, Martin – 1735 – Cross Keys, Henrietta St – DGM 1741

Coleraine, Henry 3rd Lord – 1729 – Swan, Tottenham High Cross
     – GM 1727

Crawford, John 20th Earl of – 1732 – GM 1734

Cunningham, James – 1699 – Lebeck's Head Maiden Lane

Dalkeith, Francis Earl of (2nd Duke of Buccleuchi) – 1724
     – Rummer, Charing Cross – GM 1723

Darnley, Edward, 2nd Earl of – 1727 – GM 1737

Day, Thomas – 1691 – Queen's Head, Knaves Acre

De La Faye, Charles – 1725 – Horn Tavern, Westminister

De Loraine, Earl of – 1731 – Horn Tavern, Westminister

Desaguliers, John Theophilus – 1714 – Horn Tavern, Westminister
     – GM 1719

Douglas, George – 1732 – SGW 1731

Da Bois Charles – 1700 – Horn Tavern, Westminister

Dugood William – 1728 – Three Tuns, Billingsgate

Folkes, Martin – 1714 – Bedford's Head, Covent Garden
  – DGM 1724
Geekie, Alexander – 1710 – Cardigan Head, Charing Cross
Georges John – 1719 – King's Arms, St. Paul's
Graeme William – 1730 – DGM 1739
Gray John – 1731 – St. Paul's Head, Ludgate St.
Gray Robert – 1728 – Bedford's Head, Covent Garden
Green Thomas – 1711 – King's Head, Fleet St.
Green William – 1729 – Cheshite Cheese, Arundel St
Harrington, Edward – 1734 – Queen's Head Bath
Heathcote, George – 1728 – Rummer, Charing Cross
Herbert, Lord Charles – 1673 –Stukeley
Hewer Hewer Edgerey – 1725 – Bedford's Head Covent Garden
Hackman Nathane – 1725 – Horn Tavern, Westminister
Hill, Thomas – 1725 – Queen's Head, Holborn
Hodges, Thomas – 1715 – Black Posts Great Wild St.
Hody, Edward – 1732 – DGM 1745
Hollings, John – 1726 – Rose Tavern, Temple Bar
Hunt, Thomas – 1740 – Gin & Bottle, Little Britain
Lock, William – 1754 – Queen's Arms, Newgate St
Loudon, John, 4th Earl of – 1737 – GM 1736
Earl of Leicester – 1735 – GM 1731
Lucas, Richard – 1721 – Crown & Harp, St. Martin's Lane
Machin, John – 1710 – Bedford's Head, Covent Garden
Manningham, Sir Richard – 1719 – Horn Tavern, Westminister
Markham, Sir George – 1708 – Sun, Southside, St. Paul's
Martin, John – 1727 – Golden Lion, Fleet St
Mears, William – 1686 – Crown & Anchor, St. Clement's
Milward, Edward – 1741 – Bear & Harrow, Butcher Row
Montagu, Duke of – 1717 – Horn Tavern, Westminister – GM 1721
Nicholls, Frank – 1728 – Busybody, Charing Cross
Pacey, Henry Butler – 1752 – Bear & Harrow, Butcher Row
Paisley, James Lord (7th Earl of Abercorn) – 1715
  – Horn Tavern, Westminister – GM 1725

Papillon, David – 1720 – Bricklayer's Arms, Barbican
Parker, George, David (Earl of Macclesfield) – 1722
     – Swan, Chichester
Parker, Thomas – 1747 – Crown & Harp. St. Martin's Lane
Pawlet, Edward – 1726 – Crown & Anchor, St. Clement's
Pellet, Thomas – 1711 – Bedford's Head, Covent Garden
Philips, John – 1742 – Sun, Southside, St. Paul's
Price, William – 1753 – Ship behind Exchange
Queensborough, Duke of – 1722 – Horn Tavern, Westminister
Ramsay, Andrew Michael – 1729 – Horn Tavern, Westminister
Rawlinson, Richard – 1714 – Three Kings, Spittlefields
Raymond, Robert, 2nd Lord – 1739 – GM 1739
Richardson, Richard – 1712 – Dick's Coffeehouse, Strand
Richmond, Charles, 2nd Duke  – 1724
     – Horn Tavern, Westminister – GM 1724
Rogers, Joseph – 1738 – Crown & Anchor, St. Clement's
Rutty, William – 1720 – Bedford's Head, Covent Garden
St. Albans, Charles, Duke of – 1722 – Queen's Head, Bath
Schomberg, Meyer – 1726 – Swan & Rummer, Finch Lane
Senex, John – 1728 – JGW 1723
Sharp, Sameul – 1749 – Queen's Head, Newgate St.
Sloane, William – 1722 – Dolphin Tower, St.
Smith, Edward – 1738 – Dolphin Tower, St.
Stanhope, Philip (Earl of Chesterfield) – 1735 – Stukeley
Stanley, George – 1720 – Horn Tavern, Westminister
Stevens, John – 1734 – CrownTavern, Cripplegate
Strathmore, James 7th Earl of – 1732 – Bear & Harrow, Buthcer Row
     – GM 1733
Stuart, Alexander – 1714 – The Rummer, Charing Cross
Stukeley, William – 1717 – Stukeley
Taylor, Brook – 1711 – Bedford's Head, Covent Garden
Taylor, Robert – 1737 – Crown behind Royal Exchange
Thornhill, Sir James – 1723 – Swan, East St., Greenwich – SGW 1729
Thorp, John – 1705 – Bell Tavern

Trevor, John (Lord Trevor) – 1728 – Bedford's Head, Covent Garden
Tufnell, Samuel – 1709 – Bell Tavern, Westminister
Watkins, Col. Thomas – 1714 – Rummer, Charing Cross
Webb, Philip Carteret – 1749 – Sun, Southside, St. Paul's
Western, William – 1721 – King's Arms, St. Paul's
Woodward, John – 1693 – Crown behind Royal Exchange

The specific contribution of any one of these Fellows to the design of Freemasonry is unknown. There was a slow evolution which built upon the past. The aristocratic origin of the highest officials of the fraternity was a remarkable feature, and no doubt a principal reason for its flourishing progress in that period. (The first nonoperative Mason about whom there is certainty was John Boswell, laird of Auchinleck and ancestor of Doctor Johnson's biographer, who attended the Edinburgh lodge in 1600). It is not known what contribution was made by Desaguliers, but as a chaplain to the Duke of Chandos and the Prince of Wales, he no doubt proved an effective recruiter. If he did nothing but attract the nobility and the educated to Speculative Freemasonry he left his mark.


# III


The aims of the Royal Society and Freemasonry converged in the eighteenth century, though they would diverge soon after. Both organizations deplored scholastic thought as it was promoted by ecclesiastical (specifically Catholic) authority; both sought to encourage an enlightened brotherhood of progressive and unprejudiced individuals. One can observe the confluence, oddly enough, in that supreme work of late eighteenth-century art, Mozart's *The Magic Flute*.[7] The "Queen of Superstitious Night," despite her gorgeous arias, represents the Falsehood that Sarastro and his legions must annihilate in order to effect perfect love and truth in the world. Sarastro's chorus sings (in the Auden and Kallman Translation):

To Justice and to Righteousness
   We pray, that soon may come the day
When Truth shall be revealed to all
   And every vain idol fall.

And later Sarastro adds:

   … tamed by harmony, the beast can tame
     And every elemental passion name.
  O light of Wisdom, do not blind our eyes:
     That Mind may love, and Heart may civilize.

The authors of the libretto to *The Magic Flute*, Schikaneder and Giesecke, were Freemasons, as was Mozart, and the opera has always been understood as a Masonic allegory of the coming New Age. Less obvious is the fact that the process of "civilizing" by truth recalls the purpose of the Royal Society and its Continental correspondence societies. Desaguliers had proclaimed that "by a new examen we may be led to the truth," and there he spoke not only as a scientist but as a Mason.

The mistaken theory that Freemasonry grew out of the Ancient Mysteries of Egypt was conceived and propagated out of ignorance toward the end of the eighteenth century. As a result, an aura developed around the Masons of magic and mystery if not superstition, observable already in the magus Sarastro and his secret rites. (At the opera's end he must hand on the crown to Tamino, who is no wonder-worker.) One sees the mythology at work in what is perhaps the most famous literary text depicting the rites of Masonry, the scenes in *War and Peace* which dramatize Pierre Bezukhov's attraction to and repulsion from Freemasonry. That Tolstoy is sympathetic with the aims of the fraternity is obvious from the speech of the Masonic master Bazdeev, so reminiscent of the author's own preachments:

The highest wisdom is not founded on reason alone, not on those worldly sciences of physics, history, chemistry, and the like, into which intellectual knowledge is divided. The highest wisdom is one. The highest wisdom has but one science—the science of the whole—the science explaining the whole creation and man's place in it. To receive that science it is necessary; to purify and renew one's inner self.

But Pierre's disappointment with the (purported) putative Masonic obsession with virtue and vice, and with the (purported) need for a love of death, alienates him from the Petersburg brotherhood, and causes him to conclude, as Tolstoy wrote elsewhere, that "all those Masons were fools."

What then is Freemasonry? A short definition is that it is a fraternity built around a system of moral instruction illustrated by symbols and taught by allegory. In particular it makes use of the tools of architecture and stoneworking to teach a series of moral truths. The practices are derived from historical example. The medieval workers' guilds of masons were drawn from a wide geographical region and combined with other crafts to produce single structures, such as cathedrals. The master of the work had to standardize skills, establish work patterns and schedules and recruit apprentices in addition to protecting the journeyman workers from unskilled and unfair competition. Masons had to be taught individual responsibility, and during the course of their work they needed to consult rules or "charges" explaining conditions, standards and hours of work, and the ethics of the trade, including personal standards of behavior on and off the job. Whenever a new association of builders assembled, they constructed a building called a lodge, where they could meet and work. A scribe usually assembled a "constitution" by copying one of the many old legendary histories of the craft and adding the general regulations of the guild together with the rules for that particular job. These constitutions created shared values and work standards that transcended the regional differences among such a varied work force. Copies of these Gothic Constitutions[8] of Masonry, as we have seen, provided the developers of speculative Freemasonry with a much-revered framework upon which to build a structure of moral beliefs.

The symbol of the society in this country is a square and compasses enclosing the letter **G** (in Europe and elsewhere the letter **G** is not used):

The moral teachings associated with the tools in this symbol have found their way into American idioms. If one is told to "act on the square" or to "square your actions" the meaning is clear. These are Masonic phrases that have become a part of the language. The square in this symbol reminds every Mason that as a member of society he has an obligation to see that each of his actions is up to standard (tested by the square, which was used as a measure by operative masons to make certain their work be fit for the builder's use). What makes the morality of Freemasonry so universal is that this standard is never defined; rather, the society instructs the individual that he has a responsibility to himself, his fellowman, and his God. That is the sole meaning of the square; namely, he should test his actions "by the square of virtue". Similarly, the compasses reminds a Mason that there are bounds in his relations with his fellowman that he should not cross, so "if he keeps himself thus circumscribed, he cannot materially err." The letter **G** stands for *Geometry*, which in the middle ages was synonomous with Masonry for obvious reasons, and for God. All Freemasons are required to believe in God because a man must have something greater than himself as a rule and guide. Furthermore, each member is asked to attest to his sincerity in the strongest manner possible by taking upon his Holy Scriptures three separate and distinct obligations—one for each of the three Masonic degrees—in regard to his treatment of others and of his fellow leases in particular. Freemasonry does not define the God it summons; Protestants, Catholics, Jews, Moslems, Buddhists and even Deists are all equally at ease in the fraternity.

The present tri-gradal system derives from a similar system used in the middle ages wherein a man spent seven years learning the trade as an "Entered Apprentice" and then after producing a 'masters-piece" to demonstrate his compotencies he was made a "Fellow of the Craft." From such Fellows, the "Masters" who governed the work were chosen for their expertise. The present ranks in speculative Freemasonry are Entered Apprentice, Fellowcraft, and Master Mason, and in each grade an obligation for moral behavior is taken. It is these obligations which are the strength of the fraternity. One Mason knows that he will be treated properly by another Mason, and that he will be told the truth as surely as he himself will tell the truth. As described earlier, this fundamental commitment to the truth constitutes the strongest link between Freemasonry and the tradition of progressive scientific inquiry. The hierarchial structure of Freemasonry will sound very familiar to scientists in the academy or elsewhere, who must proceed to mastery of their subject by degrees of apprentice work.

For the primary reason of progressive identification between Masons, each member must keep the secrets of the order inviolate. Unfortunately, the fraternity does not spell out these secrets and as a result a new member often keeps silent on every aspect of Freemasonry. That has done the fraternity an immense amount of irreparable harm because it has encouraged the world at large, as in Tolstoy's novel, to label the fraternity a "secret society" and imagine that it operates according to hermetic beliefs that simply don't exist. The only secrets of Freemasonry are the modes of recognition which include the exact details of the ritual within the lodgeroom, everything else is open and free for discussion including the basic rationale of this system of moral instruction.

In fact, the world would be much better off if these discussions took place. That Freemasonry is not a secret society is attested to by the fact that a Mason proudly displays a pin or ring to indicate that he belongs to the Order, the Masonic halls in every town bear the sign "Masonic Temple" and display the square and compasses in a prominent location. The meeting times are advertised either on a sign at the entrance to the city or in the local newspaper. It is far from a secret society: it is instead a "society with secrets."

The basic tenets of the fraternity are Brotherly Love, Relief and Truth. By "relief" is meant charity, and in fact Masons support aid to needy retirees, widows and orphans, homes for the elderly, burn centers, hospitals for crippled children, scholarships, etc. These charities exceed one million dollars per day in this country alone, but of greater importance is the spirit in which the aid is given. The emphasis on truth is particularly important because it results in the teaching of much needed principles: the necessity to "work diligently, live creditably and act honorably"; religious and civil liberty; a high regard for the arts and sciences; the rising to eminence on the basis of merit rather than birth; a system of government based on majority rule and one man one vote; an individual responsibility for actions.

These teachings and the strength of the fraternity had a major impact upon our forefathers during the formation of this country, both in the revolutionary period and subsequently.[9] The fraternity played a very strong part in ameliorating and healing the wounds inflicted by the Civil War[10] and in the development of educational institutions such as the University of Pennsylvania and the University of Michigan[11] in particular.

At one time in this country, Freemasonry was so strong that it counted some six million. The originators of this institution, designed originally to help solve some of the social problems of eighteenth-century London, succeeded far beyond their fondest dreams and made contributions to society which they could never have imagined. Perhaps the same is true of the founders of the Royal Society. Bishop Thomas records in his *History*[8] (1667) that "their first purpose was no more than only the satisfaction of breathing freer air, and of conversing in quiet with one another, without being engaged in the passions and madness of that dismal age." But the diffusion of scientific laws in schools, through publications, and of course through practical applications in technology, has changed the world profoundly, as well as the way that every living person thinks about the world. If Desaguliers could look upon these two civilizing currents of influence, I think he would conclude with ample justice that his efforts were not in vain.

# NOTES

1. The following was the text of a lecture given as part of a minicourse entitled "Physics and Ethics" in the Fall of 1980 at the University of Michigan.

2. The legend of Hiram is the play to which I am referring and the Worshipful Master is the title given the head of the local lodge (it comes from the old English usage of "worshipful" meaning worthy of respect and has no religious connotation). See, for example, the article on Edwin T. Booth in William R. Denslow, *10,000 Famous Freemasons*, Vol. 1 Missouri Lodge of Research. Fulton, Missouri, 1957.

3. For a detailed biography of Desaguliers see the text of an address "Life of John Theophilus Desaguliers" by John Stokes, *Ars Quator Coronati*, Volume XXXVIII (1925). pp. 285–308, W.J. Farrett. Ltd., Margate, London.

4. An excellent book on the history of Freemasonry is that resulting from the Ph.D. dissertation on this subject submitted to the Department of History, University of Connecticut: Dorothy Ann Lipson, *Freemasonry in Federalist Connecticut 1789–1835*, Princeton University Press 1977.

5. In this day of factual histories, those legendary ones may be properly regarded as being ridiculous: some had Freemasonry beginning with Adam, some with Noah, some with Euclid and some with Saint Alban, but their purpose was to depict Masonry as having an ancient and universal history (which, in fact, was true). They also claimed that the knowledge of their craft has one of the liberal sciences, which wasn't as crazy as it might at first sound, because these were highly educated men by the standards of the time. A beautiful reproduction of Franklin's 1734 reprint of *The Constitutions of the Free-Masons* by Dr. James Anderson, published in London in 1723 was printed by The Masonic Book Club, Bloomington, Illinois, 1975.

8. Jacque Chailley, *The Magic Flute, Masonic Opera*, Translated from the French by Herbert Weinstock, Alfred A. Knopf, New York, 1971.

7. There are approximately 120 of these ancient constitutions which have been preserved. The oldest of these is the *Regius Poem* (circa 1390) and is often referenced as the *Halliwell Manuscript*, after its discoverer. It has been reproduced with a modern English translation by the Masonic Book Club, Bloomington, Illinois, 1975.

8. Thomas Sprat, *The History of the Royal Society for the Improving of Natural*

*Knowledge,* London. (reprint 1972).

9. The role of Freemasonry during the Revolutionary Period is difficult to research because historians (mistakenly) did not consider fraternal associations of importance. As a result, few Americans are aware that the Indians who dumped the tea in Boston Harbor came out of the Green Dragon Tavern, the home of St. Andrews Lodge, on a regular meeting night; that this leader of the North End Caucus (refered to as the seed-bed of the American revolution) was Joseph Warren, a Grand Master of Masons in Massachusetts; that Paul Revere was the Junior Warden (and eventual Master) of St. Andrews Lodge at the time of his famous ride: that Franklin met the nobility of France as a sideliner (and later Master) in the Lodge of the Nine Muses (rather than as an official Ambassador); that it was no accident that George Washington took his oath of office from Robert K. Livingston, the Grand Master of Masons in New York, on the bible of St. Johns Lodge #1 of New York held by Jacob Morton, the current Worshipful Master of St. John's Lodge: et cetera. The true role of Freemasonry in the revolution will never be known; however, some inkling may be obtained by reading *Freemasonry and the Drums of Seventy-Five* by Sidney Morse, Iowa Lodge of Research #2, Des Moines, Iowa.

10. For a compilation of some of the documented Masonic incidents during the period of the Civil War see Allen E. Roberts, *House Undivided.* Macoy Publishing arid Masonic Supply Co., New York, 1961.

11. J. Fairbairn, Smith and Charles Fey. *History of Freemasonry in Michigan,* Volume One. pp. 117–124, Most Worshipful Grand Lodge of Free and Accepted Masons of Michigan, 1963.

# DID SHAKESPEARE CREATE MASONIC RITUAL?

## J. Fairbairn Smith. FPS

*1982Certificate of Literature*

FOR MORE than three centuries the pros and cons of the authorship of the many plays, sonnets and other writings which most literary experts believe to be the work of William Shakespeare of Stratford-on-Avon, England, has been under question. It also appears that for considerably more than two hundred years a large number of the world's leading Masonic authorities, have, with reason, maintained that Sir William also wrote the Ritual of the Craft. It must be admitted that many portions of his literary creations are more than just merely Masonically Oriented.

William Shakespeare, the World's master playwright, was a genius about whom little is known in terms of his personal life and affairs, but he did spice his dialogue with many direct Masonic quotes.

Scholars have combed the records and studied the manuscripts and have been able to piece together a comprehensive picture of his amazing career, the playwright who wrote forty dramas that are still among the most popular stage vehicles in the world today.

This situation is the result of the fact that it was not until some two centuries after his death that the world of literature recognised this literary giant and scholars awakened to the magnificent drama of his humor and plays.

## Erect New Globe Theatre

It seems most appropriate that some comment should be made at a time when the City of Detroit and Wayne State University announce a commitment to build a reconstruction of the old, famed Globe Theatre which for many years stood on the south bank of River Thames in the City of London.

Thus it was part of London Town's center of Renaissance, just as the new structure to be built on the north bank of the Detroit River will become part of the great living symbol of the Renaissance of the world's great Motor City at Detroit, Michigan, and provide another riverfront stage for a dramatist who has entertained the world for more than three centuries. Nor is this merely a Shakespearian play on words which could be "To build or not to build, etc., etc. "

Great public support has already been indicated by both industry and men of letters alike. In particular the world's first Shakespearian Congress, held in Vancouver in 1971, voiced a desire for the reconstruction of the "Globe" on the bank of the Detroit River and Mayor Coleman Young and Wayne State University President Thomas N. Bonner added their backing.

## Many Masonic Allusions

An invitation to participate in this exciting re-creation of the most renowned theatre in history is already in the hands of Detroit and Michigan Masons 125,000 strong and since Shakespeare did so much to enliven the Masonic Craft by words and phrases it would appear important, at this time, that a careful scrutiny be made of his works.

Shakespeare lived in the century that preceded the revival of Freemasonry and the beginnings of modern Craft in England in 1717.

Reading his plays and noting the Masonic allusions and passages that almost seem to stand out of the ritual and lectures, one can only come to the conclusion that Shakespeare was either a Mason or that Masons drew upon him for their material.

## Form Stationer's Company

There is one enlightening aspect of Shakespeare and his times that is preserved in the records. That is the organization of the twenty-two printers in London into what was known as the Stationer's Company.

The Crown maintained an eagle eye on printers in those days of frequent rebellion and violent civil wars for control of the Throne. Only men of repute and established loyalty and unquestioned character were licensed by the court to be printers.

It was, of course, in the days before the enactment of a copyright statute. Plays were popular and profitable. Pirating was too common to go without action. The action taken by the printers, was the formation of the Stationers' Company.

## Protects Authors

This organisation of London's legitimate and lawful printers offered protection to authors through its register. An author was protected against pirating as far as the legitimate master printers were concerned. The practice served in much the same way as a copyright law does in modern times.

This made it possible for printers to pay authors substantial royalties and this financial stimulus opened the way for Britain's great parade of literary giants.

Although there was some pirating; nevertheless, this was a powerful deterrent to outright literary robbery. The Stationers' Company was vigilant in its efforts to track down the pirating printers. The result of this vigilance was that such pirating could only take the form of sloppy and incompetent printing craftmanship.

## Master Presides

Discipline was in the Masonic method. A Master presiding over the Stationers' Company, with his two Wardens an assistants that correspond to our present lineup of officers. Master of the Stationers' Company was the highest and most sought after honor a printer could achieve.

The Stationers' Company deserves the thanks of all posterity for preserving the two score plays by William Shakespeare that stamp him as probably the greatest genius of expression that the English language has ever known.

More Shakespearean plays performed on Broadway, in London, by theatrical groups throughout the world, by college and high school groups than those by any other playwright.

## Masonically Organized

Shakespeare's genius was founded on his remarkable knowledge of people. The genius of his craftsmanship has been that his works have been cheered, patronized and honored by the poorest as well as the plainest and wealthiest.

Had it not been for the Masonic type organisation of London's printers, it is probable that these ageless masterpieces would have been lost to posterity.

In Shakespeare's play, *Henry VIII*, seldom played these days, there is a speech every Mason knows well, the lines of which carry him bodily into the lodge room. "This is the state of man; today he puts forth the tender leaves of hope, tomorrow the blossoms that bear his blushing honors thick upon him? surely his greatness is ripening, nips his root and then falls as I do:" (Act III, Scene II).

That quotation is from the first complete edition of Shakespeare's plays published in London in 1623 some 360 years ago. Did Shakespeare borrow it from Freemasonry, or did Preston, or Oliver, or some other Mason borrow it from Shakespeare to make the lecture more poetic and impressive? I cannot tell. Worshipful Brother F. de P. Castells, in his very valuable book, *English Freema-*

*sonry in its Period of Transition 1600–1700,* notes that the London Mason's Company had in connection with a "secret and mysterious association a body of speculative Freemasons, which went by the name of 'the Acception'." The records of the records of the Acception date from 1620, three years before the great Shakespeare Folio from which I have just quoted, and almost a hundred years before the formation of the Grand Lodge of England in 1717.

The first play in Shakespeare's *First Folio* of 1623 was *The Tempest.* It is both a magical and a mystical play Colin Sill has written a book, calling it Shakespeare's Mystery Play and frankly stating that a non-Mason can never see the real significance which lies locked in its speeches. Here is only one speech of many to indicate Mr. Sill's point. "This wide-chopt rascal, wouldst thou mightest lie, drowning and washing of ten tides". But there are others, like these, "Here lies your Brother"; "I'll seek him deeper that e'er plummet sounded."

And now a few from some of the other plays of Shakespeare: "I am a Brother of a Gracious Order late come from the Sea...." "And Lamb-skins, too, that signify that Craft." (*Measure for Measure*) "Your oaths are past and now subscribe your names, that his own hand may strike his honour down.... I have always sworn. If I break faith this Word shall break for me.... And profound Solomon." "Lets part the Word. No! I'll be your half. "Find out thy Brother wheresoe'er he is: Seek him with candle; bring him dead or living." *As You Like It.*

And hidden in the Prologue to the play *Troylus and Cressida,* you will find the following (if any Mason happens to know the Morse Code and is a printer sufficiently keen on Elizabethan fonts of type, he could work out for himself from the Aforementioned folio).

In 1640, when the English edition of *The Advancement of Learning* was published, its frontispiece displayed two pillars surmounted with globes; one mundane, the other celestial. Have Masons anything to do with pillars?

To answer that question from the records, the early English Masons seem to have, for the records of the Lodge of Warrington, meeting in 1646—six years, let it be noticed, after this particular English edition of Francis Bacon's work—mention that pillars were discussed in detail.

You have doubtless heard that there was a great Masonic activity in England in Queen Elizabeth I's day, even though records are scarce and meetings were not held so openly then as now. You may also have heard that the plays of Shakespeare and his philosophy are filled with Masonic symbolism. The great English author Paster Master Alfred Dodd and many others have written voluminously on the subject—texts filled with a great deal of deep and very often dry matter. Such volumes have been immensely valuable because they have uncovered much that was hidden and have thereby rounded out the data of the Craft of those days when its records were all too scanty.

Other items are as follows:

Act II, Scene 4, *Titus Andronicus:* "Both are at the Lodge."

Act V, Scene 1, *Taming of the Shrew:* "What! My old Worshipful Master!

Act IV, Scene 5, *Merry Wives of Windsor:* "Now, Whence come you?"

Act III, Scene I, *Measure for Measure:* "Lambskins to signify that the Craft being richer than innocency."

Now is the time for a rebirth and a revitalization in Freemasonry. So true is this that perhaps never before has the Fraternity presented such a potent mystery and challenge to the outside world. Its purpose and history have aroused the attention, and awakened the interest of those outside the Order ,who would seek to wrest from the past the secrets of its origin and development.

# IOWA'S MASONIC MAGAZINES:

# THE BATTLING EDITORS

## Keith Arrington, FPS

*1983 Certificate of Literature*

THE MEN may be more interesting than their magazines. This is a war story, the story of battles fought in the pages of three nineteenth century Masonic periodicals and of the protagonists who wielded the vicious pens.

Brother Albert Pike, Sovereign Grand Commander of the Supreme Council, A. & A. Scottish Rite for the Southern Jurisdiction, was introduced to the grand Lodge of Iowa in session at Davenport in 1871 by Past Grand Masters Theodore S. Parvin and James R. Hartsock. He was most cordially welcomed by Grand Master John Scott.

This event presented three of the combatants in the story to follow. Each was a rugged individualist, a pioneer who had made his own way from early life. Joining these giants of Iowa Masonry there was to he a midget, Sidney Smith, fifty inches tall and Junior Grand Warden in 1886. His role in the battles was peripheral: he, though inclined to be impartial, was handed stones to cast.

Iowa Masonic archives do not contain much information on James R. Hartsock. His Masonic career ended in disgrace. As

Joseph E. Morcombe wrote in his *History of the Grand Lodge of Iowa*, "After events were untoward and sad and no other Masonic hand has before essayed."

Born in 1818, Hartsock came to Iowa Territory from Pennsylvania in May of 1838, moving to Iowa City in 1842. In 1861, he was appointed postmaster by President Lincoln. After six years, political changes forced him from the job, but he was reappointed by President Grant and held the job until 1872. He was for many years active in state and national politics. He was among those most prominent in the organization of the Republican party when the slavery question disrupted the Democratic party. Hartsock was sergeant-at-arms when the Iowa senate met for the first time in the new capital at Des Moines.

John Scott and T. S. Parvin were both Ohioans. Born in 1824, Scott was admitted to the bar in that state in 1845 and then migrated to Kentucky. Enlisting in the Kentucky volunteers during the Mexican War, he was captured and a prisoner of war for ten months. Returning to Kentucky, he was editor of the Kentucky Whig at Mt. Sterling. He moved to Nevada, Iowa, in 1856, organized and was first Master of Lodge No. 99. In Grand Lodge he was Senior Grand Warden in 1859, Deputy Grand Master in 1867 and Grand Master in 1869 and 1870. With Dr. E. A. Guilbert and William Langridge, he served as Custodian of the Work in 1860.

Upon his retirement from the Grand Master's office, he announced that he desired no further Masonic honors, and did not attend Grand Lodge for a number of years.

Scott's membership in the Scottish Rite is pertinent to the telling of the story. Of this he wrote: "We are by no means proud of it, and have never written '32nd degree' as description of our Masonry, and yet our date in the Scotch Rite is earlier than that of anyone in the West, as far as we know. Parvin is one of the oldest. He had the Rite from Pike. Pike had the Rite from Mackey. We had the Rite from Mackey, June 15th, 1856. This was three years before Parvin got the Rite at the hands of Pike."

The office of Grand Secretary naturally threw Theodore S. Marvin into the several controversies, but he possessed the scrappy self confidence which always welcomed the opportunity to do battle. A young lawyer-school teacher, the future Grand Secretary came to the new Iowa Territory in 1858 as the personal secretary to the first Governor, Robert Lucas. He immediately entered into the political, cultural and educational scene in the frontier towns and was instrumental in organizing two of the four Iowa Lodges which received their charters from the Grand Lodge of Missouri. Serving as Grand Secretary from the organization of the Grand Lodge in 1844 until his death in 1901, with one year out to be Grand Master; being credited with starting and building the great library collection of the Grand Lodge. Marvin unquestionably exerted more influence on Masonry in Iowa than any one man in its history.

The Hartsock–Parvin battle was the real story of *The Western Freemason*. The controversy was over Iowa's ritual: what it should be and who was to decide it. It also was a conflict of personalities.

Just where it all began is difficult to determine. Certainly there was conflict between the two at the organization of the Grand Lodge in 1844. At that time, Parvin desired and expected to be elected Grand Secretary and to see Ansel Humphreys elected Grand Master. Hartsock also had his eye on the position of Grand Secretary and did some politicking to try to capture the job.

Three "Mormon" lodges which had been working under dispensation from the Grand Lodge of Illinois hoped to become a part of the new Grand Lodge of Iowa. In consideration of his help for their cause, Hartsock was promised their support for his election as Grand Secretary. In the shuffle, Hartsock was defeated but so was Ansel Humphreys. Parvin and Oliver Cook were elected to the two posts. The "Mormon" lodges were not permitted in and, in time, disappeared.

"Uniformity of the Work" was the big issue of the time when James Hartsock introduced his *Western Freemason*. A scant two decades had passed since the migration of pioneers from the east had carried Masonry into the new Territory and with it a duke's mixture of ritual. No attempt will be made here to tell the complete story of Iowa ritual, though bits of the story are vital to the feud between James R. Hartsock and Theodore S. Parvin.

*The Western Freemason* was the creation of Hartsock, the "first Mason initiated west of the Mississippi river and north of the Missouri line." His raising was at the river town of Burlington in December of 1840. This was Parvin's lodge and in it twenty-two men were raised during the first year.

Hartsock was gone from Iowa during some of the following years, spending at least part of this time in Louisiana. Somewhere along the line he picked up some ritual which was different from that taught in Iowa. Ansel Humphreys, who had served for some time as a Master of a lodge in Connecticut, probably was primarily responsible for the ritual as Iowa had it.

Described as "Past High Priest of Louisiana and present Grand High Priest of Iowa," Hartsock was listed as editor when the first number of *The Western Freemason* was published at Iowa City in April, 1857. The thirty-two page, six-by-nine journal was offered for one dollar per year, "in advance." Actually, it seemed that several thousand copies were sent out, unsolicited, in the vain hope that everyone would mail their dollars in.

The name of the publication was justified "upon the frontier of civilization and being perhaps the first and only periodical of the kind west of the Mississippi river."

By the time the fourth issue appeared, John Kennedy, the printer, had gone out of business. The change to a new printer was to the benefit of the paper with a neater printing job and a change to a single rather than a double column format.

An additional change was that the cover now listed T. S. Parvin and J. F. Sanford, Grand Master, as corresponding editors. On the back cover of this issue was an advertisement for Iowa Medical College at Keokuk with J. F. Sanford, Dean. This college offered "entire course $80. Matriculation fee $5. Dissecting fee $5. Gradu-ation fee $25."

In light of the events to come it is worth noting that at the Grand Convocation in 1857, G.H.P. Hartsock presented to P.G.H.P. Parvin a gold jewel in appreciation for "invaluable services rendered." And, in the August *Western Freemason*, Hartsock gave high praise to Parvin, the Grand Secretary, for the "zeal, research and devo-tion he has brought to the management of the affairs of the Grand Lodge. To him the Grand Lodge is indebted for the proud position she now sustains as one of the most flourishing Grand Lodges in the United States." And, significantly, "He has become one of the ablest Masonic jurists in the land. We regard his decisions and opinions (as a general thing) on jurisprudence as law."

The enlisting of Parvin as a contributing editor and the flattery printed about him do not exactly jibe with what Parvin wrote in *The Evergreen* in 1872: "It was generally believed through the state at the time that *The Western Freemason* was started to secure the over-throw of the "work" then practiced by Grand Master Sanford, and to introduce what was then and since known as "the Hartsock work."

Parvin continued: "That the editorship of the fourth volume was assumed by the writer for the sole purpose of setting aside the Hart-sock work we never denied and always affirmed and, in this, we were successful. While Brother Harts sock succeeded only as Grand Master and editor, the overthrow of his work was consummated by the Grand Lodge authoritatively and permanently through the labors of that journal as their conductor. This success was, however, greatly due to the large and enlightened corps of assistants the edi-tor had, in the persons of Brothers Benton, Guilbert, Scott, Langridge and others. *The Western Freemason* accomplished the purpose for which it was started and continued, and would have itself continued but that its publishers went to the war and the editor, while giving his time and labor would not give his money—for he had none to give. It was not supported by the lodges, chapters and commander-ies and it proved a losing concern to publishers and editors."

James Hartsock was elected Grand Master in June of 1858. John Scott became Senior Grand Warden and Dr. E. A. Guilbert, Junior Grand Warden. Soon, *The Western Freemason* began to carry the official rulings of the Grand Master on jurisprudence and to relate his travels around the state. During his first year as Grand Master—he served two terms—Hartsock visited 116 of the 147 lodges, teaching his variation of the ritual as well as examining the record books of the lodges. This was quite a feat when you consider the conditions of travel at that time.

It would seem that the Grand Master believed in what he was doing. He was putting all of his energy into establishing in every lodge in the state a Uniform Ritual. The ritual he was teaching was the ritual that he knew and the ritual he believed to be correct.

By January of 1859, Editor Hartsock was forced to admit to his readers "We fear we have too many irons in the fire," and announced that his partner would take charge of the department during his temporary absence. It was inevitable, in light of the financial plight of the paper, that the Editor's swan song came in the twelfth number of the third volume. The paper was to be published by "Sir Kts. Calvin and Ball." Calkin, Hartsock's partner in the photography business, had done work on the paper before.

In October, the magazine moved to Muscatine under J. W. Eystra, with T. S. Parvin as editor. In his typical fashion, the new editor shot some barbs in the first issue: "We have always believed that *The Western Freemason* was prematurely ushered before the public and had the founder consulted the wants of the fraternity or the wisdom of its rulers, one stone would never have been presented for inspection."

Never one to hide his light under a bushel, Grand Secretary-Editor Parvin wrote: "I have given a quarter of a century of the best period of my life to Masonry. I have enjoyed of the honors an over-partial brotherhood can bestow, have passed every round of our mystic ladder, and for fifteen years stood upon the top-most (secretariat of a young but full-grown Grand Lodge) and viewing the field of labor on all sides have no place to seek, no power to covet, no friends to promote, and hence no selfish ends to advance; but shall labor assiduously to extend the area of knowledge of my brethren, not of ritual only—a very small matter—but the sum total of Masonic literature." Of the magazine he said, "The work is designed primarily for home consumption."

New publisher Eystra printed a notice to subscribers: "In no instance will the magazine be sent without advance payment." The May issue, number eleven of the volume, carried the publisher's note: "The publisher must be paid or the Craft cannot expect to retain his services." While a next issue was referred to, it did not appear and *The Western Freemason* vanished from the scene. It had been a readable magazine, a good magazine when you consider the inexperience of the editors and publishers. It offered a variety of Masonic information in its pages, in contributed articles along with some copied from other sources. It deserves to be remembered for more than the quarrel for which it provided the forum.

During his short tenure as editor of the magazine Parvin wrote several articles on Uniformity of the Work. Speaking of "younger brethren who go ahead too fast to look back unless arrested by some stumbling block wisely fallen in their path" he speaks of the laws of the order in Iowa on the work and points out that the subject "at a very early day arrested the attention of the fathers of Masonry before the boys in the order were born. Every step taken in the last ten years has carried us further from the goal of our ambition." He then traced "the work" from a period prior to the organization of the Grand Lodge.

Parvin stressed that Grand Lodge law made the Grand Lodge and not the Grand Master, the custodian of the work. He related that the first five Grand Masters had exemplified the Webb Work (as restored by the Baltimore Convention) in open Grand Lodge. Even Hartsock, acting as Deputy for Grand Master McCleary, had "worked the old, alias Humphrey, alias Webb work." For the first thirteen annual communications, the work taught was the same. In

1856, Hartsock was able to "engraft many of his views upon the work adopted" at a sparsely attended Grand lodge of Instruction held at Iowa city during severe winter weather. Parvin refused to teach or accept this changed work. Grand Master Hartsock has set at naught the work of the Grand Lodge while professing in his inaugural "to build upon the foundation laid by his worthy predecessors, and as far as possible establish a perfect ceremonial uniformity."

The Grand Secretary commented: "The Grand Lodge of Iowa, heartily sick of the manner in which the 'work and lectures' have been hawked about as merchandise, at its last session put a stop upon the "one man power" and elected 'Custodians of the Work' consisting of Brothers John Scott, E. A. Guilbert and William B. Langridge." Thus gradually the "bastard work" of Hartsock was cleansed from Iowa ritual.

A third combatant, with his own private battle with Parvin and the Grand Lodge, appeared in the pages of *The Western Freemason* in 1858. John Scott contributed two articles, one being a caution to watch the ballot box and the other a discourse on what Masonry is.

Scott's magazine, created solely for the purpose of arguing and publicising his case, was *The Lodge*. It was introduced in October of 1892 at Nevada. Iowa, being published monthly, until the following April, when it became a quarterly. Only one volume of twelve issues was published, ending in March 1894.

"A monthly journal devoted to the interests of Freemasonry, the publication is a business matter and is conducted on business principles. A copy of Mrs. Scott's "Indian Corn as Food" will be sent postpaid as a premium for a club of ten subscribers." Seventy-five cents a year paid for the sixteen page octavo size paper. Advertising was carried in each issue.

Very little news or other literary matter found space in any number of the publication, its columns being crowded with statement and restatement of Scott's arguments.

"Cerneauism" was the disturbing factor. "Cerneauism" had invaded Iowa, was feared by some who Scott termed "high riters" and was being ruthlessly combated. The so-called Cerneau Scottish Rite was flourishing in Ohio at the same time. Considered clandestine by the established Scottish Rite bodies, this variation was said to have been implanted in the United States in 1807 by Joseph Cerneau and was sometimes referred to as the Americanized Scottish Rite.

Enough Iowa Masons joined this clandestine Scottish Rite to alarm T. S. Parvin, who was Sovereign Grand Inspector General for Iowa of the A. & A. S.R. of the Southern Jurisdiction. A new Chapter 37 was added to the Code of the Grand Lodge, declaring membership in the Cerneau Order a Masonic offense.

Scott contended this was of no concern to the Grand Lodge. He argued that the Grand Lodge should be concerned only with Lodges and Grand Lodges, that other bodies were simple social organizations which Masons had a right to join if they chose. His repeated thesis was that only Lodges and Grand Lodges are Masonic, that all other bodies are creatures which have attached themselves to Masonry. And, that the consideration of these bodies had no place in Grand Lodge.

Invective and condemnation of Grand Secretary Parvin and Grand Master Phelps occupied so much of Scott's time and space that he didn't get around to stating the facts of his quarrel with them.

In like manner, the Grand Secretary censored and abbreviated the Grand Lodge proceedings to the extent that the clear facts are not available there.

In any event, some Iowa Masons were expelled for membership in this "clandestine" Scottish Rite Order. The Grand Master issued an edict forbidding the election to office in the lodge of members of the Cerneau order. Grand Master Phelps later claimed: "So far as I know not a single Master of a lodge belongs to that order." Scott retorted: "Many know that there are Cerneaus holding important offices in Iowa lodges and that Grand Master Phelps had knowledge of these facts and that he has not performed the duty of enforcing this "law of the Grand Master."

John Scott, as Worshipful Master of Lodge No. 99 at Nevada, appeared at Grand Lodge in 1891. He was not a Cerneau member at any time. Apparently he did lift his powerful voice in protest against the Grand Master's actions in regard to the Cerneaus. He appeared to be fighting for a principle that he believed in and in defense of those Masons he felt had been wrongfully expelled or "black listed."

As a result, the Grand Master arrested Scott's Jewel of office, deposing him from the Mastership and refusing to permit him to represent his lodge in the Grand Lodge sessions. However, Past Grand Master Scott was able to take his seat. Nevada Lodge re-selected John Scott as Master in 1892, but he still was not permitted to take his seat as Master.

Twelve issues of a magazine devoted exclusively to this theme, particularly when the problem was not clearly stated, became tiresome. Invective and name calling got in the way of honest argument of a just cause.

The final battle was fought at Grand Lodge in 1893. A hotel room was rented at Davenport as headquarters for "the repeal of Chapter 37" Candidates for Grand Master and for Grand Secretary in opposition to Phelps and Parvin were run and, though making a good showing, both failed of election. Repeal of Chapter 37 was defeated—Scott claimed votes that had been promised were switched at the last minute.

The illustration of the ritual at Grand Lodge by the Custodians was novel, according to Scott. "Had the Custodians and some of the visitors known it then would have greatly enjoyed the fact that the floor work was done mostly by Cerneaus: not the clandestine sort, but real Joseph Cerneau Scottish Riters!"

It was after this session that much of the steam went out of *The Lodge*. Scott still presented his old arguments, but other material did get into the magazine occasionally. He never again returned to Grand Lodge. There was only a veiled hint in the twelfth issue of the magazine that this might be the last published. Scott, too, it seemed, had wearied of constant reiteration of his "facts." A wealthy man, he later served in the State Senate and was Lt. Governor.

Sidney Smith wrote of The Smallest Masons in the second number of his *Iowa Masonry*. "Robert H. Huzza, of Lodge 483, Brooklyn, N.Y., is said to be the smallest man ever made a Mason. His height is 33 inches. Charles S. Stratton. "General Tom Thumb." was 35 inches high and a 32nd degree Mason.

"Sidney Smith, the editor and proprietor of *Iowa Masonry* is fifty inches tall. He was made a Mason in September, 1879, and has received all the degrees save the thirty-third. He is a Past Master, High Priest, Prelate, and Past Junior Grand Warden of the Grand Lodge of Iowa (1886). He is a confirmed old bachelor 34 years of age, and wedded only to Masonry." Before the year was out, however, little Sidney took a bride at Little Rock, Arkansas.

Twenty-five thousand copies of the first issue of *Iowa Masonry* dated January 1892 were sent out, claimed by Editor Smith to be the largest edition of any Masonic periodical ever published. The neatly printed octavo size journal sported a green cover with a sketch of the Iowa Masonic Library building adorning it. A frontispiece carried photos of all of the elective Grand lodge officers for the year. The sixteen page monthly carried advertising and the price was one dollar per year.

Although Sidney Smith was a resident of Sac City, he evidently thought that Cedar Rapids, with the presence of the Library and the office of the Grand Secretary, was the more logical place of publication. A typesetter telegrapher and newspaper man, Smith hoped to "faithfully reflect the official and social proceedings of the craft of Iowa in particular, and the rest of the Masonic world in general." To this end he did have the promise of T. S. Parvin, the Grand Secretary, for a series of articles under the title of "An Hour Among the Old Records." The regular series promised failed to materialize beyond three efforts in that direction by Brother Parvin. This was quite like the record Parvin established after promising to supply articles for E. A. Guilbert and *The Evergreen*.

A poem opened each number of the magazine, in the custom of the day. These and the short stories which were often carried were often the work of Lura E. Brown, who became Mrs. Sidney Smith.

Short news items, in keeping with the stature of the editor, on the various bodies, on Masonry and on most any other subject regularly filled pages of the publication. There were a few longer articles, mostly clipped from other sources. No signed articles by the editor appeared. His contribution seemed to be in collecting and assembling the material, although he did have editorial comment on occasion.

It was often difficult to tell whether Sidney Smith was doing the writing or if it was from the pen of T. S. Parvin. Certainly, Parvin's views were reflected in the reporting, especially when mention was made of the controversy between Parvin and Past Grand Master John Scott, which was then in progress.

Numbers ten and eleven of the journal were combined, because of a delay brought on by illness in the editor's family. Publication ceased with the completion of the first and only volume in December, the editor observing that the venture had not been so profitable as had been hoped. At this time, John Scott, its *The Lodge*, commented: "Coming from the shadow of the Grand Secretary's office was too heavy a load. Had it been sent out from Sac City, it might have lived for many a year. Brother Smith is deservedly very popular among the brethren and had he felt able to walk alone he might still have been on foot."

# WHY SAINT ALBAN?

## Wallace McLeod, FPS

*1984 Certificate of Literature*

THERE ARE in the world some twenty-three Masonic lodges named after or connected with St Alban. Since 1954 they have held an annual gathering. The thirtieth such meeting took place in Thornhill, near Toronto, Canada, on 8 October 1983, with representatives of eleven lodges in attendance: No. 4999, St. Albans, England; No. 7, Newark, New Jersey; No. 56, Floral Park, New York; No. 38, Guilford, Connecticut No. 6, Bristol, Rhode Island; St. Albans Lodge, Foxboro, Massachusetts; No. 677, Youngston, Ohio; No. 28, Jackson, Louisiana; No. 20, Marshall Michigan; No. 514, Thornhill, Ontario (the host lodge); and No. 106, Montreal, Quebec. The following paper is based on an address delivered on that occasion.)

## Life of Saint Alban

Why Saint Alban? Well, the first stage in our quest is to find just who the man is. In 1485 William Caxton published a collection of the lives of the Saints, under the title of *The Golden Legend*. We might summarise one of the stories it includes. A certain law in force in the Roman Empire stated that no man was permitted to receive the honour of knighthood, save only at Rome, and then at the hands of the Emperor himself. And so it was that about the year 295 a deputation of young noblemen went from Britain to the capital. They included Amphibal, the son of a Welsh prince, and Alban, the son of a lord of the city of Verulamium. While they were in Rome, Amphibal was converted to Christianity, and left the brotherhood of apprentice knights. A Great day was set, and the others were all knighted by the Emperor Diocletian, after which a tournament was held, where Alban won the palm of honour. The blazon on his shield was a cross of gold against a blue background. (This is still used as part of the lodge seal of St. Alban's. No. 514.) After the tournament all the British knights returned home, except Alban, whom the Emperor kept in his service, on account of his manliness and prowess, for the term of seven years.

In due course a rebellion broke out in Britain, and a Roman army was sent to suppress it, with Alban as chief of the knights. At this same time there was a persecution of Christians in Rome, and the people of the faith were scattered, each one to his own country. And so it befell that Amphibal, who had gone to Rome with Alban, returned home to Britain, and came to the city of Verulamium, where he found Alban as lord of the city, prince of the knights, and steward of the land, having a great multitude of servants. Amphibal was clothed as a Christian priest, and could find no lodging in the city. He recognized his former friend Alban (who did not however recognise him), and sought hospitality of him. This was granted. They fell into conversation, Amphibal told Alban of his faith, and Alban had a vision, and in short was converted to Christianity and was baptised.

After they had communed together for six weeks and more, the magistrate heard that a preacher of the new religion lay concealed at Alban's house, and he summoned them to appear before him. Amphibal had to go to South Wales, and to facilitate his escape Alban exchanged clothes with him. Amphibal departed garbed as a knight, whilst Alban, robed as a priest and wearing a cross, went to the judge. The judge cross-examined him closely, and when he learned his true identity, asked him where his teacher had gone, and directed him to renounce Christianity. This Alban declined to do. Then a great crowd of pagans came forth and tried to force him to offer sacrifice to their false gods, but he steadfastly refused. The judge cross-examined him closely and on the rack and scourged. The torturers beat him so long that their hands grew weary. He was kept in custody for six months and more, and during that whole time there was neither rain nor dew, nothing but the blazing sun, so that neither trees nor fields brought forth any fruit. The judge was afraid to sentence him to death, because he held the Emperor's commission. Finally the emperor sent one of his viceroys to Britain, with orders to kill all the Christians except for Alban; he alone had the option of abandoning his faith. If he refused, he was to be beheaded by another knight; and the priest that had converted him was to suffer the foulest death that could be imagined.

Alban was brought forth from prison, but when he refused to relapse into paganism, sentence was passed. First it was decreed that, when Amphibal was found, he should be scourged, and after bounden to a stake all naked, and then his navel be opened and his bowels to be fastened by that one end to the stake, and he then to be driven to go round and about the stake till all his bowels were wounden out about the stake, and after to have his head smitten off....

Alban was to be simply beheaded. On the stated day, a great crowd assembled, and he was led forth to Holmhurst Hill for execution.

The people were so great a multitude that they occupied all the place.... And the heat of the sun was so great that it burnt and scalded their feet as they went, and so they led him till they came to a swift running river, where they might not lightly pass for press of people, for many were shifted over the bridge into the water and were drowned, and many, because they might not go over the bridge for press, unclothed them for them to swim over the river, and some that could not swim presumed to do the same, and were wretchedly drowned.... And when Saint Alban perceived this thing he bewailed and wept for the harm and death of his enemies…, and kneeled down holding his hands up to God beseeching that the water might be lessed and the flood withdrawn that the people might be with hind at his passion.

In answer to his prayer the waters withdrew. At this miracle the knight who was escorting him threw down his sword and acknowleged his error. The pagan mob seized the new convert, and pulled out all his teeth, and beat him, breaking all his bones, and left him lying on the sand. When at last they reached the place of execution, there was a great multitude, nigh dead from the heat of the sun and for thirst. Saint Alban prayed for relief for them, and at once a cool breeze sprang up and a fountain gushed from the top of the hill. Then the pagans fastened his hair to the branch of a tree, and they found a man to cut off his head. And at once the executioner's eyes fell out of his head and lay upon the ground. Then the knight who had been left for dead came crawling up the hill, and reverently loosed Alban's head from the bough. At this act of devotion he was restored to health, and took and buried the body and raised over it a fair tomb.

Many people were converted to Christianity when they saw this array of miracles They carried word to Amphibal in Wales, and he returned to suffer the martyrdom to which he too had been condemned. And the pagans, persevering in their malice, threw stones at his dead body; and when a quarrel arose among them, a certain Christian man was able to steal the body away and hide it.

And soon after their deaths the Lord showed forth another miracle, and this was that "the visages of the tormentors were disfigured, their hands, arms and other members dried up, and the judge lost his mind and was mad."

## The Influence of Saint Alban
Like many lives of the saints, this is a pretty good story, full of bloodthirsty episodes, and reaching its climax in a suitable punishment for the villains, and an appropriate triumph of the faithful. It

shows by example the virtue of steadfastness, and one can readily see why it became popular. Of course the full version of the story contains a certain amount of preaching, which has been curtailed in the version you have just heard. It would be inappropriate to enquire whether every detail of the life is true, because its function is to inspire people, not to recite history.

According to tradition, Alban died at some time about 303–305, being the first one in the realm to suffer death for the new faith, and he is therefore known as the protomartyr, or "first martyr," of England. The story has it that his death took place at the Roman city of Verulamium, 20 miles northwest of London. He was soon canonized as a Saint, with his festival being set on 22 June. By 429, a century and a quarter after his death, there was a church dedicated to him near his tomb; and Verulamium soon took the name of Saint Albans. In 793 King Offa is said to have founded a new church here, and a monastery. During the Middle Ages this grew into a great Benedictine Abbey, which was one of the richest in England until King Henry VIII dissolved the monasteries in 1536. Here too was built one of the largest Gothic churches in the world, still in use after nine centuries.

The monastery was of course a centre of literacy, and one of the necessary activities of the monks was to keep the memory of Saint Alban green. And so we know of at least five lives of the Saint that were composed by or for members of the house and disseminated to the world at large in the years between 1166 and 1439. The story was also picked up in other circles, and thereby hangeth a tale.

## The Old Charges

We modern Freemasons are descended, not as we are told in our ritual from the workmen at King Solomon's Temple, but from the operative stone masons of Britain in the Middle Ages. At some time soon after 1350 these stone-masons began to congregate themselves into formal bodies that were known as Guilds or Lodges; they served some of the functions of the modern trade union. We know quite a bit about what they did, and we also know something of how they were governed-particularly the Lodges. It seems that each of them had a handwritten scroll containing the laws and regulations of the masons, and also giving a traditional history of the craft of building More than a hundred (actually 113) of these old manuscript constitutions have survived, and the strangest thing about them is that they all go back to a single, original, that was written not too long after the year 1350. (The coincidence of date is striking.) This was copied and recopied, edited and revised, dozens of times between 1350 and 1750: and it looks as if every lodge of stone-masons had to have its own copy.

These old manuscript constitutions are still reflected in modern Freemasonry today, in various ways. The oldest of them closes with the words, "Amen, Amen, So mote it be! So say we all for charity!" So evidently a little of our traditional Masonic language is derived from them. Again, if you look at the Book of Constitution of your Grand Lodge, you will find a section with a title that runs something this: "The Charges of a Free-Mason, extracted from the ancient records of Lodges beyond Sea, and of those in England, Scotland, and Ireland, for the Use of the Lodges in London: to be read at the making of New Brethren, or when the Master shall order it." Have you ever looked at them? We don't use them very much any more, but they're still worth reading. They have been reprinted in every book of constitution of modern Freemasonry ever since the first one, in 1717. And the Rev. Dr. James Anderson, the editor of that volume (the most influential book on Masonry every written) "borrowed" large parts of them from the old manuscript constitutions of the operative stone-masons.

But we said that the old texts included a traditional history. And it too is occasionally reflected in our ritual. It tells how the seven liberal arts and sciences (you know, Grammar, Rhetoric, Logic, Arithmetic Geometry, Music, and Astronomy) were found before Noah's flood by the three brothers Jabal, Jubal, and Tubal-cain, together with their sister. You will find the story recorded in the Book of Genesis. And then how they wrote their sciences on Two Great Pillars. And then it recounts how masonry was used at some of the great architectural programmes of Biblical times: at the Tower of Babel, and at the building of King Solomon's Temple; and how Solomon was helped by Hiram King of Tyre, and by his principal architect. And then we are told how the Art was brought to Western Europe; first it came to France, and from there it was brought to England. And in due course Prince Edwin called a great assemblage of masons in York some time about the year 930, and established the code of regulations that continued in use through the Middle Ages.

## Saint Alban in the Old Charges

That is not real history. It is real propaganda, that was intended to give the masons a proper sense of their own worth by showing how the Craft went back to Biblical times, and counted even monarchs themselves among its members. But it was heard and believed by our operative brethren. Now of particular interest to us today is the story of how masonry came to England. The version which had the widest currency runs like this.

England in all this season stood void of any charge of masonry, until the time of Saint Alban. And in his time the King of England, that was a pagan, did wall the town about that is now called Saint Albans. And Saint Alban was a worthy knight, and chief steward to the King, and had the governance of the realm, and also of the making of the town walls. And he loved well masons, and cherished them much. And he made their pay right good, standing as the realm did then, for he gave them two shillings and sixpence a week, and threepence for their nuncheons. And before that time through all the land a mason took but a penny a day and his meat, until Saint Alban amended it. And gave them a charter of the King and his council for to hold a general council, and gave it the name of an assembly. And thereat he was himself, and helped to make masons, and gave them charges as you shall hear aftenpards. (Reconstructed text of the Standard Original Version.)

Now, can you see what has happened? The man who made the earliest full version of the old manuscript constitutions composed the traditional history basing himself in the first instance on the Volume of the Sacred Law, the only book ever seen by most people in those days. But he had to find somebody famous to bring Masonry to England. Who better than a notable martyr of the church, a man who had a city named after him. Surely that must have meant that he was himself a builder? Obviously the natural choice! (It may mean that our writer lived somewhere near the monastery of Saint Albans, but of that we cannot be certain.)

**Lodges Named for Saint Alban**
And again the fact that lodges are named after Saint Alban is interesting. He is not regarded today as one of the patron saints of Masonry. They are Saint John the Baptist, Saint John the Evangelist, Saint Barbara, and the Four Crowned Martyrs. But it looks as if someone in the early days of the premier Grand Lodge recalled that Saint Alban was a part of the traditional history, and determined that his name should be perpetuated. There is in London, England, an old lodge, founded in 1728, meeting at Freemasons' Hall, under the name of St Alban's, No 29, but of course that will not be its original name. Lodges were originally named for the tavern in which they met, and the practice of taking permanent names did not become common until the 1760's. Thus, we know that Lodge No 29 was originally known as the Lodge that met at the Castle and Leg in Holborn. In due course it moved to St Alban's Tavern on St Alban's Street, and in 1771 it took the name St Alban's Lodge. Quite possibly it was the earliest lodge to be distinguished in this way. Others soon followed. Lodge No 176, in Birmingham, England, became known as St Alban's Lodge in 1784. St Alban's lodge, No 62, in Brooklyn, New York, was warranted in 1797.

It's interesting to learn where lodges get their titles. There are in Ontario more than forty which are named for saints. The reason for some of them can be guessed. For example, thirteen are named for St John, the traditional patron of Masons. There are seven St Andrew's lodges, and I'd bet there is a Scottish connection in most of them. Six are named for St George, and it would hardly he surprising if they all claimed a link with England. There are three St. Clair lodges, and the St Clairs (or Sinclairs) were in early days the hereditary Grand Masters of Scotland. There are in this jurisdiction two lodges carrying the name of St. Alban: one, No 200, at Mount Forest (instituted in 1868), and one, our host, No 514, near Toronto (instituted in 1913). Why were these names chosen. Was it because one of the founders came from St Albans in England? Or was there a connection with one of the English lodges of that name? Or did the name perhaps come from a church? (The cornerstone of St Alban's Church, Ottawa, was laid with Masonic honours in 1867). Or is it possible that one of your founders was aware that this saint had a place in the Masonic tradition?

## Conclusion

Those of you who belong to these lodges, and to others of the same name, hold high your heads with pride. Not only do you commemorate a man who preferred to suffer death rather than betray the sacred trust reposed in him. You also bear testimony to a Masonic tradition that goes back more than 600 years. St Alban has had a demonstrable connection with the Craft since 1350, though latterly it is not much remembered. The name should constantly remind you that you are part of a continuous chain of good men thousands of them, going back through the impenetrable mists of time. The vast majority are no longer with us, for they have been summoned to the Grand Lodge Above, but they have left their deeds behind, as monuments for us to emulate. And we may perhaps imagine that though dead they still speak to us through these monuments; and maybe even (who knows?) from on high they look down with interest on the deeds of us, their successors. It is pleasant to think so anyway. It we bear that picture in mind, perhaps we may, without irreverence, apply to ourselves the words of the apostle.

Wherefore seeing we also are come passed about with so great a cloud of witnesses, let us lay aside every weight, and the sin which doth so easily beset us, and let us run with patience the race that is set before us.

Run with patience, brethren, the race that is set before us. There is lots to be done. Do you make a daily advancement in Masonic knowledge? Do you support the charitable and benevolent activities of your lodge, and of your grand lodge? Do you visit your sick and shut-in members? Do you have an instructional programme in your lodge for your candidates? Is provision made for the training of your officers? Do you investigate the situation of those who come up for suspension N.P.D.? Do you tend the widows of your brethren? In short, do you show by your actions that you believe in the three Tenets or Fundamental Principles of Brotherly Love, Relief, and Truth? "Business?" said Marley's ghost. "Mankind was my business!" The Brotherhood of Man! Run with patience, brethren, the race that is set before us. Think about it.

## SELECTED REFERENCES

William Caxton, *The Golden Legend, or Lives of the Saints*, edited by F. S. Ellis (London, 1934), volume 3, pages 236–253.

J. R. Clarke, Douglas Hamer, W. McLeod, "Letters to the Editor: Saint Alban and Saint Amphibal, " *AQC*, volume 92 (1979), pages 218–221.

W. McCleod, "Saint Alban and Saint Amphibal in the Mediaeval Masonic Tradition: A Review Article," *AQC*, volume 89 (1976), pages 113–122.

W. McLeod, "Alban and Amphibal: Some Extant Lives and a Lost Life," *Mediaeval Studies*, volume 42 (1980), pages 407–430.

Herbert Thurston and Donald Attwater, *Buwler's Lives of the Saints, Complete Edition reused and supplemented* (Westminster, Maryland, 1956), volume 2, pages 612–614, "St Alban, Martyr."

# SIR CHRISTOPHER WREN

## Louis Williams, FPS

*1985 Certificate of Literature*

## I – ST. PAUL'S CATHEDRAL

SOARING MAJESTICALLY heavenward, three hundred and sixty-five feet above the formerly murky streets of London, is the golden Cross that surmounts the glorious dome of St. Paul's Cathedral. It is of little consequence that in size this great Cathedral is the third largest in the world, being exceeded only by the Cathedrals of Milan, Italy, and Seville, Spain. Of more importance is its quality, and here it ranks with the finest, being the greatest example of church architecture in the British Isles, and with a very few on the European Continent as being the best in the world.

St. Paul's Cathedral was the product of one great genius. Sir Christopher Wren. It was the major work of his life, although he produced many others. He stands almost alone as Britain's greatest architect, rivaled only in part by Indigo Jones, who lived one generation ahead of Wren. That he surrounded himself with other great artists, whose work contributed greatly to the overall production, is only further proof of the ability of Sir Christopher.

What stunning forces of nature combine to make a great genius of one man, while leaving his fellows unknown? What combination of genes, of birth, of heredity, of environment, of motivation, will make one man a da Vinci, a Shakespeare or an Einstein; and leave his blood brother an ordinary man? We may search the learning of all the anthropologists, the geneticists, the philosophers,—and never find the answer. This is one of the world's great mysteries.

This was true of Christopher Wren, born in Wiltshire in 1632, the son of a poor and relatively obscure Church of England rector. However, when only 2 years old, his father was appointed as rector of the royal palace at Windsor, then occupied by Charles I. Here, in the atmosphere of learning, of rivalry and of aristocratic tastes may have been nurtured the intellect that eventually flowered into the genius that could design a St. Paul's.

The facts of Wren's life which are available to us are very few indeed, considering the mark left by the man. But compare this to Shakespeare, the greatest genius ever born, who had died only sixteen years before Wren was born, where the controversy over the facts of his life and the authorship of the plays continues unabated to this day.

Wren's life was devoted to just one thing—the pursuit of scientific knowledge in its highest dimension of excellence, and this probably does nor lend itself to a colorful biography. What little we do know is chiefly derived from a book written by his eldest son, also named Christopher, whose *Parentalia* was supposed to be a record of Sir Christopher's life and works, but was very meager in intimate biographical data.

Remember at this time England was experiencing governmental chaos. Henry VIII had thrown off the Catholic yoke in 1535, one hundred years earlier, and religious wars flared between Catholics and Protestants, Puritans and Presbyterians, Episcopalians and Dissenters for two centuries thereafter. Elizabeth I had reigned from 1588 to 1603, and England's maritime power dated from the defeat of the Spanish Armada in 1588. Shakespeare, representative of the greatest flowering of literature in any country in any century, died in 1616. Charles I was hanged in 1649, when Wren was seventeen years old. Cromwell ruled from 1649 till his death in 1658, and Charles II ascended the throne in 1660. Before and during Cromwell's regime the country was in constant civil war.

But all this seemed to have little effect on the even tenor of Wren's life. He entered Westminster School in London, and at fourteen became a student in Wadham College, Oxford, receiving his Bachelor of Arts at nineteen and his Master's at twenty-one. He then became a fellow of All-Soul's College, still in Oxford, where he remained until appointed Professor of Astronomy at Gresham College, in 1657 (age 25) and to the same post at Oxford in 1661 (now being 29).

In the meanwhile, he was really making a name for himself in collegiate and scientific circles. The great diarist, John Evelyn, met him at Oxford in 1654. when Wren was 22, and wrote in his diary that he had been introduced to "that miracle of a youth, Mr. Christopher Wren." For by this time Wren had invented several astronomical and pneumatic instruments, had written a treatise on spherical geometry, and an algebraical tract on the Julian period. Shortly he published his hypothesis on the evolution of comets; a study on Saturn and its rings; had made a model of the moon: and had discovered a method to control and measure a charge of dynamite; and a practical graphic method of computing eclipses. Had he stayed in the field of astronomy, he would have become one of the world's most renowned but his real genius was destined to unfold itself in another field. However, he did help organise the Royal Society for the Advancement of Science, and served as its President in 1681–83.

If ever Wren had a hobby outside his work, it is never mentioned. His mind was apparently set on one thing, his work. In the architectural field alone, which he entered when he was about 30, he produced enough actual work to have kept five other less qualified men busy. At the age of 37 he took time to marry, had two children, of whom only one survived, his first wife dying after 6 years of marriage. A year and a half later, in 1677, he remarried, but the second wife died 3 years later, leaving two more infant children. From age 48 onward, he remained single, married only to his work.

Wren's entry into the field of architecture may have been pure happenstance. He was secure in his post as Professor of Astronomy at Oxford, but like most scientists he was undoubtedly dabbling in many other fields. So far as we know he had no formal training in architectural design or building construction, but seems to have been self taught, which is all the more remarkable, and a tribute to his depth of knowledge and perception. He had apparently ridden the whirlwinds of political change through the 1650's without damage, and upon the accession of Charles II in 1660 he was very much in royal favor, and in 1661 was appointed assistant to the Surveyor General of the Royal Works, a post he himself assumed upon the death of the holder in 1669. He was knighted by King Charles in 1673. The post of Surveyor General virtually made him supervisor of all building in England. He held this post till 1718, when at age 86 he was dismissed through Court intrigue. But by then it mattered little. He had been Chief through six of the most important decades in English building history, and had served his country well.

Wren first entered the architectural arena in 1663 at the age of 31, when his uncle, the Bishop of Ely, asked him to design and build a Chapel for Pembroke College, at Cambridge. This, his first commission, was completed two years later, in 1665. In the same period, in 1664, Bishop Sheldon of Oxford asked him to build a Theatre there, which was completed as the Sheldonian in 1669. Here Wren solved his first big construction problem. The span of the auditorium was too wide for ordinary ceiling beams. Yet a ceiling had to be supplied on which the pictorial artist could display his fantasies of Cupids, gods, and nymphs gambolling in the clouds. To solve this, Wren produced an architectural first by suspending his ceiling from the beams of the roof structure.

Fate often intervenes to determine the course of our lives. About as important as any other factor in life is to be the right man in the

right place at the right time. To be the right man one has to be prepared when the time and place conjoin. These factors worked for
Wren, and he was prepared. His experience in his first two ven-
tures into architecture apparently showed him the need for more
study and preparation. In addition, in 1663, he had been placed
on a royal commission to study the restoration of "Old St. Paul's."
of which more explanation later.

So Wren decided to take leave from his pending assignments,
and devote a year to study in France, where the greatest artists of
the day, including Bernini, were working under the aegis of the
greatest patron of all, the "Sun King," Louis XIV. Bernini, one of the
great sculptors and artists of all time, Chief Architect of St. Peter's
in Rome, designer of the Papal Throne and high altar in St. Peter's,
and the stately Colonade that surrounds the square, together with
many of Rome's fountains, including the Trevi fountain, had just
fallen out of favor with Pope Innocent X, and had accepted Louis
XIV's invitation to come to Paris in that same year that found Wren
there, 1665.

Again, this was fortunate timing, for the Great Plague was
sweeping over England, and 200,000 of London's million citizens
died in 1665 alone. What a loss England and the world would have
suffered if Wren had succumbed; but he didn't, and he returned to
London in 1666, renewed in spirit and in mind, and ready for the
great decades to follow.

He was immediately commissioned to remodel "Old St. Paul's",
on which his great predecessor, Inigo Jones, had labored before his
death in 1652. The story of St. Paul's we will relate later, but Wren
had prepared a plan accepted by the Commissioners, to remodel
and rehabilitate the existing structure, when again the timing of
fate solved the problem. During the first week of September, 1666,
the Great Fire ravaged the City of London. Over one half of the City
was destroyed, including 87 of its churches. The task of reconstruction was truly enormous. Wren, equal to the challenge, produced
the first Urban Renewal plan in history for within five days after the

fire had ended, he presented an elaborate plan for redesigning and rebuilding the City. Finances and lack of vision prevented its adoption, but Wren was made one of 6 commissioners given the task of overall supervision of reconstruction.

In addition to his work on St. Paul's, he designed and rebuilt the following churches: St. Stephen: St. Benet: St. Lawrence; St. Bride's; St. Magnus; Christ Church; St. Martin: St. James, St. Vedast, St. Clement and St. Mary-le-bow. Many presented unusual problems of odd shaped lots, and hemmed in spaces. Yet each design was different and suited to its needs. Wren was an architect who featured elaborate spires, and impressive domes, and his imagination had ample opportunity to express itself. The interior design of St. Clement's; St. Jances; and St. Lawrence; the exterior of St. Benet's: the dome of St. Stephen's; and the spires or steeples of St. Bride's and St. Mary-le-bow, the latter of which contains the famous Bow Bells, are particularly noteworthy. Most of these were completed by 1685, and their glittering spares and domes were giving the City of London a skyline surpassed by no other city in the world.

To particularly commemorate the Great Fire and to mark the rebirth of the City, the commissioners decided on a suitable memorial. Accordingly Wren and his noted student assistant. Hooke, built a Doric column 200 feet high, which was six years in building and which still stands at Fish Street and Puoding Lane, where the Great Fire was supposed to have originated. The original plan called for the column to be topped with a golden phoenix rising from the flames, but eventually they settled for the simpler design of a flaming urn.

While all the churches were a-building, and while St. Paul's was being planned and built, Sir Christopher was by no means neglecting other projects. 1668 saw a new building for Emanuel College, Cambridge; 1670 a new gateway to the City called the Temple Bar, later removed intact to a country park outside London; 1675 the Royal observatory at Greenwich, occupying the site and marking Longitude 0d, which was not accepted internationally until 1884.

The year 1671 had seen the design for a new Library for Trinity College, Cambridge, and a new Tower for Christ Church: Oxford; 1677 the Town Hall at Abingdon; 1682 the Royal Hospital at Chelsea: and 1690 Wren's famous design for Hampton Court Palace for William and Mary, where for the first time in architectural history staircases came into their own, and the grand staircase at Hampton Court was nor only an innovation, but a magnificent design in its own right. 1690–1704 was occupied by the re-design of Kensington Palace, for William and Mary, to which in 1714 he added an Orangery for Queen Anne. 1695 found Wren designing Morden College at Blackheath; 1696–1715 covered the building of the Royal Naval College at Greenwich, with another of Wren's classical domes.

Nor was the New World entirely neglected. In 1693, William and Mary, the reigning English monarchs, and Wrens royal patrons, issued a charter for a new college for Virginia, to be built near Jamestown, and named after them. This was the second college in the American Colonies; Harvard being the first. Sir Christopher was commissioned to design their new building, and for its support William and Mary ceded 20,000 acres of land in the colony of Virginia. The foundation was laid in 1695 near Jamestown, but in a community later to be called Williamsburg after the King. After completion it served as an academic hall, president's house, faculty apartments and student dormitory for the new college, which had at that time from 50 to 100 students.

This building was called Old Main, and served as meeting place for the House of Burgesses for a time in the early 1700's. It passed through the usual experience of fires, vandalism, neglect and decay. It was only a shell when restored by John D. Rockefeller, Jr. in 1928, but the restoration was made on lines as near the original as research could determine. Since then it is known as Wren Hall, and those of you who have visited Williamsburg will remember that it anchors the west end of the restoration area at the end of the Duke of Gloucester Street, the Capitol being at the other end. Wren Hall is now the oldest academic building in use in the United States.

His fame was such that, although he seemed not to admire politics, he was induced to stand for Parliament, and represented several boroughs in that august body—Plympton in 1685. Windsor in 1689, and Weymouth in 1700. Probably each term continued for several years, but on this point his biographers are silent.

During almost all of this period Wren had designed and was building his masterpiece, St. Paul's. In June, 1675, the first stone was laid; in 1708 the last stone was placed at the apex of the dome by his son Christopher. What a lifetime of activity. Wren was one of the few men in history, if not the only one, who had lived to see a great Cathedral of his own design carried to completion.

In 1714, four years after St. Paul's was finished Queen Anne died, and a new royal line was instituted under the Hanovers, beginning with George I. Through court intrigue, he was dismissed by George I from his post as Surveyor General in 1718, at the age of 86. Five years later, when 91, and after a last visit to St. Paul's, he caught a chill, and died in a chair by his fireside on February 25, 1723. He was buried in a crypt in his beloved Cathedral, and his son caused to be lettered as his epitaph on the stone above the crypt the now famous Latin inscription, -

*Si monumentum requiris, circumspice.*

"If you seek his monument look around you!"

Such are the bare details of a long life filled with great activity, and with accomplishments granted to few men in the world's history. As an architect he brought to his profession a profound knowledge of the principles of his craft: an artistic taste seldom equalled; an inexhaustible fertility of invention: and a constant pursuit of excellence. Great generals who conquered empires mat have gained more lasting fame; the great religious leaders of the centuries may have influenced more people: but great builders like

Sir Christopher Wren have contributed much to our lives, our pleasure and our inspiration.

## II – MASON OR NO?

IN A previous issue of this magazine, we discussed the life of Sir
Christopher Wren, England's most distinguished architect, and his
great contribution to the rebuilding of London after the Great Fire
of 1666. Now we examine a question that has troubled many generations of our Masonic forebears.

What was Sir Christopher Wren's connection with the Craft of
Masonry? Was he a Speculative Mason? Was he a Grand Master,
as Dr. James Anderson asserted in his famous "Constitutions of
1738"? Let us examine the facts, and draw therefrom appropriate
inferences.

Throughout the years of organized Masonry, since 1717, there
have been three schools of Masonic historians. The first we might
call the "Claim everything in sight" school, founded by Dr. James
Anderson with his fanciful histories of the Craft, tracing our ances-
try back to Adam as the first Grand Master. Preston and Oliver followed him blindly, perpetuated his flights of imagination until they
gained an aura of responsibility, and even Mackey, great historian
as he was, fell partially into the trap.

Then came the natural over-reaction. Beginning with Gould
came the "hard rock bottom fact" school, who rejected everything
about Masonic history that couldn't be proved by evidence admis-
sible in a court of law. Unless supported by written or other indis-
putable evidence this group refused to accept previous Masonic
beliefs. This school of historians served a very useful purpose,
debunking Masonic tradition, and forcing Masons to face up to the
hard and sometimes unpalatable facts of Masonic truth. Even yet
their task is not complete, for we still find Masonic writers repeat-
ing the old hoary legends as if they were the gospel truth.

Most modern Masonic historians, after a calm and unemotional survey of the past, have joined the "reasonable inference" school, a group which looks dispassionately at fact and fiction, sorts out the fact, and from that try to accept a reasonable line of logical inference. The Regius Manuscript (circa 1390) contains the earliest written account of Masonry as we know it today. Does it follow then that Masonry began in 1390? Of course not. Experts believe the Regius itself, and the Cooke Ms. which followed about A.D. 1401, were both copied from earlier writings. It thus follows that Masonry, Operative, that is, was in existence for a century or more, and long before the unknown scribe set down the story in his medieval poem we call the "Regius."

Any Masonic fact, thus known, must be projected back into its historical origins, applying the same tests that every reliable historian applies when he sets down the story of ancient and medieval history. Happily for modern Masonic historians, there is enough fact and reasonable inference to satisfy anyone as to the history of our early Operative Masons, and its source as the genesis of our modern Speculative Fraternity.

Now, after this longwinded buildup of historical analysis, we return to our original question as to the membership of Sir Christopher Wren in our great fraternity. Let's first look at the setting and environment. He was born in 1632, almost a century before the Grand Lodge was organized in 1717. He died in 1723, 91 years of age. He was an organizer of the Royal Society for the Advancement of Science while still a professor at Oxford, and its President in 1681–83. He was a close friend of the leading citizens of England, and this included Dr. Desaguliers, also a fellow of the Royal Society, one of the organizers of the Grand Lodge, and its third Grand Master in 1719. He was a friend of John Aubrey, of Dr. Robert Plot, of Elias Ashmole, of whom more hereafter, and he was unquestionably well known to if not a friend of Dr. James Anderson one of the organizers of the Grand Lodge, and the author of its "Constitutions" of 1723 and 1738.

Why, then, do we not have a better record of Wren's membership in the Craft, if he were indeed a member? Why was it not more often mentioned by his friends and Masonic acquaint lances and fellow Masons of the period? These are pertinent, and very potent questions, and deserve an answer. Strangely enough, our predecessors of 2½ centuries ago were not as careful as we are today to preserve every scrap of writing, every minute of a meeting, every chance remark concerning every great man. Even today we are overwhelmed with the millions of tons of paper work, and have to resort to microfilm to preserve even the tiniest part of the records of our own daily lives. And from the old days, if any record at all is left of any person or event, we're just lucky.

Even the intimate details of Sir Christopher Wren's daily life are strangely incomplete. True, he left his many architectural monuments for our wonderment, yet so important a date as placing the capstone on St. Paul's is in dispute, some authorities saying 1708 and others 1710. His own son, Christopher, claims he laid the stone in July, 1708. But Thomas Strong, the Chief Mason on St. Paul's, claims Edward Strong, either a brother or nephew, placed the capstone on October 25, 1710. Young Wren wrote the earliest biography of his father's life, called *Parentalia*, published in 1738 by the grandson, Stephen Wren. It is completely silent on Sir Christopher's Masonic membership, if it ever existed. But then it is also silent on hundreds of other details we should like to know about, and was described by a later biographer, one James Elmes, as "a miserable compilation, a bungling per" formance."

And so it goes. But despite the fact that young Christopher, the son, said nothing about his father's Masonic affiliations, he does quote his father at length on his father's dissertation of how Operative Masonry came into being, and how the great European Cathedrals were built by great transient groups of Operative Masons.

Elias Ashmole has left us in his diaries, the first recorded instances of the making of a Freemason in England, the dates being 1646 and 1682. He was the creator of the Ashmolean Museum at

Oxford. This proves nothing except that Masonic records of the day were mighty rare, and any Masonic writing worthy of note. Next comes Dr. Robert Plot, curator of Ashmole's Museum, himself not a Mason, but whose *Natural History of Staffordshire*, published in 1686, remarks about the Society of Freemasons in that area of the Midlands of England.

These three short mentions of Masonry, together with John Aubrey's remark hereafter are the only written evidences coming from the 17th Century in England to prove that there were any lodges of organized (or slightly disorganized, if we face the facts) Speculative Masonry in existence in the period covered by the building of St. Pauls, 1675–1708. Aubrey has a very important message quoted from his original Ms. in the Bodleian Library at Oxford, entitled the *Natural History of Wiltshire* written in 1691, which says, and here is an exact quote from the Ms., with all the deletions and additions. This Ms. was completed in 1686, but the author later made corrections. On folio 73 he had inserted a discussion about the origin of the fraternity in his original draft. Then in 1691 he wrote a note on the back of folio 72, and this note he also later corrected. Here is the passage which concerns us on the back of folio 72;-

> Memorandum. This day, May the 18th, being Munday, 1691, after Rogation Sunday, is a great convention at St. Paul's Church of the fraternity of the adopted Masons, where Sir Christopher Wren is to be adopted a brother, and Sir Henry Goodric, of the Tower, and divers others. There have been kings of this sodality.

This entry, hidden away in an unpublished Ms., was not mentioned until 1844, a century and a half after the fact. Are we to ignore it? In Gould's marvelously pragmatic History of Freemasonry, first published in 1885, and which started the iconoclastic historical trend referred to above, he spends some 25 pages in analyzing the facts and inferences relating to Wren's membership, and completely discounting Aubrey's statements above, avers that

Wren was never a Mason. Gould deduces that lack of proof is failure of proof. Gould relies on the failure of Desaguliers; of Martin Folkes, Deputy Grand Master in 1725; of Martin Clare, Deputy Grand Master in 1741, but whose chief claim to fame rests in his purported authorship of the *Defence of Masonry*, which appeared in answer to Prichard's attack, *Masonry Dissected* in 1730; and of Richard Rawlinson, Grand Steward in 1734, all Fellows of the Royal Society with Wren, and all outstanding and well known Freemasons, to ever mention that Wren was a Mason.

Gould also makes much of this. In his *Constitutions* of 1723 (published the year of Wren's deaths, incidentally), Anderson mentions Wren only as "the ingenious architect" of St. Paul's. But in his 1738 issue, 15 years later and 15 years after Wren's death, his memory and his imagination greatly improve, and among other statements he has the Lodges meeting and electing Wren Grand Master in 1685, Deputy Grand Master to the Duke of Richmond as Grand Master in 1695, with the Edward Strongs, Sr. & Jr., (who were the actual operating masons on St. Paul's) as Grand Wardens; makes Wren Grand Master some time later, until 1708, when he so neglected his office that the lodges fell into disarray, whereupon the four immemorial lodges were forced to meet and reorganize the Grand Lodge in 1717. Anderson's historical references have been so completely refuted that one can place no reliance whatever in his statements.

In the *Postboy*, a London newspaper of the period, and in one other, published the week following Wren's death, mention is made of the burial "of that worthy Freemason, Sir Christopher Wren." Other contemporary notices of his death and burial fail to state his Masonic affiliation. Many other Masonic books of the period 1723 to 1738 fail to include Wren in any list of Freemasons.

From all this silence Gould concludes that Aubrey's diary mentions an initiation that never happened; that the two newspaper obituary notices were in error; and that Anderson was certainly engaging in his usual flight of fancy in 1738, after exercising restraint in 1723; and that the failure of Wren's friends to acknowledge Wren as a member clinches the argument. *Coil's Encyclopedia* (Macoy, 1961) quite strongly affirms the Gould view.

The reader must judge for himself. Consider the almost complete lack of written proof concerning any Masonic matter in the period before 1717, and this author is inclined to give Aubrey more credit than Gould has given. That Aubrey's mention laid unnoticed in a handwritten manuscript in a large library until 1844 is only more proof of its authenticity, to my mind. Wren was 85 when the Grand Lodge was formed in 1717. Little wonder that he would take no part in it. Certainly he was not Grand Master, for there was none until 1717. That he never participated in a meeting after his initiation in 1691 is no proof of his non-membership, for there are no records of any such meetings in the following years till 1717. That he was plenty busy with his work is amply shown. He worked daily with the Strong family, two brothers and several sons, all operative masons of great skill, undoubtedly possessed of whatever masonic secrets operative masons had at that time in London.

It is the well considered belief of the author that notwithstanding the very well constructed and logical arguments of Gould, Coil and others, that we have over-reacted to the evidence, and have failed in the logical inferences that may be drawn from it in view of the current conditions of the times, and the almost complete absence of any Masonic record.

Wren was in constant contact with Operative Masons, on St. Paul's and his many other projects. Lodges of that day held no stated or regular meetings,—kept no formal records. The initiation ceremony was informal with little ritual as we know it today, but only a few signs, words, and possible grip. The lectures or story of the Craft at most such ceremonies was an ad lib rendition by whoever chanced to preside. What more natural than that the great architect, the great leader of all building in the city at that time, should be honored with speculative membership, as others had been before, and as many many others were to be so honored before the organization of 1717?

I can well believe that Wren was a knowledgeable operative Mason, and an initiated Speculative Mason, who thereafter had little or no time to devote to active participation in any recorded work of the Craft.

If Wren were a Mason, we may well take pride in his contributions to the life of his time. If he were not, and this I will not concede, he did his work as a just and upright Mason should, and covered himself, if not the Craft, with the utmost glory. In Part III of this study, to be published in a later issue of this magazine, we will tell of Sir Christopher's vicissitude and ultimate triumph as he designed and built his greatest achievement, St. Paul's Cathedral.

## III – ST. PAUL'S CATHEDRAL

FROM THE early days when it was first a cluster of huts on the mud-banks of the Thames, London claimed St. Paul as its patron saint. Picking out the highest point in the vicinity, subsequently called Ludgate Hill, a wooden church was built by Ethelbert, King of Kent, (A.D. 560–616), and the history of the church begins with the consecration of Mellitus as bishop of the East Saxons in A.D. 604.

Before the century was over the first St. Paul's had been destroyed by fire as have all of its successors except the present one, and it has had narrow escapes. This first church was replaced by another of stone in 675–685, and became a favorite shrine for pilgrimages. Sometime during the ninth century, during one of the numerous Viking invasions, this second church too was burned. It was then rebuilt in 962. In 1087, following a few years upon the Norman conquest of 1066, this church built by the Saxons in 962 was also burned, perhaps accidentally. Immediately William Rufus (the Red), son of William the Conqueror, whom he had just succeeded as king, began rebuilding on a vast and imposing scale a tremendous cathedral known through the six succeeding centuries as "Old St. Paul's."

This enormous structure was many years a-building, and quite naturally was built in the Norman, or roundarched style. It occupied several city blocks, and while a small fire in 1136 delayed the work on one portion, the main cathedral was completed about 1200, the great spire begun in 1220, and the whole finished and dedicated in 1240. A large addition was begun in 1258 and completed in 1314, making Old St. Paul's the third largest church in Christendom, exceeded in size only by the cathedrals of Seville, Spain,—still the world's largest—and Milan, Italy. It was 596 feet long, and the enormous spire, the loftiest ever built, soared 489 feet into the heavens. In addition to the cathedral proper, the adjacent grounds contained a bishop's house, a deanery, a chapter house, and a Cathedral School. All in all, it was truly an imposing development.

Throughout the years, Old St. Paul's fell upon both good and evil times. We can readily understand that the constant battle going on between Church and State, usually between the English monarch and the Pope or his English legate, could not fail to affect the largest church in London, and the diocese of London's archbishop. In 1377 John Wyclif was tried here for heresy, and when John of Gaunt, son of Edward III, appeared in his defense, the ignorant and superstitious peasants rioted, and the trial was abandoned. All of which goes to prove that riots, even court room riots, are not a modern invention.

In the 14th Century, the floors were paved with marble, and much gold decoration added, until the interior appearance became sumptuous indeed. Many heresy and witchcraft trials were held, and the unhappy victims were taken nearby and burned at the stake.

On November 14, 1501, Arthur Prince of Wales, the son of Henry VII, married Katherine of Aragon, daughter of Ferdinand and Isabella, in a wedding ceremony of great magnificence in Old St. Paul's. Widowed six months later, within seven years she sealed her doom by marrying his brother, Henry VIII, and became the first of his six wives. She was faithful and true, but put aside when Henry became enamoured of Anne Boleyn. The refusal of the Pope to sanction a divorce was the final reason for Henry VIII's repudiation of the Catholic Church, and radically changed the course of English and European history.

Old St. Paul's was in the very center of the fight. It was switched from Catholic to Protestant under Henry VIII, back to Catholic under his daughter Mary I, called Bloody Mary because of the large number of Protestants she beheaded as heretics; and back to the Church of England under Elizabeth. During this period the Cathedral was robbed of most of its treasures, the high altar pulled down, and most of the tombs despoiled. Elizabeth often attended services here, and when the dean, preaching on Ash Wednesday, 1565, left his prepared sermon to attack the use of images in some ad lib remarks, Elizabeth interrupted him in the midst of his sermon by saying, "To your text, Mr. Dean, to your text: We have heard enough of that."

During this period of the Reformation, the use of the Cathedral became truly scandalous. The naves and bays of the church were used for trade stalls; merchandise of all kinds was sold throughout the building; the nave became a public thoroughfare through which even horses were driven, and beggars and rogues made it into a flophouse, and slept and ate in its precincts. Perhaps the worst abuse of all came during the Puritan regime of Cromwell (1653–1659) when his forces used the Cathedral for a barracks, and stabled their horses in the aisles, using all the finely carved woodwork for campfires.

It was during these very decades, the Cathedral having deteriorated to the point of danger, that many steps looking to its restoration were taken. In 1628 Inigo Jones, England's great architect second only to Wren, and reputed but not proved to be a Mason, planned and completed extensive repairs, including a new west entrance. He spent 100,000 pounds and that was far from petty cash in those days. The Civil War which deposed Charles I and led to his execution put an end to Jones work, and the Cathedral was used as barracks and stable by the Puritans as I have previously described.

With the accession of Charles II in 1660, the Cathedral was in the final stages of decay, and scarcely worth repair. Nevertheless, in 1663 a Royal Commission for this purpose was appointed, and Wren commissioned to produce plans. He did, and proposed a dome to replace the old spire which had been so battered by wind, lightning and fire through the years it was a worthless wreck. Perhaps recognizing his inadequacy as an architect, Wren studied in Paris in 1665, and returned to London to embark on the project. But the Great Fire of 1666 solved many problems by destroying Old St. Paul's past any hope of redemption.

In 1668 Wren was commissioned to design an entirely new building, subject to approval of King and commissioners. Wren was now the King's Surveyor General, and occupied a position of great authority and prestige, including the need to supervise the rebuilding of about half of London destroyed by the Great Fire, including the 55 churches to be rebuilt. But Wren went to work with a will, and in 1670 produced a plan now named the "New Model," whereby the fifth church was to be built on the historic site. This plan called for a Greek cross design, with a great central dome and four even aisles or sides. King Charles II quickly approved, but the commissioners thought it too unorthodox, and refused their approval.

Then Sir Christopher embarked upon his second design, much bolder and more radical but in which design he lengthened one side to form a nave, providing a traditional Latin cross. In order that all might visualize what he proposed, and to forestall their petty objections, Wren built a model of his proposal which was fashioned of oak and was about 20 feet in length, costing 600 pounds, and taking 9 months to fashion. This design, named the "Great Model," he presented to the commissioners in 1673. Once again the King enthusiastically approved, and once again the commissioners rejected the design as not traditional. We may imagine the frustration which Wren must have felt after two splendid and imaginative designs were thus foolishly rejected by those who knew far less about the subject than he. Wren knew he had designed a cathedral of supreme beauty and great originality, but some of his critics thought it too reminiscent of St. Peter's and too "popish" in flavor. This "Great Model" is still on display in the present Cathedral.

But swallowing his pride, Wren again set to work, and in 1675 produced the third design, subsequently named the "Royal Warrant" design. Here the Latin cross was retained, the dome greatly reduced, and a steeple or spire placed on the modified dome. This the commissioners approved, and the King, a pretty good judge of human nature, in approving the design and issuing the royal warrant for its construction, authorized Wren to make such variations as might be necessary as the work progressed, thus giving Wren the last word, and enabling him to accomplish his original purposes. As the years went by, and the work progressed, he made radical changes, and the finished product not only embodied his great dome, one of the finest in the world, but eliminated the spire, and brought the cathedral almost entirely back to his second design of the "Great Model."

The foundation stone was laid June 21, 1675. Tradition reports that it was laid with Masonic ceremonies, although no direct proof exists, but almost all authorities report this fact. As the rubble from the fire was being cleared from the site, Wren asked a labourer to bring him a stone that he might mark the center of the new cathedral. The man brought him an old broken grave stone, which had inscribed upon it the Latin motto "Resurgam"—"I shall rise again." This was such a wonderful sign that Wren caused this motto to be lettered on the south entrance to the structure.

As the work proceeded through the years, Wren surrounded himself with many great artists and artisans. Hooke, a great architect, and Hawksmoor, who served as clerk and after Wren's death, himself became England's leading architect, assisted with the plans. Thomas Strong became Master Mason throughout the entire project, assisted by various members of his family, his son Edward, or nephew, claiming that he placed the capstone in 1710. (Christopher Wren, Sir Christopher's son, claimed he placed the capstone in 1708, and the dispute is still unsettled.) Grinling Gibbons carved much of the stone work, with a grace and delicacy that has never been surpassed. He also did the carved woodwork of the choir and pulpit,—work said to be the finest woodcarving every produced. Francis Bird did a magnificent marble font, and the huge "Conversion of St. Paul" on the west entrance. Jean Tijou, imported from France to fashion the ironwork, produced entrance gates and stair balustrades of unexcelled beauty. Sir Charles Thornhill, a renowned artist, painted the murals on the inside of the dome, and these are the only items of artistry in the Cathedral which Wren felt were not quite worthy.

Work progressed slowly, but not by comparison with the other great cathedrals of the age. In fact, St. Paul's is said to be the only great Cathedral ever built during the lifetime of the same architect and the same Master Mason. Finally, the capstone was laid in 1708 or 1710, and Wren was present at the dedication. He made numerous visits to it in after days, and it was after one such visit in his 91st year, that he quietly died.

St. Paul's is not noteworthy alone for its size, but for a rare combination of size and beauty. Its great dome, with the golden cross 365 feet high, provides an airy spaciousness of unusual power. The dome itself was an engineering triumph of the day, as conceived by Wren. The outer sheath is lead over framework, but the gigantic stone lantern and cross which surmount the dome are supported by an inner brick cone from which also the inner dome is suspended.

The elaborate western facade is Renaissance, with two porticoes of columns, one above the other, and twin towers, one at either end. Just below the inner dome is a gallery, 100 feet above the floor, now known as "The Whispering Gallery," for it was quickly discovered that the acoustics of the inner dome were such that a whisper could be heard across its width. The high altar with its baldachin or ornamental superstructure is breathtakingly beautiful. The choir and organ, with Grinling's woodcarvings, is unsurpassed. Various smaller chapels occupy strategic places, including All Soul's, St. Dunstan, Modern Martyrs, Lady Chapel, Chapel of St. Michael and St. George, Order of British Empire Chapel, and most interesting of all to us, the American Memorial Chapel.

During World War II German bombers destroyed many blocks of London, and St. Paul's was not spared. Only a constant fire watch prevented hundreds of incendiary bombs from wreaking great destruction. Nothing, however, could prevent the damage of two major bombs, one of which almost destroyed the altar, since beautifully restored, and the north transept; and the other going through a portion of the Cathedral from roof to basement crypt. The first bomb, which destroyed the altar and the north transept, also destroyed Jesus Chapel, which occupied that portion of the north transept behind the great altar. When it was rebuilt after the war, the church and national authorities decided to build a chapel in memory and in honor of the American soldiers who had died in defense of Britain, some 28,000 in number. Accordingly the space was filled with a tastefully designed but simple small altar, backed by elaborately gilded oak paneling, surmounted by a golden American eagle. Behind this rises three beautiful stained glass windows, containing scenes from the life of Christ symbolizing the Service Sacrifice and Resurrection of the Christian soldier. Opposite the altar stands a glass case containing the American Roll of Honour, on which are inscribed the names of the 28,000 American war dead. It was presented on July 4, 1951 by then General Eisenhower. The Chapel was dedicated by the Bishop of London on November 26, 1958, in the presence of the Queen and the then Vice President of the United States, Richard M. Nixon.

St. Paul's has never rivaled Westminster as a place of burial of England's noted citizens. But it does contain several important tombs. Most apropos, of course, is Sir Christopher Wren's tomb with its legend, *Si monumentum requiris, circumspice*—"If you seek his monument, look around you." John Donne, the great English poet and writer, dean of Old St. Paul's from 1621 till his death in 1631, is buried here, and strangely enough, his tomb and marble effigy was the only one to come intact through the Great Fire of 1666, and occupies a prominent place in the new structure. The Duke of Wellington, victor over Napoleon at Waterloo, has an imposing tomb of Cornish porphyry on a foundation of granite. Lord Kitchener of World War I is buried in All Soul's Chapel.

But the most beautiful, and perhaps the strangest tomb of all is that of Horatio, Lord Nelson, victor over the French and Spanish fleets at the battle of Trafalgar in 1805, and who died on his flagship, aptly named Victory, on the day of the battle, from an enemy shell. The story of his life, as written by Robert Southey, is one of the great biographies of all time, read by every English schoolboy. Following his death as England's greatest naval hero, he was buried with appropriate pomp and ceremony in St. Paul's. The strange part about his tomb is that the black marble sarcophagus, of the utmost beauty, grace and refinement, was designed and carved by an Italian artist to serve as the tomb for Cardinal Wolsey, who died almost 300 years before, and who as Bishop of London, had his see at Old St. Paul's. Having as cardinal temporarily thwarted Henry VIII in his determination to divorce Catherine of Aragon and wed Anne Boleyn, Henry partially retaliated by confiscating his prepared sarcophagus during Wolsey's life, and stored it in Windsor Castle, where it lay forgotten for almost 300 years, until found and restored to serve as Lord Nelson's tomb.

Every great cathedral, every great church, has its points of interest. St. Paul's combines far more than its share, because even among great cathedrals it is still outstanding. And irregardless of whether or not Sir Christopher Wren was ever initiated as a speculative Mason; regardless of whether or not the foundation stone of St. Paul's was laid with Masonic ceremonies,—the fact remains that St Paul's fulfills the highest function expected of any church and likewise expected of every Masonic lodge namely—"Erected to God, and dedicated to His service."

# OF OATHS, VOWS, & OBLIGATIONS

## L. L. Walker, Jr., MPS

*1986 Certificate of Literature*

*A paper prepared for the Texas Lodge of Research,
AF&AM, Dallas. Texas, 15 September 1979*

## Introduction

PERHAPS NOTHING else so thoroughly characterises Freemasonry as does the oath, or "obligation," which accompanies each of its Three Degrees. These oaths together form the nucleus of the Masonic fraternal structure, and enunciate in pragmatic terms the duties, responsibilities and limitations of the fraternal relationship which they establish.

By their very nature they give substance to the long-held popular conception of Freemasonry as a secret society. In consequence, they have been the principal cause of the estrangement, and at times animosity, of the Church at Rome, as well as the object of misunderstanding and distrust by some branches of Protestantism.

It is not the purpose of this paper to investigate the historical development of Masonic oaths. This has been done by Knoop and Jones and other competent investigators. Neither is it the purpose of the paper to examine the relationship of Freemasonry and organized religion, or to consider any of the tensions which have prevailed between Catholicism and the Masonic Order by reason of these oaths. This has been done and is being done by Mellor, Carr and others.

The purpose of the paper is no more than to consider the character of Masonic oaths in the legal, religious and ethical context of all oaths and vows, and to establish the fact that they derive their form and language, if not their precise content, from the social, political, religious and intellectual milieu out of which modern Freemasonry itself sprang. In seeking to realize this purpose we shall exercise appropriate discretion. Because there are things we can not properly say, the fullest understanding and appreciation of this paper requires a rather accurate recollection of the content of the obligations of the Three Degrees. Those who do not have that recollection are at a disadvantage, but it is hoped that the general discussion of oaths, vows and obligations will be of sufficient interest in itself to engage the attention of anyone, even though the ultimate purpose of the paper is not fully realized.

## Of Oaths, Vows and Obligations

The word "oath"—is found throughout the Teutonic languages, but without discernable etymology. In its most basic meaning an oath is an external pledge or asseveration, made in verification of statements made or to be made, coupled with an appeal to the sacred or venerated object, in evidence of the serious and reverant state of mind of the party, or with an invocation to a supreme being to witness the words of a party and to visit him with punishment if they be false.[1]

In a more strictly legal sense, an oath is a solemn appeal to the Supreme Being in attestation of the truth of some statement, and an outward pledge that one's testimony is given under an immediate sense of responsibility to God.[2]

From the foregoing it will be seen that belief by the witness in Deity and an appeal to him as an avenger of falsehood are the essentials of the oath. For this reason oaths in Christendom, since the time of Justinian, have included an appeal to God, Jesus Christ, the Virgin Mary, the Four Gospels, the Archangels Michael and Gabriel, or some combination of these. About A.D. 802, during the reign of Charlemagne, the feudal oath of fealty came to include the phrase Sic me adjuvet Deus. These words came into English as the familiar and long-prevailing "So help me God," the so-called words of adjuration.

Further, at some time in the Middle Ages there arose the practice of using the Holy Bible as the external symbol of the witness's acknowledgement of the obligation of the oath. This usage might include either touching the Bible or kissing it to seal the oath taken. Such an oath, ratified by contact with the Holy Bible, either by touching or kissing, is called a corporal oath. The practice called "kissing the book" prevailed in the law courts of Great Britain and Ireland into the present century when an Act of Parliament superseded that practice with one requiring the witness or deponent to hold a New Testament in his upraised right hand. Other provisions were made for non-Christians, Quakers and others.[3]

A public oath in this country is customarily taken with the right hand upraised. This is the Scottish form, so recognised by the laws of Great Britain. Swearing in this manner is, as a general thing, an American statutory requirement. As a principle of American law, however, no special form need accompany the administration of an oath, unless required by statute, provided that some formal act be done to impress the witness with the distinction between sworn statements and bare assertions.[4]

To take an oath is to swear. The word "swear" is an Anglo-Saxon word which, like the word "oath," is without helpful etymology. The word means not only to take an oath, or to declare on oath the truth of statements made: it also means to become bound by an oath duly administered.[5]

As we shall see later, because of religious scruples, or because of professed lack of religious beliefs, not all persons are prepared to swear. In lieu of swearing such persons are allowed to make affirmation in any mode which they may declare to be binding on their consciences, so long as the affirmation takes the form of a solemn and formal declaration or asseveration.[6] An affirmation, then, is defined as "a solemn and formal declaration or asseveration that an affidavit is true, that a witness will tell the truth, etc., this being substituted for an oath in certain cases."

A vow is a solemn promise, especially one made to God or to some deity. It is as well an act by which one consecrates or devotes himself to some act, service or condition. In its broadest sense, it is a promise of fidelity or constancy, behind which lies the idea of personal consecration.

While oaths and affirmations are primarily identified with the law of the state, vows are associated with the church and with religion. We see that the three terms—oath, affirmation and vow—have in common the characteristic of solemnity. As acts, they are set apart from the common things of life. In the widest possible sense, each is an asseveration; that is, each affirms or avers positively and does so in a solemn manner. The distinction seems to lie in the fact that an oath or affirmation is an act of verification which Deity is adjured to witness, while a vow is an act of consecration to which the Deity is a party.

It will be perceived that an oath, affirmation or vow creates an obligation on the part of its maker. The word "obligation" is derived from the Latin ligate, to bind, which word is also the root of the anatomical term "ligament."

An obligation is the bond laid upon one to act in a certain way or to do a certain thing in consequence of his oath, vow or contract. The binding power may arise from the external compulsion of law, either through statute or through contract, or it may come from internal moral constraint. In the latter case religion interprets the obligation as having its ultimate ground in the moral goodness and sovereignty of God as man's creator, while acknowledging its immediate source in the moral nature of man. In either case, the obligation is the bond. In the law, the witness, whether he swears or affirms, is bound to tell the truth. In religion, the votary is bound to live, act or speak in accordance with his vow.

From these definitions it would appear that there is little difference between obligation and duty. The distinction seems to be in the fact that, while obligation implies restraint under immediate circumstances, duty is impulsion from within on wholly moral grounds.

Having now defined the principal terms being used in this paper, it will be well to consider some classification of oaths. There may be a number of classifications, depending upon the purpose of a given writer, but for our present purposes we will enumerate four; judicial oaths, oaths of allegiance, official oaths, and extrajudicial or voluntary oaths.

A judicial oath is one taken in judicial proceedings, before an officer in open court. The most familiar such oath to the average American is that administered to witnesses and deponents: "Do you solemnly swear that the testimony you are about to give in this case is the truth, the whole truth, and nothing but the truth, so help you God?" Of like nature, if less familiar, is the oath administered to jurors upon their being impaneled, one form of which is as follows: "Do you, and each of you, solemnly swear or affirm, that in Case No. ___, styled _____ you will a true verdict render according to the law as it is given you in charge by the court, and to the evidence submitted to you under the rulings of the court, so help you God?"

It will be seen that these oaths are administered in the form of interrogatories in the second person. This seems to be the form of most Judicial oaths in this country, although in Great Britain the juror's oath is a declaratory statement in the first person.

So far as we in the English-speaking countries are concerned, judicial oaths have their origin in the Anglo-Saxon practice of compurgation, wherein a defendant called "oath-helpers," or compurgators, who swore to their belief in the defendant's oath. Their oath was, "By God the oath is clean and unperjured that he hath sworn." They did not swear directly to the truth of the defendant's testimony, but that they believed his oath, under which the testimony was given.[8]

An oath of allegiance is that oath by which one swears fidelity to one's government, sovereign, or sovereign state. For example, in Great Britain the oath is to the sovereign by name, her heirs and successors: "I, A.B., do swear by Almighty God that I will be faithful and bear true allegiance to her Majesty Queen Elizabeth the Second, her heirs and successors, according to law."

In our own country the object of allegiance is not the President, or the Congress, but the Constitution. This fact will be remembered by the millions of men who have, in this century, been inducted into the armed forces of this nation. That oath is presently in this form:

> I, A.B., do solemnly swear (or affirm) that I will support and defend the Constitution of the United States against all enemies, foreign and domestic; that I will bear true faith and allegiance to the same; and that I will obey the orders of the President of the United States, and the orders of the officers appointed over me, according to regulations and the Uniform Code of Military Justice; that I take this obligation freely, without any mental reservation or purpose of evasion; and that I will well and faithfully discharge the duties of the office upon which I am about to enter: So help me God.

Oaths of allegiance are of very ancient origin. We know the very words spoken by the youth of Athens, five hundred years before Christ, as they stood before the altar and pledged themselves to their state. But we are mostly concerned here with the words of oaths as they have come down to us in the English language, and so we will mention only two: the oaths of homage and of fealty. We shall not try to define the terms; we will say only that they are concepts basic to the entire English system of land tenure.

In the act of homage, the tenant knelt before his lord, placed his hands between the lord's hands, and said, "I become your man from this day forward of life and limb and earthly worship, and unto you shall be true and faithful and bear to you faith for the tenements that I hold of you, saving the faith I owe the king."[9]

In the oath of fealty the tenant placed his hand on the Book and said, "Hear this my lord that I shall be faithful and true unto you and faith to you shall bear for the lands that I hold of you, and that I shall lawfully do to you the customs and services which I ought to do, so help me God and his saints."[10]

An official oath is one taken by an officer when he assumes charge of his office, whereby he declares that he will faithfully discharge the duties of the same, or whatever else may be required by statute in the particular case.[11]

The history of official oaths in America may be said to have begun with the inauguration of our first President. There being neither rules nor precedent for the ceremony, Robert R. Livingston, Chancellor of the State of New York, was designated to administer the oath. Samuel Otis, Secretary of the newly elected United States Senate, stood with him, holding the Holy Bible on a red cushion. George Washington stood before them and placed his left hand upon the book. Livingston raised his right hand and Washington did likewise, whereupon Livingston then asked: "Do you solemnly swear that you will faithfully execute the office of President of the United States and will, to the best of your ability, preserve, protect and defend the Constitution of the United States?"

At this juncture Washington might have said no more than "I do." Instead, he said. "I solemnly swear," repeated Livingston's words in the first person, and added the words, "So help me God." Before Otis could raise the book, Washington bowed and kissed it.[12]

Official oaths since that time have customarily been in the declaratory form in response to the question of a competent officer, and in the first person, accompanied by the act of touching, holding or kissing the Holy Bible.

The last of our four classifications is the extrajudicial oath, which is exactly what the name suggests: an oath not taken in any judicial proceeding, or without authority or requirement of law, though taken formally before a proper person.[13] Such an oath, since it is outside the processes of the law, may be called a voluntary oath.

The person taking the oath comes of his own volition, appearing willingly before a body not vested with authority to command his presence. The breach of such an oath does not come within the purview of the law. Further, since an extrajudicial oath is one not prescribed by law, it may be taken in such form and manner, and may be administered by such person, as the administering body may prescribe.

The breach of a judicial oath may be perjury; of an oath of allegiance, treason: of a public oath malfeasance; all of them public wrongs defined by statute. On the other hand, although the breach of an extrajudicial oath is likewise a wrong, it is a violation neither of right nor of law, and therefore without judicial remedy. The only remedy lies with the institution which has administered the oath. If the oath has incorporated in it a sanction—that is, a part which ordains a penalty for its violation—then the institution may proceed against the violater in accordance with that sanction. Such sanctions however, are necessarily moral and social in their nature.

Having examined some kinds of oaths and examples of them, we should now consider vows, to see how they both resemble and differ from oaths.

It should first be said that a vow has no standing in the law. A vow resembles an extrajudicial oath in that the breach of neither can result in judicial remedy. A vow also resembles what has been called a "promissory oath." This kind of oath is defined as "a solemn appeal to God, or in a wider sense, to some superior sanction or a sacred or revered person in witness to the inviolability of a promise or undertaking."[14] This similarity of vow and promissory oath has been given ecclesiastical recognition in Chapter XXII, Article V, of the Westminster Confession of Faith, 1647, in this language: "A vow is of the like nature with a promissory oath, and ought to be made with the like religious care, and to be performed with the like religious faithfulness."[15] We may perceive from this that there has not always been a clear line of demarcation between oath and vow. However, we would turn to our earlier statement and say again that an oath is an act of verification which Diety is adjured to witness, while a vow is an act of consecration to which the Deity is a party.

Of vows, the most familiar are those of marriage and ordination, and the language thereof varies widely among the religious denominations, depending upon their respective liturgical traditions. Then too, marriage vows may be administered by either civil or religious authority marriage being essentially a civil status.

Religious vows are ordinarily thought of as being in perpetuity, even though we know that the law may dissolve marriage and that the church may absolve from orders. But we may say that vows are perpetual in duration, as distinguished from the judicial oath, let us say, where the obligation extends no further than the cause or matter at bar. Further, the votary binds himself not to the state or to the individual, but, in Christian vows of the more familiar kind, to God in his Trinitarian manifestation.

There is one other vital distinction between oath and vow. While the judicial oath, the oath of allegiance and the official oath have behind them the sanction of the law, the extrajudicial oath and the vow ultimately have no other sanction than that of the conscience itself. However the institution may proceed against him, one suffers no consequences for the violation of an extrajudicial oath or vow except in the pangs of conscience. Yet, such is the power of conscience in the moral composition of most persons that it compels to right action with no less force than the law. Indeed, conscience anticipates the law, for the morally sound individual is disposed to act in an equitable manner whether or not the law has spoken. We may reasonably say that whenever a society is responsive to the public morality every enactment of positive law is called forth by the public conscience.

Conscience we understand to be that sense of right and wrong inherent in every person by virtue of his existence as a social entity. Good conscience is a synonym of equity, of fairness, of right conduct; the guarantor of sound morality. There may be some truly amoral persons without any sense of moral responsibility, but it seems more likely that those persons who claim to be amoral do so to spare themselves the self-confronting moments of moral decision.

It has been well said that it is a basic article of social morality that men should keep their oaths. We can scarcely conceive of a society in which such is not the case.

Oaths and vows are administered on the theory that the man who is under an immediate sense of responsibility to God will speak the truth or discharge a duty with greater fidelity than will the man who speaks or acts under no such responsibility. The fear of divine retribution thus impels truthful speech and honest action. This fear of divine retribution has been much more real in some ages than in others, but it probably is true that even in the most cynical of times those who were not devout were at least like the medieval barons who lived licentiously, acted wantonly, defied the Church—and endowed perpetual Masses for their souls.

Because there have always been enough people who "fear God," society has been able to rely on the internal moral restraint thus generated as the surety for a formal system of truth and fidelity. This may explain why our society still incorporates oaths and vows into its laws and customs.

At various times in history down to and including the present, there have been sects who have looked with disfavor upon the practice of swearing, relying upon the words of Jesus (Mt. 5:34) and the Epistle of James (Jas. 5:12) In English law, such people, among which Quakers and Moravians, have been called non-jurors. Foremost among these non-jurors have been the Quakers, that sect so obnoxious to English churchmen of the 16th and 17th centuries. Since they refused to take an oath they were not competent witnesses in any judicial proceeding, and it was not until the reign of William III that they were granted this privilege, and then only with respect to civil proceedings. Much later, all restrictions were removed and a form of affirmation established, not only for Quakers, but for all other non-jurors.

The norm for English-speaking Protestantism, however, is rob-ably expressed in Article XXXIX of The Thirty-Nine Articles of Religion of the Church of England. Published A.D. 1571:

> As we confess that vain and rash Swearing is forbidden Christian men by our Lord Jesus Christ, and James his Apostle, so we judge, that Christian Religion doth not prohibit, but that a man may swear when the Magistrate requireth, in a cause of faith and charity, so it be done according to the Prophet's teaching, in justice, judgment and truth.[16]

The words of the Scripture seem plain enough on their face to have justified the exclusion of swearing, but the Church of Rome in time developed its own self serving exegesis by which to reserve to itself sole competency to administer oaths. Further in this direction and at a later time in history, Rome, having excommunicated Elizabeth I, by Papal bull undertook to absolve her subjects from their allegiance to the Queen. To this arrogance a memorable reply was made by one Thomas Preston:

> ... it clearly followeth, that the Pope hath no authoritie to absolve from the oath of a true temporal allegiance, unless hee also have authoritie, as he hath not, to declare that true temporall allegiance is not in that particular case lawful, or necessary, and consequently, not a sufficient matter to be sworne, whereas true temporall allegiance is not only always lawful, but also necessary, and commanded by the law of God and nature.[17]

Thus, we see, on the one hand, religious acceptance of the temporal oath, and, on the other, the origins of a principle of law that ecclesiastical authority cannot absolve one from such oath. Although not until much later, there also developed the principle that civil courts have no authority to release one from his religious vows, marriage excepted.

Now, because this work has been undertaken by way of stimulating thought about the oaths and obligations of Freemasonry, we must begin to see how what has been said is directly applicable to that subject.

The first observation to be made is that the administration of oaths is not a practice peculiar to the Masonic order. The second is that Masonic oaths do not differ materially in form from any other oaths. The third is that, while the specific content of the oaths is peculiarly Masonic, the vocabulary is that common to oaths and vows in the English language for the better part of a millenium. The fourth observation is that the manner in which the oaths are administered, while it does reflect in detail the peculiarities of the Order, is not essentially different from the manner of administration of oaths in other times in other places.

Because of our traditional origins in time immemorial, there is a disposition among Masons to suppose that if a practice is typically Masonic it is also Masonically archetypical. Such is seldom the case, and certainly not the case with oaths. Whether the antiquity ascribed to Freemasonry is that of history or of legend, Masons cannot seriously hope to antedate the words of scripture by which we know that the practice of oath-taking was already old when the children of Israel were wanderers in the wilderness:

> Moses said to the heads of the; tribes of the people of Israel, 'This is what the Lord has commanded: When a man vows a vow to the Lord, or swears an oath to bind himself by a pledge, he shall not break his word; he shall do according to all that proceeds from out of his mouth. (Num. 30:1–2, RSV)

From the several different kinds of oaths heretofore quoted it will have been noted that their form is very much the same, regardless of purpose. Each oath prescribed by law contains prescriptive words of performance by which the oath-taker binds himself to witness, to render verdict, to serve, to be true, or to do or to say whatever other thing may be required of him. Each also contains some words of adjuration, whether those words be, "I do swear by Almighty God," or "In the name of Almighty God, and as you shall answer to God at the great day of judgement," or "So help me God," or some other. Whether the words of adjuration come at the beginning, the end, or at both points, they are indispensible to the oath.

Following this same form, Masonic oaths likewise have words of performance and words of adjuration. The commitment is to the laws of the Order and—because it lies at the very heart of the whole enterprise—to fraternal responsibility. Had the oaths contained no more it may be that Freemasonry would never have come into conflict with the Church. But the oaths do contain something more, and it is that "something more" which has occasioned the historic conflict.

The oaths contain a vow of silence concerning the secrets of Freemasonry, together with a penal clause said to be applicable in the event of violation. The penal clause is couched in highly figurative and dramatically imaginative language, and it is the unwarranted—literal interpretation of this language, as much as anything else, which has been responsible for the generations of distrust. Let it be said that no Masonic Lodge can or does lay hands upon an erring brother and impose punishment after the manner of the ancient synagogues under Hebrew criminal law, nor, presumably, has such ever been the case. The sanctions are wholly moral and ethical, and if the offender suffers for his transgressions it is in the knowledge of the disapprobation of his brethren.

Given the historical position of the Church at Rome (and of elements of Protestantism, to a lesser degree) extra-ecclesiastical oaths, oaths over which the church had no control, seemed to fly in the face of scripture and of canon law. Then too, the Church's willingness to literally interpret Masonic penal clauses, despite the evidence to the contrary, served further to exacerbate the relationship of Craft and Church.

The language of every oath is different, depending upon its purpose, but the language of every oath echoes to some degree the language of every other, for that language is drawn from a common English vocabulary. The same words are heard in different contexts "true," "truth," "faith," "faithful," "allegiance," "obey," "obedience," "defend," "obligation," "lawful," "lawfully," "freely," "mental reservation." These words, or their cognate forms, are common to some or to all of the oaths heretofore cited. It is to be expected that these words, or some of them, should be heard in the oaths of Freemasonry.

We have observed that the acts of raising the right hand and of touching, holding or kissing the Holy Bible or one of the Testaments are two of the time-honored elements of oath-taking still practiced to this day. Judicial oaths, oaths of allegiance and public oaths are customarily taken in this country while standing, although we know that oaths of homage and fealty, and almost certainly the oath of allegiance to a sovereign in times past, were taken while kneeling. The vows of marriage taken in the liturgical churches, are taken kneeling at the altar or prie-dieu. Likewise, at ordination, even in non-liturgical churches, the ordinant customarily kneels, at least for the imposition of hands. The manager of administering Masonic oaths conforms to these ancient and revered customs and practices.

Thus, we see that Masonic oaths are not unique in themselves. In the practice itself, in the form or structure, in the vocabulary, and even in the general manner of administration, Freemasonry conforms, as one might expect, to the usages and customs of the past, both civil and religious.

There is one further matter which merits our consideration. We have throughout this paper spoken of "Masonic oaths," yet the word "oath" is rarely used by Masons. The word most commonly used is "obligation," and its use gives to the word almost esoteric meaning. Whereas generally the obligation is the binding power of the oath or vow, in Masonry it takes on the meaning of the oath itself; it is the act performed and the words spoken. Almost secondarily, it is the duty imposed, the responsibility incurred. More properly we should speak of the obligation of the oath, thus clearly distinguishing the act from the binding power of the act. But the word is too much a part of Masonic speech, and it will continue to mean what we want it to mean.

Also, we early defined the term affirmation. We did so because it is a concomitant of oath, and the relationship of the two terms must be understood. However, affirmation has no place in Masonry for the simple reason that the Order requires an oath to be sworn and unlike the law, offers no alternate form. Non-jurors, therefore, cannot be Masons.

We have spoken of vows at length, but, until now, without saying what relationship vows have to Masonry. Perhaps you will have perceived that the Masonic obligations—what we have called oaths—do partake of some of the characteristics of vows. The Masonic obligations are promissory oaths and therefore, according to the *Westminster Confession*, "of like nature" with a vow.

Those obligations are in perpetuity, making them again of like nature to a vow. But of vows, we have noted that they can be terminated. An oath of allegiance is essentially one in perpetuity, but even such an oath can be forsworn and one may assume a new allegiance without violence to the conscience. The obligations of Freemasonry, to an even more marked degree than the familiar vows, are perpetual. These oaths—vows, we might say in this context cannot formally be forsworn. Formal membership in a Lodge of Masons may be terminated, but the obligations of the oaths remain. Neither legally enforceable nor religiously binding, they exert their own sanction through the power of man's conscience.

To illustrate the degree to which this sanction of the conscience has been misunderstood, we would quote from Dorothy Ann Lipson's excellent work, *Freemasonry In Federalist Connecticut, 1789–1835*:

> In the discussion Amasa Walker of Massachusetts summed up what seemed to be a widely shared conviction: "The opposition to these oaths is the sure foundation of anti-masonry.' If a basic article of social morality required men to keep their oaths, Anti-masons were faced with the immediate contradiction of persuading Masons to disavow their oaths. If Masons could be convinced that oaths are neither morally, legally, or religiously binding it should be the most effectual measure we can possibly take to destroy the institution.[18]

The Anti-masons failed in their efforts to destroy because, giving high value to their own principles, they failed to realize that the kind of man who becomes a Mason is the kind of man who feels the obligation to do "according to all that proceeds from out of his mouth."

## REFERENCES

1. *Black's Law Dictionary*: "Oath", p. 1268f

2. Ibid.

3. Stringer, F.A.: Oaths and Affirmations, Preface

4. Black's Law Dictionary: "Oath," p. 1268f

5. Ibid.

6. Ibid

7. Ibid.

8. Maitland, F W.: *The Constitutional History of England*, p. 115

9. Ibid. p. 26

10. Ibid, p. 26

11. *Black's Law Dictionary*: "Oath " p. 1268f

12. Freeman, Douglas Southall: *George Washington*, Vol. VI, p. 192

13. Black's Law Dictionary: 'Oath," p. 1268f

14. Ibid.

15. Schaff, Philip: *The Creeds of Christendom*, Vol. III, p. 651

16. Ibid., p. 513f

17. Preston, Thomas: *Roger Widdingtons Last Rejoynder*, p. 307

18. Lipson, Dorothy Ann: *Freemasonry In Federalist Connecticut*, p. 302

## BIBLIOGRAPHY

Coil. Henry Wilson, Sr. *Freemasonry Through Six Centuries*, 2 vol. Fulton. MO, Missouri Lodge of Research, 1966.

Durant, Will and Ariel. *The Age of Reason Begins* N.Y. Zircon and Schuster, 1961.

Elton, G. R. *Reform and Reformation, England, 1509–1558* Cambridge, MA, Harvard University Press, 1977

Freeman, Douglas Southall. *George Washington, 7* vol. Vol. VI, President and Patriot N.Y. Charles Scribner's Sons, 1954

Friedman, Lawrence M. *A History of American Law* N.Y., Simon and Schuster, 1975.

Hyman, Harold Melvin. *Era of the Oath: Northern Loyalty Tests During the Civil War and Reconstruction* Philadelphia, University of Pennsylvania Press, 1954

Human, Harold M. *To Try Men's Souls: Loyalty Tests in American History* Berkeley, University of California Press, 1960

Lipson, Dorothy Ann. *Freemasonry In Federalist Connecticut, 1789–1835* Princeton, Princeton University Press, 1977

McGrath, John J., Editor. *Church and State In American Law — Cases and Materials* Milwaukee, The Bruse Publishing Co. 1962

McKelvey, John Jay. *Handbook of the Law of Evidence*, Third Edition St. Paul, West Publishing Company, 1924

Maitland, F. W. *The Constitutional History of England* Cambridge, Cambridge University Press, 1908

Plucknett, Theodore F. T. *A Concise History of the Common Law* Rochester, The Lawyers Co-Operative Publishing Co., 1929

Preston, Thomas. *Roger Widdingtons Last Reioynder, 1619 English Recusant Literature, 1558–1640*, Vol. 280 Selected and edited by D.M. Rogers London, The Scolar Press, 1976

Schaff, Philip. *The Creeds of Christendom*, 4th edition, 3 vol., Vol. III Grand Rapids, Baker Book House, 1977 (Paperback edition)

Stringer, F. A. *Oaths and Affirmations In Great Britain and Ireland*, Third Edition London, Stevens and Son Limited, 1909

*Black's Law Dictionary*. Revised Fourth Edition St. Paul. West Publishing Co., 1968.